90 0507395 9

KW-467-393

ABOUT THE AUTHORS

DR QUENTIN BERESFORD is a specialist in public policy,
and author or co-author of six previous books including
Our State of Mind: Racial Planning and the Stolen Generations,
a prize-winner in the 1998 WA Premier's Book Awards.
DR HUGO BEKLE'S speciality is environmental geography,
in particular Western Australia's unique wetlands and
bio-diversity. ASSOCIATE PROFESSOR HARRY PHILLIPS is
widely known for his knowledge of Australian and Western
Australian politics, and his many works include *Representing
the People: Parliamentary Government in Western Australia*.
JANE MULCOCK is undertaking doctoral studies in anthropology at The University of Western Australia. Together they
make a formidable team to discuss the very topical subject
of salinity.

THE
SALINITY CRISIS

**LANDSCAPES, COMMUNITIES
and POLITICS**

QUENTIN BERESFORD, HUGO BEKLE,
HARRY PHILLIPS and JANE MULCOCK

University of Western Australia Press

First published in 2001 by
University of Western Australia Press
Crawley, Western Australia 6009
http://www.uwapress.uwa.edu.au

Publication of this book was made possible with generous funding from the
Co-operative Research Centre for Dryland Salinity at The University of Western
Australia and the School of Community Services and Social Sciences,
Edith Cowan University.

National Library of Australia Cataloguing-in-Publication entry:

The salinity crisis : landscapes, communities and politics.

    Bibliography.
    Includes index.

    ISBN 1 876268 60 3. ✓

    1. Salinization - Australia. 2. Salinization - Control -
    Australia. 3. Soil salinization - Western Australia. 4.
    Landscape changes - Australia. 5. Biological diversity -
    Australia. 6. Australia - Rural conditions. 7. Australia -
    Environmental conditions. I. Beresford, Quentin, 1954- .

577.57

Cover image: Salt scald near Beverley, Western Australia

Produced by Benchmark Publications, Melbourne
Consultant editor: Jan Anderson, Melbourne
Designed by Ron Hampton, Pages in Action
The map on page 8 is by Ophelia Leviny
Typeset in 10.5pt Adobe Garamond by Pages in Action, Melbourne
Printed by Frank Daniels, Perth

Contents

Preface

'State agencies estimate that one hectare [of land in Western Australia] an hour is being lost to salinity.'
The Sunday Times, 4 March 2001

The outlook for much of Western Australia's Wheatbelt over the coming decades is a bleak one. The spread of salinity throughout this vast region represents an environmental crisis with no parallel in the State. Until very recently, the problem was largely ignored by the political system. Yet, concern about salinity has been a public issue since the turn of the twentieth century. Fifty years ago a few even foresaw the crisis we now face.

It took seven decades to develop the Wheatbelt into one of the State's major export-earning regions, and during this time reactions to salinity have ranged from the dire warnings of experts, denial by farmers, and indifference from politicians at Federal, State and local levels. However, in recent times a growing sense of urgency has crept into public debate and private responses to the problem of salinity.

Explaining these complex and often contradictory reactions to salinity is the underlying purpose of this book. It is an attempt to bring a series of social science perspectives to a topic of increasing public importance but which has usually been the province of the physical science. Our major concerns, therefore, are with the social, political, and environmental dimensions of this problem. However, we appreciate the extensive work which various branches of the physical sciences have brought to bear on understanding the causes and manifestations of salinity, and we have drawn upon this work where necessary.

We believe an environmental crisis on the scale of salinity requires an explanation. This book is the first attempt in Western Australia to bring a multidisciplinary perspective to the problems that salinity poses. Our approach is to draw out the larger issues embedded in these problems: What are the origins of the current crisis? How will salinity impact on the populations and landscape of the Wheatbelt region? Why has it paralysed decision-makers for so long? What should we learn from its spread throughout large parts of the region?

In attempting to answer these questions, we have structured the book into four parts. The first part, comprising Chapter One, provides an overview of the current salinity crisis showing its multidimensional character. Part II—comprising Chapters Two, Three and Four—provides a largely narrative history of the spread of salinity, and the scientific and political responses. The origins of salinity as an environmental crisis are located in the history of government policy and ideology which favoured a development-at-all-costs approach to the State's future. Chapter Four in this part takes the story up to the attempts by the Court–Cowan Coalition Government to formulate the first systematic political strategy to deal with the crisis: efforts which at the time of publication, were under review by a new Labor Government.

Part III of the book—comprising Chapters Five, Six and Seven—takes up the major contemporary issues posed by salinity. Its impacts on affected communities are dealt with in Chapter Five through a case study of the town of Katanning. This is followed by a chapter examining the evolving environmental damage and the attendant focus on preserving remaining biodiversity, and one examining the uncertainty surrounding the available measures to control salinity's spread. Part IV comprises Chapter Eight—a conclusion reflecting on the lessons raised by the prospect of losing a part of the Wheatbelt equal in area to a small European nation and resulting from the imposition of a European farming system.

For ease of reading, wherever the state of Western Australia and the government of Western Australia are specially referred to, typographically they are shown as 'the State' and 'the State Government' respectively.

We greatly appreciate the commitment of Edith Cowan University to this applied social research on salinity, which is a topic of vital community interest. We would particularly like to thank the Dean of the Faculty of Community Services, Education, and Social Sciences, Professor Susan Holland, and Professor Bill Louden. The project was also facilitated by the University's award of several research grants and time release for Dr Beresford and Dr Bekle to concentrate on the research and writing.

The book could not have been written without the cooperation of many people, all of whom share a passionate interest in, and concern about, Western Australia's salinity problem. Special assistance was provided by Mr Keith Bradby, Mr Marty Ladyman and Dr David Bennett, who helped throughout the project by providing extensive interviews and insights, and access to materials and on-going encouragement. In a variety of ways, each of these people has worked for decades at the front line of salinity and their experience proved invaluable.

Several people read the draft in its entirety, providing editorial and professional feedback. In this regard we would like to thank Professor Phillip Cocks, Dr Graeme Robertson, Mr Keith Bradby, and Ms Marilyn Beresford.

Many of the staff associated with Agriculture WA, the State Salinity Council, Environmental Protection Authority, CSIRO, WA Conservation Foundation, Department of Conservation and Land Management, the Water and Rivers Commission, the Department of Land Administration, Greening Australia, the Salinity Forum Inc., Men of the Trees and the Battye Library provided time and expertise. There are too many people to thank individually, but they can be assured that we value their contributions. However, we would like to thank Mr Alex Campbell, Mr Don Crawford, Dr Richard George, Mr Simon Eyres, Dr Tom Hatton, Mr Ben Carr, Mr Greg Keighery, Ms Rachel Siewert, Mr Robert Sippe, Dr Paul Vogel, Mr Rod Short, Mr David Hartley, Dr Don McFarlane, Dr Don White, Dr Richard Harper and Dr Bob Hay.

Other people who lent valuable assistance include the Hon. Phillip Pendal, MLA, the Hon. Hendy Cowan, MLA, the Hon. Monty House, MLA, the Hon. Christine Sharp, MLC, Associate Professor Glen Phillips, Associate Professor Arthur Conacher, Dr Duncan Bythell, Dr Peter Bedford, Mr Harvey Morrell, Mr Colin Nicholl, Mr

Pat Cuneen, Mr Barry Oldfield, Mr Clive Malcolm, Mr Ted Rowley and Ms Donna Weston. John Bartle's preparedness to share his vision for the future of the Wheatbelt was much appreciated. Associate Professor David Pannell's extensive work on salinity was invaluable.

We are especially indebted to Mr Noel Nannup for sharing his extensive knowledge of Noongar culture and history.

We wish to thank all those people who participated in the Katanning case study. They were very generous with their time and interest, and in many instances gave detailed interviews. The following gave extensive assistance: Margaret Scott, Jenny Gardner, Fred Armstrong and Lynne Coleman. Whilst most people interviewed agreed to be named in the study, some, understandably, wished to remain anonymous.

While appreciative of the support from all of the above, all responsibility for matters of interpretation rest with the authors.

The West Australian newspaper made available its extensive collection of photographs, and we would like to thank Ms Gail Knight and Mr David Taylor for their assistance.

The photographs we have used come from a variety of sources, and these are shown in the captions. In all cases, we wish to thank the relevant parties for their permission to use them.

The staff at UWA Press have our gratitude for their commitment to this project and for providing such a high level of professional guidance.

Finally, we would have been lost without the expertise of Mrs Janice Bryant and Mrs Bruna Bekle who provided patient and skilled word processing. Mrs Bekle also provided assistance with research in several chapters.

Quentin Beresford,
Hugo Bekle,
Harry Phillips and
Jane Mulcock

AUGUST 2001

Abbreviations and Acronyms

ACF	Australian Conservation Foundation
Agriculture WA	Western Australian Department of Agriculture
BCE	Before the Common Era (a replacement of BC)
BSc	Bachelor of Science
CALM	Conservation and Land Management
CAMBA	China-Australia Migratory Bird Agreement
CP	Conditional Purchase (Block)
CSIRO	Commonwealth Scientific and Industrial Research Organisation
DCE	Department of Conservation and Environment
EPA	Environmental Protection Authority
ESD	Ecologically Sustainable Development
ICM	Integrated Catchment Management
JAMBA	Japan-Australia Migratory Bird Agreement
KCCG	Katanning Creek Catchment Group
KSMS	Katanning Salinity Management Strategy
LCDC	Land Conservation District Committee
MLA	Member of the Legislative Assembly
MLC	Member of the Legislative Council
NHT	Natural Heritage Trust
PGA	Pastoralists and Graziers Association
RAIC	Rural and Agricultural Industries Commission
RTP	Rural Towns Program
TAFE	Technical and Further Education
WGLR	Working Group on Land Release
WISALTS	Whittington Interceptor Salt-Affected Land Treatment Society

Conversion Tables

	Metric Unit/Imperial Unit	Imperial Units	Metric Units
(a) LENGTH, MASS, AREA AND VOLUME			
Length	millimetre (mm), inch (")	1 cm = 0.394"	1" = 2.54 cm
	centimetre (cm), foot (ft)	1 m = 3.28 ft	1 ft = 30.5 cm
	kilometre (km), mile (mile)	1 km = 0.621 mile	1 mile = 1.61 km
Mass	tonne, ton	1 tonne = 0.984 ton	1 ton = 1.02 tonne
	kilogram (kg,) pound (lb)	1 kg = 2.20 lb	1 lb = 0.454 kg
Area	hectare (ha), acre (ac)	1 ha = 2.47 ac	1 ac = 0.405 ha
Volume (dry measure)	cubic metres (m³), bushel	1m³ = 27.5 bushels	1 bushel = 0.0364 m³
Mass per unit area		1 tonne/ha = 0.397 tons/acre	1 ton/acre = 2.52 tonnes/ha
		1 kg/ha = 0.893 lb/acre	1 lb/acre = 1.12 kg/ha
Volume (dry measure) per unit area		1m³/ha = 11.13bushels/acre	1 bushel/acre = 0.09 m³/ha
(b) CURRENCY			
Australian	dollar ($) (post-1966) pound (£) (pre-1966) = 20 shillings (s)	$1.00 = £0.50 $1.00 = 10 s	£1.00 = $2.00 1 s = $0.10
(c) SALINITY			
Salt concentration	Perth's seawater = 35,000 mg/L		

SALINITY—
A MULTIDIMENSIONAL CRISIS

'Australia is the greatest clearer of native vegetation in the developed world, and the sixth-largest overall.'

Source: Australian Conservation Foundation, March 2001; as quoted in *The West Australian*, 10 July 2000.

The Salinity Crisis—An Overview

Of the elements sustaining human life on earth, the quality of soil and water are two of the most crucial. Poor management of the soil–water system can threaten the survival of human populations by making it much harder to produce food. In fact, according to the International Food Policy Research Institute, there is growing concern in some quarters that a decline in long-term soil productivity is already seriously limiting food production, especially in the developing world.[1] There is no more damaging threat to the maintenance of soil–water systems than the spread of salinity; literally the salting of the earth. In many areas of the world large concentrations of salt have accumulated over millennia by rainfall, the weathering of rocks and the deposit of wind-borne ocean salt. Nature evolved effective means to prevent this salt from leaching out of the earth; mostly, native vegetation with its deep-rooted systems acted to keep underground water tables from reaching the surface. Interference from humans, however, has widely upset this equilibrium (see the salinisation diagram on page 13). Disturbing natural vegetation systems in the name of agriculture is as old as human history and, consequently, so is the spread of salinity.

Salinity is thought to have been a major contributing factor to the demise of the world's earliest urban society. Established in the lower reaches of the Tigris and Euphrates rivers in the second half of the fifth millennium BCE, the enterprising people who became known as the Sumerians settled a perilous land. Consisting of a flat, dusty and dry alluvium plain, interspersed with swamps, its only great advantage for agriculture was the easy access of water from the river system. Through use of irrigation, the Sumerians transformed their parched plain into 'a land of extensive grain and forage fields and date palm plantations'.[2] In fact, the prominent civilisation they constructed in Mesopotamia was built upon agricultural productivity, as there were no other major resources to exploit.

In spite of their achievements, the Sumerian civilisation began an irretrievable decline during the third millennium BCE. According to Hillel, land degradation through silting and salinisation was probably the major cause.[3] The deforested upper reaches of the Euphrates were prone to erosion—the soil carried down the river raised the river banks above the plain, causing flooding in times of high rainfall. The second severe problem was salt. The irrigated plains so energetically cultivated by the Sumerians had no natural or artificial system of drainage, and excess water seeped into the ground, causing the water table to rise and bring salt to the surface, killing wheat and other cereal crops.

The experience of salinity in southern Mesopotamia had universal lessons. One historian has pointed out that the combined effects of irrigated agriculture applied in a region already prone to saline groundwater created a bind for farmers, the dimensions of which have not changed across the millennia: 'The subsistence farmer ... is typically caught between short-term uncertainties as to the adequacy of irrigation supplies to support this year's crop and ultimate salinisation of his land as the long-term consequences of over-watering.'[4] Furthermore, the experience of ancient civilisations shows that 'the general elevation of groundwater levels in a region, even if for a time farmers manage to adapt to it, increases the likelihood of an ultimate, general agricultural collapse.'[5]

In the modern era, dryland salinity has become a major worldwide problem. According to the International Food Policy Research Institute, nearly four million acres of farmland are lost to excessive salt every year.[6] Salinity is particularly a problem on irrigated land which produces about 40 per cent of the world's food. Poorly designed irrigated systems leach salt out of the soil while salinity in dry-land areas is the consequence of a rising water table, which brings salt to the surface. Dryland salinity has been a major problem in the Dakotas of North America and the western prairies of Canada. The salt lies underground from the weathering of ancient rocks. The perennial grasses which covered these regions were well adapted to absorb as much of the available moisture as possible.[7] However, the imposition onto these landscapes of large-scale wheat farming upset this balance. The shallow-rooted wheat crops allowed seepage of moisture underground, causing the water table to rise and bring salt with it to the surface. The resulting environmental damage has seen over a million hectares (1991 estimate) lost from production and a growing death-rate among a range of wildlife.[8]

SALINITY ACROSS THE AUSTRALIAN STATES

Like North America, Australia has a major problem with salinity. However, in ecological terms, salinity is only part of a much wider problem of land degradation which includes soil erosion, soil acidity and declining soil structure. While each is a distinctive manifestation of land degradation and has varying effects on the landscape, each is caused by poor land management practices and especially the wholesale clearing of native vegetation for agriculture. These problems were given scant attention by most Australians until the late 1980s. Few conservationists had the issues of land degradation at the top of their list of priorities. Rarely did the problems rate a mention in the media and few Australians 'connected to the problems' as affecting their future.[9] Even in the mid-1990s, public awareness re-mained low. Coverage of rural issues in the mainstream media was marginalised. According to regional journalist Tim Hughes, much of the mainstream media have steadily abandoned interest in, and commitment to, rural Australia:

> Newspapers have long since abandoned having a team of country correspondents whose news was used with frequency … Nowadays, when 'shareholder value' is often more important to news-

paper management than its masthead being a journal of record, the inevitable budget cuts means stringers and contributors will go first; plane fares and hire cars, essential but costly tools to get around the bush, are next.[10]

Not surprisingly, a survey of Australians' environmental concerns, undertaken by the Australian Bureau of Statistics and reported in 1998, found land degradation rated second last—behind air pollution, pollution of the ocean and destruction of forests.[11] In other words, loss of contact by urban dwellers with the bush has meant many more Australians have been denied enough opportunity to understand rural issues.

However, media interest in salinity changed dramatically during 2000. In February of that year, a front-page banner headline in *The West Australian* blared: 'Salt Levy: You Will Pay for This.' Below the headline was a dramatic colour photograph of a lone horseman riding across a paddock turned frost-white with salt.[12] The article raised the suggestion that the problem was now so bad in the State that a levy might have to be raised on citizens to fund a rescue. A similar theme appeared in the influential *Bulletin* magazine when, in June 2000, it ran a lengthy feature article on the problem, headlined 'The Salvation of a Continent'. Readers were told that time was fast running out to save large parts of the Australian landscape. To fix the readers' minds on a problem most had not seen, let alone understood, the author conjured up a suitably dramatic metaphor: Australia was little more than 'a gigantic pool of toxic waste with a threadbare blanket of shagged-out soil', the consequences of which had reached a threatening state: 'Right now, a vast lake of poison beneath our feet is rising to the surface across millions of hectares, killing everything in its path.'[13] These reports followed earlier ones in *The Australian* which highlighted new concerns over the threats to Adelaide's water supply from salinity and to the uncertain future of agriculture in large parts of the Murray–Darling Basin.[14] As media interest now signifies, land degradation—and especially salinity—has emerged as the nation's worst environmental problem. They have also become politicised issues with growing demands upon government for action.

Causes of Salinity

'Most of the salt responsible for salinity in Western Australia originated in the ocean. Salt, mainly sodium chloride, has been carried inland by the prevailing winds and deposited on the land in small amounts (20–200 kg/ha/year) in rainfall and dust. The amount of stored salt in the soil profile is least in the high rainfall areas (generally moderate relief and well drained) and highest in low rainfall areas (generally flat and poorly drained).

'Primary salinity develops naturally, mainly in areas where rainfall is insufficient to leach salts from the soil profile and evaporation is high. Over thousands of years, salt slowly accumulated beneath the south-west of Western Australia, causing changes in biological systems and landscape form and function.

'Secondary salinity (which takes the form of either dryland or irrigation salinity) is the result of clearing native vegetation and replacing it with shallow-rooted crops and pasture that use less water, causing changes to the hydrology of the landscape. The indigenous vegetation of Australia is perennial and deep-rooted, well-adapted to surviving both floods and drought and effective in its use of water. Annual crops and pastures do not use as much of the incoming rainfall and this unused water either runs off or infiltrates beyond the root zone and accumulates as groundwater (recharge).

'Much of the land in the south-west agricultural region was prone to salinity prior to clearing. It has been estimated that the region has an average of about 2,000 tonnes of salt stored below every hectare in the soil profile between the surface and the bedrock, with as little as 300 t/ha in uplands and as much as 10,000 t/ha in saline valleys. In many areas, this accumulation of salt has become mobilised with the rise in groundwater levels, emerging where water is forced to the land surface. This secondary salinity is the threat addressed in this strategy.

'As saline groundwater comes close to the soil surface*, salt enters the plant root zone leading to the death of native plants and crops and pastures that are not salt tolerant. Plants also suffer from increased waterlogging. Saline groundwaters discharge at the soil surface and are concentrated by evaporation, damaging soils on-site and down slopes, eventually draining into streams, rivers and lakes, degrading wetland habitats and water resources. Seepage areas and scalds are the surface expression of salinity, although salt can also be present in areas where only marginal reductions in yield can be seen. Most early settlement in the south-west agricultural region occurred in the valleys near water courses. These areas, including most of the towns in the region, are now in the areas at highest risk of salinity.

'The primary cause of salinity is under-use of annual rainfall and the relatively impermeable and flat nature of many Wheatbelt groundwater systems. Generally speaking, groundwater continues to rise at an average rate of 20 centimetres per year in the south-west agricultural region as it is recharged by rainfall. The rate of groundwater rise and the spread of salinity can only be slowed or reduced by either reducing the amount of rain that reaches the groundwater or finding ways to remove groundwater in an environmentally sound and practical way.'

Source: The State Salinity Council (2000). The Salinity Strategy. Natural Resource Management in Australia. Perth, Government of Western Australia, pp. 14–15.

* Soil salinity becomes a problem when the underground water table is less than 2 metres from the surface.

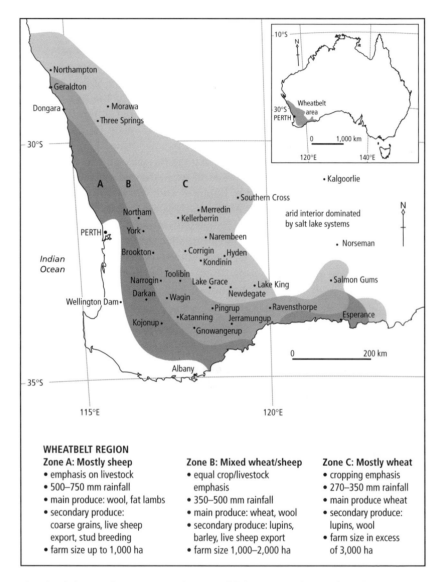

WHEATBELT REGION

Zone A: Mostly sheep
- emphasis on livestock
- 500–750 mm rainfall
- main produce: wool, fat lambs
- secondary produce: coarse grains, live sheep export, stud breeding
- farm size up to 1,000 ha

Zone B: Mixed wheat/sheep
- equal crop/livestock emphasis
- 350–500 mm rainfall
- main produce: wheat, wool
- secondary produce: lupins, barley, live sheep export
- farm size 1,000–2,000 ha

Zone C: Mostly wheat
- cropping emphasis
- 270–350 mm rainfall
- main produce wheat
- secondary produce: lupins, wool
- farm size in excess of 3,000 ha

The Wheatbelt in south-western Australia. As rainfall decreases to the east, farms become larger and there is a greater emphasis on wheat production.

TABLE 1: Extent of dryland salinity in Australia, 1982–96 ('000 hectares)

	NSW	Vic	Qld	SA	WA	Tas	NT	Aust
1982	4	90	8	55	264	5	0	426
1991	20	90	8	225	443	5	0	791
1996	120	120	10	402	1804	20	Minor	2476

Source: Conacher, A. and Conacher, J. (2000). *Environmental Planning and Management in Australia.* South Melbourne, Oxford University Press, p. 57.

For the purposes of coherence, and in recognition of its distinctiveness, this book focuses on salinity. All states experience the effects of salinity. As Table 1 shows, rates of dryland salinity have grown dramatically since the early 1980s.

Major salinity problems occur throughout the Murray–Darling Basin which features dryland and irrigation salinity, across the Mallee region of north-western Victoria/south-western New South Wales, and irrigation salinity in areas including the Riverina plain stretching into New South Wales from north-central Victoria, and the Riverland region around Renmark in South Australia. These regions include some of the most productive agricultural lands in Australia.

Along the Murray River itself, large irrigation developments in the 1870s were followed by the construction of weirs and dams to ensure a reliable supply of water. By the turn of the twentieth century major Red Gum forests, valued as an important source of timber for firewood and building, were cut within several kilometres of the river, while on the vast floodplain area Black Box woodland and salt-tolerant shrubs were cleared to make way for pastures and crops. The transformation of the Basin into one of the major foodbowls of the nation has come at a heavy cost to the region's environment. As the Murray–Darling Basin Commission acknowledges, agricultural production along the Basin's rivers 'cannot be sustained unless the waterlogging and salinisation resulting from irrigation and clearing can be controlled'.[15] Equally alarming, is the rise in the salination of the Murray itself due to a

TABLE 2: Extent of salinity in Australia

State	Hectares salt affected (1996)	Hectares at risk (incl. areas already affected)
WA	1,804,000	6,109,000
SA	402,000	600,000
Vic	120,000	Unknown
NSW	120,000	5,000,000
Tas	20,000	Unknown
Qld	10,000	74,000
NT	Minor	Unknown

Source: www.science.org.au/nova/032

combination of saline groundwater flowing into the river, and run-off from saline irrigation areas.

Throughout the Basin, in both dryland and irrigated areas, the effects of salinity are becoming more starkly apparent. For example, evaporative basins created to dispose of saline water throughout the floodplain area of South Australia have resulted in extensive areas of dead trees, giving these basins 'an appearance of bleakness and decay'.[16] Salt-induced death of River Gum and Black Box has occurred around weirs and dams due to the resulting rising water table. Many of the original species of native vegetation have been eliminated as salt levels have increased beyond their tolerance, while the diversity of river life is also being affected.

Australia-wide, recent estimates put the area of affected land at 2.5 million hectares with another 10 million at risk.[17] However, other estimates suggest that over 15 million hectares will become saline before stabilisation is reached.[18] The Australian Academy of Science produced the figures shown in Table 2.

On such a scale, salinity represents a massive, multidimensional problem with major economic, social and environmental consquences. The full extent of these consequences is only now beginning to be conceptualised, and much remains speculation. A growing body of environmental scientists see a crisis looming: agricultural industries forced into retreat; country towns facing large infrastructure damage and, in some cases, their viability under serious threat; diminished bio-diversity with extensive species loss; and dislocation to human popula-tions in the most affected areas. The worst of these effects may be only twenty years away, which makes remedial action all the more urgent.

The seriousness of these findings raises fundamental questions about Australians and their landscape: Why has Australia been farmed in such a destructive manner? What role did governments play in this process? What is required to turn the situation around? This book examines these and other issues through a study of the Western Aus-tralian Wheatbelt. The approach is a multidisciplinary one: history, politics, anthropology and environmental geography are brought to bear in an effort to understand how the problem arose, its impacts on communities and landscapes, and the responses from government.

WESTERN AUSTRALIA'S SALINITY CRISIS

In terms of extent and severity, Western Australia's Wheatbelt (see the map on page 8) is one of the worst examples of dryland salinity in the world. Stretching approximately 400 kilometres north of Perth and eastwards for 700 kilometres, the Wheatbelt has a little-known, but unenviable, reputation: in no other region in the world is there thought to be an area as large which has been cleared of its natural vegetation in so short a period—most of it in the sixty years between the 1920s and the early 1980s.[19] This vast area of vegetation was torn down so quickly that its original name, the Mallee Belt, has long been forgotten. In its place, shallow-rooted cereal crops, particularly wheat, and pasture for sheep, form a largely featureless landscape. As a result of the large-scale clearing, the region now contains 70 per cent of the nation's dryland salinity. The most recent estimates indicate that:

> Almost regardless of what treatments are implemented in the short-to-medium term, an additional 2 million hectares of agri-cultural land in WA will become salt affected. Beyond that, a fur-ther 2 million hectares is at stake, with its preservation depending

on the extent of treatments that are implemented. However, the medium-term loss of 2 million hectares is already not practically preventable.[20]

Other estimates put the area at risk even higher. The National Land and Water Resources Audit estimates that 6.5 million hectares of agricultural land will be subject to shallow water tables and salinity over the next fifty years.[21]

Although public awareness of salinity has risen considerably in recent years, the full impact of the salinity crisis does not appear to be understood fully in either the general or farming communities. This was the finding of a survey of community opinion recently undertaken by researchers at the University of Western Australia in three samples— farmers, people from rural towns, and people from Perth—the conclusions from which showed that:

> The awareness of agricultural problems was only moderate in all samples, and their attitudes towards conservation may be influenced by their lack of knowledge about environmental damage resulting from farming activities. This is particularly so for the city population who, although generally aware that farming activities are causing degradation problems, were significantly less aware that salinity was affecting biological diversity, buildings and roads. Farmers were significantly less aware that agricultural activities are damaging river systems and wetlands.[22]

Conceptualising what will happen to the landscape, to agricultural industries and to local communities is a challenging task. For all the potential seriousness of the problem, its human dimensions have been little studied by either government agencies or academic researchers. One of the statistics widely quoted indicates that over 30 per cent of the region will become saline within the next couple of decades. This figure marks a substantial upgrading of the seriousness of the problem. In the 1970s, it was commonly thought by officials that salinity was a minor problem and would affect about 1 per cent of the

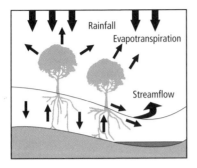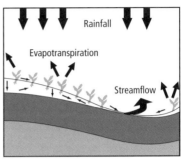

This diagram shows the process of salinisation in the Wheatbelt, resulting from a rising water table. Annual crops and pastures use far less water from rainfall than does deep-rooted native vegetation. (*Courtesy of the State Salinity Council*)

area; in the 1980s this was revised to be about 8 per cent. Now it is accepted that salinity in the Wheatbelt is rapidly shaping up as one of the nation's greatest ecological disasters. As CSIRO scientist Tom Hatton bluntly explains: 'An area the size of a small European nation will have been rendered useless.'[23] Restoring this area will be a major challenge. Hatton writes: 'If 50 to 80 per cent of the Wheatbelt were restored to woodlands, the salinity spread might be stopped—but even with this level of regeneration, it would take several hundred years.'[24]

WHEATBELT ENVIRONMENT AND PHYSICAL SETTING

Covering approximately 30 million hectares, the Wheatbelt extends from about latitude 27 degrees south (near the Murchison River) to the South Coast at Israelite Bay (150 kilometres east of Esperance). Its boundary divides the farming areas from the inland pastoral areas.[25] The inland extent of the Wheatbelt is a little east of Southern Cross and is mainly controlled by the decline in the amount and reliability of rainfall.

Until very recently, few Europeans appreciated the intrinsic beauty of the region like zoologist Barbara York Main. Writing in the

1940s, she has left an evocative account of natural bushland in the central Wheatbelt at a time when large tracts of such bushland still existed, including a description of the varied landforms and vegetation during the approaching hot, summer easterly wind:

> From the eastern, timbered, low hills and flats and wide gullies the wind moved ever westward across sandplains, whirring through their scrubby thickets. It tumbled along and across the low-lying stretches of timber [insinuated between the sandplains], tipping the umbrella tops of the eucalypts, whistling through their spokes, tearing at their crumpled, leafy vanes. Locked boughs groaned together, ribbons of bark unravelled and were plaited and unplaited by the fingering wind. On and on the wind rushed; over dry saltlakes, through wooded flats, over sandy rises and gravelly hillocks; sometimes it lifted over granite domes which rose above the general level of the countryside … It is a well-treed landscape but each shrub and tree is specially equipped to withstand the drying effects of sun and wind, of a long, rainless summer.[26]

Traditionally, the country which Barbara York Main wrote about was occupied by the Noongar people, the collective name given to Aboriginal people whose country lies in the south-west corner of Western Australia. Noongars were divided into about fourteen different groups, each with strong traditions of territorial occupation.[27] Aboriginal management of country was closely tied to the fire ecology of native vegetation. Each Aboriginal group was responsible for burning its own country, and would have known each part of it in great detail, its fire history, and when it was due for burning.[28] Controlled local fires were lit in the scrubland communities during the hot, dry summer period, starting towards the end of December and continuing into January, providing a form of environmental control.[29] The 'burns' were used to drive game, such as kangaroos and Western Brush Wallabies, into the open so they could be speared more easily. As fire swept through selected patches of bush, many reptile species, such as the Sand Monitor (the locally named Racehorse Goanna, or Bungarra), and small marsupials fleeing the flames were killed by women and children with clubs and sticks. As soon as the fire passed, the group searched the ashes for burnt lizards (for example, the Shingle-back Lizard) and snakes. Burning not only reduced undergrowth, but also stimulated the lush regrowth of grasses and young plants. This new food source attracted kangaroos in late winter and early spring, improving opportunities for Aboriginal hunters.

Fire is the most obvious Aboriginal influence on the vegetation, where many of the species (particularly eucalypts and some edible plant foods) are assisted in their regeneration and germination by fire or its associated effects, including smoke and ash. Once rain falls, germination of seeds released after fire enables these plants to take advantage of the minerals stored in ash.[30]

In fact, the region inhabited by the Noongars supported over 4,000 species of vascular plants. This unique range of vegetation is a product of the combination of climatic, physical and environmental factors in what is one of the oldest landscapes on earth. An estimated 600 million years of continuous erosion has shaped this ancient, relatively flat, but occasionally undulating, granitic rockmass that forms part of the vast Great Western Plateau.[31] This plateau has been transformed by wear and modification of bedrock into wide, shallow, flat-bottomed valleys with divides of long, gently sloping rises, up to ridges.[32]

The flora of this undulating landscape varied according to climate and soil types. Many of the blocks of land taken up for agriculture in the early days of European settlement were selected on the basis of the type of vegetation they supported.[33] The centenary historian of Western Australia, Sir Hal Colebatch, has left the following description of vegetation types:

> The forest country runs through the wheat belt like broad ribbons, following the low places. Towards the edges of the forest as the ground rises, mallee thickets are usually found, thence, as the ground rises and the soil becomes lighter, brushwood thickets predominate, until on the highest elevations is the sand plain or heath-like country.[34]

Further out still was the 'salt-pan' vegetation, which Colebatch described in the following manner:

> Salt-pan vegetation covers the flats adjacent to the 'salt lakes'. These are formed by the drainage waters from the interior of the wheat belt which flow into depressions from which there is no outlet. As a result of evaporation during the summer, accumulations of salt, gypsum, etc., are formed. Around these are the flats on which samphire and salt bush grow.

The mostly flat and gently undulating country in the Wheatbelt made it highly suitable for cropping. Initially, the woodlands were selected and cleared because of their heavier and more fertile soils, and better rainfall. Woodlands are made up of various species of eucalypts and are generally described as having less than 30 per cent canopy cover, with an understorey of grass or hard-leaved shrubs. The trees are 10 to 20 metres tall, and comprise the following notable species: York Gum, Salmon Gum, Gimlet, Red Morrel, Black Morrel, Yorrel, Flat-topped Yate and Wandoo. York Gum is usually associated with the species called Raspberry Jam, and this country was valued for the natural grass it offered.[35] With the availability of the fertiliser known as 'superphosphate', Salmon Gum and Gimlet country became the principal area of wheat production.

Only a relatively small area was cleared by the turn of the twentieth century and the isolated Salmon Gums and York Gums were so numerous that no-one thought to try to preserve them.[36] These trees merely indicated where clearing should begin, as they grow on the best agricultural land. The Christmas Tree was the only species that had any protective legislation, due to its attractive flowers. In some parts of the landscape, the trees were quite stunted or so widely spaced that the woodlands have taken on a 'park-like' appearance. Wandoo woodland and mallee (stunted eucalypt) scrubland communities occur in drier areas of the eastern Wheatbelt, on less fertile soils. They often contain plants that are toxic to livestock. When bushfires burn through mallee country, there is usually a rapid regrowth of *Acacia* species called mulga.

As for its plant life, the Wheatbelt has a tremendous diversity of terrestrial and aquatic animals, many of which inhabit areas low in the landscape, including those that are naturally saline. The region supports the largest number of endangered mammals; for example, the Red-tailed Wamdenger, and Western Mouse. It also has major populations of other once-widespread species, such as the Numbat.[37]

The region's uniqueness underlies a fragility, especially to imposed agricultural systems. Wheatbelt soils have a low organic and mineral content, and are naturally infertile due to the long period of erosion of, and removal of, nutrients from the ancient landscape. By comparison with the rest of the world, these soils have a low phosphorus content and are not naturally suited to agriculture.

Two types of soils exist in the Wheatbelt: light, sandy soils located high in the landscape on elevated sandplains; and heavier, clayey soils that occur on the sides and floors of valleys and in low-lying parts of the landscape, where the overlaying sand and gravel have been removed and soil has formed either from fine deposits over old clay or from fresh granite rock. Areas of sandy soils account for about two-thirds of the entire Wheatbelt, and have now become more productive with the addition of phosphates and trace elements, such as copper, zinc, molybdenum, and manganese, in various fertiliser mixes. Growing nitrogen-fixing legumes, like lupins, also assists in overcoming nutrient deficiencies. Ironstone gravel occurs in variable amounts in the surface and subsurface of light soils and can make up 90 per cent of the weight.[38] With the application of fertiliser and sufficient winter rainfall, these gravelly soils are still able to produce crops and pastures. Erosion by wind on the sandier soils, and by water on the more rigidly structured soils, is also a significant problem.

In the early years of land clearance, the Department of Land Administration (formerly Department of Lands and Surveys) used the terms 'first class', 'second class' and 'third class' to describe the agricultural potential of new land in the subdivisions to be opened for farming.[39] First class land refers to the heavy, more fertile soils of the Wheatbelt, carrying York Gums and Salmon Gums and other local tree species. Second class land has grey to brown, sandy or sandy loam surfaces, with tough, sandy clay subsoils. This land supports the mallee form of various eucalypts, with Wandoo being associated with better rainfall. Third class land comprises the sandplains or scrubplains, with sandy and ironstone gravelly soils covered with shrubs up to three metres high. Such areas account for about half the Wheatbelt and are recognised to be of little value without trace elements and nutrient supplements. This early system of classifying soils highlights the fact that natural vegetation cover was considered to be a good indicator of the soil type and its agricultural capability.

The region's Mediterranean climate of cool, wet winters and hot, dry summers, made it attractive for broad acre farming and especially wheat. Early settlers recognised that the bright, dry summers minimised the risk from disease and made harvesting easy and cheap.[40] Most of the wheat is grown inland from the 500-millimetres isohyet,[41] but the rainfall pattern held hidden threats ignored by those who cleared and developed the land. Winter is dominated by rain-bearing cold fronts, and dry easterly winds prevail over summer. The growing season in the Wheatbelt is from May to October, during which time most of the region's rainfall—between 150 and 500 millimetres—is received. The coverage of native vegetation was crucial to maintaining the balance of the landscape during this time of concentrated rainfall, as its roots deep into the ground soaked up the moisture, preventing seepage into the water table below.

The environment of the Wheatbelt is one of remarkable contradictions. Its ancient, and in large parts, infertile landscape supports a gallery of unique wildlife. However, this wildlife exists in an incredibly finely balanced ecosystem, relying on an inter-relationship between natural vegetation and drainage systems to keep at bay a threat which lies within—the salt stored by the accumulation of the natural movement of ocean winds. Yet, it was only Aboriginal people who appreciated the beauty of this intrinsic, fine balance. Mostly European settlers did not. Few could see beyond its immediate challenges to the richness of its life-forms. Indeed, from the early days of European settlement, the typical view held that this was a land not worth preserving in its natural state. Casting European eyes across it, they judged it an 'uninviting landscape',[42] as did young English biologist Charles Darwin, who visited King George's Sound in 1836 on board the *Beagle*.

The early settlers found the lakes in their new surroundings quite unfamiliar and hardly worthy of preservation. The following is the account by an astonished early visitor to Western Australia:

> At home, a lake is known only as a sheet of water which seldom or never is dried up, and it is naturally associated in one's mind with pleasant and picturesque scenery, but here it is quite different … there is an air of desolation about these lakes which strikes the spectator at once … It is complete still life without one point of interest in it, as far as striking scenery goes, and totally different from anything I ever saw outside Australia.[43]

This inability to value the intrinsic qualities of the landscape was openly acknowledged. The Commissioners considering the opening up of the mallee country between Salmon Gums and Esperance in 1917 were of the view that 'the country in its virgin state is admittedly unattractive'.[44]

As late as the 1950s, similar sentiments were still being expressed. Hollywood celebrity, Art Linkletter, who took up farming near Esperance, has left the following account of his first visual encounter with the landscape he was to settle:

> As we came in from the coastline, I had my first view of Esperance from ten thousand feet. Seeing it for the first time I contemplated asking the stewardess for an airsick bag. My queasiness came not from turbulence in the air but from the forbidding character of the land. Away from the coast, it is an expanse of dismal, grey-brown soil pockmarked with what proved to be salt pans. Nowhere was there a splash of pasture green, and a strong wind was blowing dry, fine grit called bull dust over the bleak landscape.[45]

These attitudes form part of the explanation for the widespread clearing of the Wheatbelt.

ENVIRONMENTAL IMPACTS

Salinity is rapidly changing the face of the landscape in large areas of the Wheatbelt. Tom Hatton, who arrived in Perth in 1997, was aghast on his first trip through the region. He saw 'a vast landscape of cropping pastures dotted with saltpans and creek lines littered with dead trees'.[46] Struggling to find the words to explain the immensity of the problem to his colleagues in the eastern states, he says simply: 'Nothing in the east looks like this. It's truly unique.'

The scale of the clearing that occurred in the Wheatbelt is simply immense. Only 11 per cent of the original native vegetation cover remains.[47] Over recent years, much of this has been subject to pressures for clearing, and remains vulnerable to the further spread of salinity. It is not surprising therefore, that in February 2000, the prestigious scientific journal *Nature* named Western Australia's South-West, encompassing the Wheatbelt, as one of twenty-five global environmental hotspots singled out for its spectacular, internationally significant biodiversity and the extinction threats facing it.

According to work recently carried out for the State's Salinity Council, salinity is set to unleash biological devastation on the remaining flora and fauna of the region: hundreds of species of plants, birds, fish and animals are teetering on extinction. This will occur in a region which contains a baffling range and diversity of species; one of the richest in the world. Yet, the decline and almost certain loss of large numbers of species in the years to come has hardly rated a mention in the recent debates about the problem. Nor has the potential effectiveness of recent Federal Government biodiversity legislation in providing a framework for the protection of this area. In many ways, the protection of the remnant flora and fauna of the Wheatbelt is an early test case of the legislation and the capacity of the State Government to provide the on-going management needed. These issues are discussed in Chapter Six.

The environmental effects of salinity have spilled over into the region's rivers and streams. Observations and studies showing a connection between clearing and salination of waterways date from the turn of the twentieth century and were fully documented by the early 1980s.[48] Presently, more than one-third of the region's water resources are unusable due to increased salt levels, and stream salt loads are expected to increase five-fold over the next fifty years.[49]

ECONOMIC IMPACTS

Salinity will impact on the economics of agriculture in the region, and especially on the wheat industry. Only recently have there been any comprehensive studies which try to predict the extent of its impact. The National Land and Water Resources Audit of Dryland Salinity in Western Australia identifies broad economic impacts comprising risks to agriculture, infrastructure, and biodiversity.[50]

The State Government estimates that, at the current expected rate of the spread of salinity, an average of $30 million will be lost in the value of land each year for the next thirty years.[51] However, the national audit of dryland salinity estimates annual losses currently at $80 million per year, rising to $120 million per year over the next fifty years. [52] No matter which is the more accurate estimate, many of the region's farmers are starting to experience an economic crunch:

> In the past, landholders largely adapted to the cost of salinity by increasing production on unaffected land. They did this with improved technology, farm rationalisation, higher yielding varieties and other agricultural systems advances, or simply clearing more land and thus perpetuating the cycle. This will be increasingly difficult in the future as the resource base continues to deteriorate.[53]

Environmental activist, and now government policy officer, Keith Bradby, has been working with farmers in the Wheatbelt for more than two decades. He has seen the crunch coming: 'There's a lot of desperate blokes out there. What do you say to a farmer whose house is salt crusted up to the fourth layer of bricks. These people have now got salinity in their face.' Bradby can recall the attitude prevalent among farmers ten to fifteen years ago: 'Why should I fix salt when it's more economical for me to buy the farm next door and have two farms which are partly salty.'

Yet, as Bradby drives throughout the Wheatbelt today, the signs of change are everywhere: belts of trees growing along the creek lines and intersecting paddocks; remnant bushland fenced off; and contour banks carved into hill tops. But will these attempts to counteract salinity be enough to stave off major economic damage to the region? Bradby remains sceptical: 'In most areas, the changes are not making a fundamental difference.' This is also the conclusion of agricultural economists, David Pannell and Elizabeth Kington. Their study of the Upper Kent River Catchment concluded that although there was a high level of farmer attendance at Landcare events, and a high level of awareness about dryland salinity, the adoption of preventative practices was not on a sufficient scale to prevent continuing increases in salinity in the catchment area.[54]

Many farmers have been slow to respond with remedial measures. According to salinity consultant Mr Marty Ladyman, one-third, or less, of farmers are doing anything about salinity: 'Many are saying the right thing, but doing little.' Research conducted for the National Dryland Salinity Program explained the dilemma many farmers found themselves in:

> There is ample evidence that many farmers are aware of the consequences of land degradation and have a strong sense of responsibility to care for their land, but nonetheless continue to allow their land to degrade. The reason for this may be their inability to translate their awareness into action.[55]

Productivity gains in the wheat industry continue to underpin high returns and therefore limit incentives to engage in long-term investment to reduce the risks from salinity. The incentives are further diminished by the changing demographic profile of large parts of the region with many of the younger farmers leaving. Worsening the situation is the high debt structure of up to half the region's farmers, leaving them with limited capacity to fund remedial measures such as tree planting, or drainage.

Yet, there are deeper issues in the response of farmers to the crisis of salinity. The Industry Commission, a Commonwealth advisory body on economic issues, argues that a cost–benefit analysis of environmental repair flowing from land degradation may not, in many instances, favour extensive investment on the part of farmers: 'sometimes the highest returns can be obtained by slowing the rate of spread rather than halting or removing the degradation and sometimes by allowing degradation to increase'.[56] Evidence suggests that these economic realities are driving the practices of some farmers. Research conducted by McKenzie indicates a 'concern that some farmers are overcropping and overstocking in order to generate sufficient cash flows to remain economically viable'.[57] This may be a rational response to the longer term problems posed by salinity but it clearly contributes to a worsening of the problem.

More complex still is the extent to which farmers, as a group, are capable of fundamental change in the way they farm. Research shows that, in general, most farmers are cautious in adopting new farming methods:

> They come to any innovation with scepticism, uncertainty, prejudices and preconceptions and with an existing farming system that may or may not be operating as they would wish, but at least it is operating. Unless they are new to farming, they will have trialled other innovations in the past and concluded that some of them fell far short of the claims made for them. They will be particularly wary of a system that is radically different from that with which they are familiar and comfortable. They will almost certainly hold an attitude that the people advocating such a radical system do not understand the realities of farming, or at least of their farm.[58]

As salinity is the product of a farming system based on annual crops and pastures, adapted for wheat and sheep, overcoming farmer resistance to change is crucial in any long-term solution to salinity. Yet, this will be no easy task.

Two principal economic issues confront the future of agriculture. The first is the extent to which the industry will suffer from declining rates of productivity in the coming years, arising out of damage to crops from increased levels of salinity and/or from diminished access to productive land. Surprisingly, there are no available studies to show this impact. The second issue is a more fundamental one: to what extent is the industry compatible with ecologically sustainable development? In other words, in the face of the salinity threat can the industry—or at least significant parts of it—justify its continued existence?

Concerns over the lack of agriculture's sustainable basis date back several decades. In 1982, for example, G.A. Robertson, Chief of the Agriculture Department's Division of Resource Management, gave a talk on farming practices at the Esperance Civic Centre pointing out that more appropriate farming systems needed to be developed in much of the Wheatbelt: 'It is quite apparent that we have not developed an appropriate stable farming system for the south coast nor indeed for many areas north of here ... A system more attuned to the environmental conditions of the region, a system that will be stable in the long term.'[59]

Two decades later, the challenge to devise an environmentally sustainable farming system remains, but the issues have become even more urgent. In the year 2000, CSIRO called for 'a revolution in land use' in Australia based around the following considerations:

– Current farming systems are the fundamental cause of the dryland salinity problem;
– Under best management practice, the leakage from most agricultural land still far exceeds the capacity of the landscape to shed the excess water;
– For most of the country we do not have profitable systems to replace existing land use;
– Even if we did introduce very different farming systems immediately, it would be a long time before we saw an improvement in salt trends.

Current government mechanisms to address such deficiencies lack clear definition and force. In 1992, Federal and state governments adopted a National Strategy for Ecologically Sustainable Development which committed them to safeguarding the welfare of future generations; to protecting biological diversity; and to maintaining essential ecological processes. However, as the Industry Commission has pointed out, these are little more than fine sounding words: 'they do not define what should be done with any precision. Moreover there are significant differences of opinion as to what needs to be done.'[60] The crux of the problem is the ambiguity of the term 'sustainable'. According to one critic, this ambiguity serves the broader political purpose of maintaining 'an uneasy alliance between naturally hostile groups'; that is, conservationists and the developers of commercial agriculture.[61] These groups have conflicting philosophical interests which have been obscured by the prevailing rhetoric of ecologically sustainable development. The wheat industry is a particular case in point. Although the wheat industry is the major contributor to the current and future salinity crisis, we do not know what an ecologically sustainable wheat industry might look like and, even whether it is feasible. Yet, at the very least, the community is entitled to ask at what point will the continuation of the industry in its current form conflict with the emerging goals of valuing and maintaining the remaining natural ecosystems of the region: the rivers, wetlands and remnant vegetation? The efforts of Agriculture Western Australia to deal with sustainability are examined in the last chapter.

Such a consideration is even more relevant in light of a recent proposal by the Industry Commission for a statutory duty of care to be applied to the environment.[62] This was indeed a far-reaching suggestion, challenging the traditional approach to land degradation that comprises a combination of volunteerism, education and cooperation.[63] The fact that such a proposal has been considered by a mainstream economic advisory body illustrates the extent to which a rethink of land-use patterns is occurring in Australia. The proposed 'duty' advocated by the Commission would 'require everyone who influences the management of the risks to the environment to take all "reasonable and practical" steps to prevent harm to the environment that could have been reasonably foreseen'. To give effect to its proposal, the Commission maintains that duty of care towards the environment should represent an extension and codification of the common law duty of care which is concerned with minimising any harm that one person may cause another. The codification of this duty 'will clearly establish in the minds of all concerned, that protecting the environment is a continuous legal and social responsibility'.[64] Whether or not the proposal will find support in government, it resurrects the question of the role of law and of obligation in the protection of the environment,[65] for which the ongoing threat of salinity in the Wheatbelt serves as a graphic example.

For many, issues of duty of care and ethical responsibilities to the environment are, at best, marginal concerns. However, the futures of the cereal and pastoral industries are clouded in more immediate uncertainty. This concerns the issue of funding a reversal of current levels of salinity and its future prevention. A case could be created to view government funding for salinity as a subsidy to these industries; in other words the industry could not exist—at least in its current price structure—without such funding. From this perspective, the cereal and pastoral industries might be argued to be uneconomic and concerns might be raised internationally by countries that Australia has severely criticised for providing subsidies to its agricultural industries. At the very least, sustainable agriculture may be necessary to gain advantage in some markets. As the Western Australian Government's own *State of the Environment Report* argues:

> Demonstrating sustainability is becoming an increasingly important economic driver, necessary to access international markets and receive premium prices. Those countries and industries that can show that their products are safe to eat and have been produced to ecologically sustainable, best practice principles (in other words, Clean and Green) are likely to enjoy an increasing market advantage.[66]

Some researchers are approaching the revolution called for in Australian agriculture as an exciting challenge. John Bartle, Director of the

Department of Conservation and Land Management's Farm Forestry Unit, envisages a very different landscape in the Wheatbelt from that which now exists. He sees the landscape covered in rows of new perennial crops linked to emerging industrial products in the transportation fuel and electricity industries. It is a bold vision coupling salinity control with the needs of a more environmentally friendly, twenty-first century economy. Importantly, it is an optimistic vision in an otherwise pessimistic outlook of worsening salinity problems. An outline of this vision for the Wheatbelt is included in Chapter Seven.

Apart from its major impact on agriculture, salinity has several other economic impacts. The national audit on dryland salinity estimates that approximately 20 per cent of all road and rail networks are currently affected, a figure which could rise to 40 per cent by 2050.[67] The cost of repairing the road system alone is estimated to be currently in excess of $500 million. By 2050, this cost is estimated to rise by a further $288 million. Protection of native vegetation also incurs economic costs, estimated at more than $60 million a year.[68]

SOCIAL IMPACTS

The Wheatbelt has already extracted a huge toll in human hardship and suffering. Many of the 'new-land' farmers of the 1950s and '60s were forced off their land crippled by debt, poor prices, and unviable blocks. Now, salinity is beginning to have direct impacts on communities: farms cannot sell because they have become too saline; houses and businesses in country towns are suffering structural damage, as is the surrounding infrastructure such as roads and recreational facilities.

The emergence of salinity as a major threat to rural communities has come on top of a range of external factors underpinning rural decline in large parts of the Wheatbelt. In her study, McKenzie found that many farmers were struggling to remain optimistic in the face of the power of global markets, demographic change, declining government services and the pressure to get big or get out.[69] Not surprisingly, the fabric of rural communities is taking a battering. Many farmers 'expressed regret and concern about the dwindling rural population and the shriveling sense of community'. Salinity intensifies this loss of confidence while, at the same time, undermining the social value of farming as an occupation. Research by Hammill shows that the rise of urban-based environmental concerns regarding land degradation is having a damaging psychological impact on farmers.[70] Having perceived themselves for years as engaged in a 'morally good' enterprise of growing food 'to feed the masses', farmers now feel targeted as the environmental destroyers. Changing government policy has heightened the sense of uncertainty about their place in the world. Whereas for decades they were told to clear as much of their land as possible, now they are being compelled to protect at all costs what little remains. This loss of a sense of purpose may result in frustration, despair and anger in some farmers before a sense of acceptance is reached. Some may not be able to rise to the challenge of developing new farming systems or rural enterprises. As salinity spreads it may also become harder to sustain the commitment of some Landcare groups to the value of the work in which they have been engaged. However, the human face of salinity remains unpredictable and, to date, largely unknown. It would be surprising if an environmental threat on the scale of salinity did not impact adversely on many people, notwithstanding the stronger sense of community which has traditionally characterised rural communities.

Country towns face an equally uncertain future. Little public attention has been given to their plight but as many as forty are facing substantial damage to buildings, roads, airstrips and railway lines from salinity. Many locals are reported to be reluctant to talk about the full extent of the damage for fear of adverse impacts on property values.[71] Others remain in denial about the extent and severity of the problem.

The geographic location of many Wheatbelt towns in low parts of the landscape made sense in the early decades of the twentieth century when they were planned around the building of the railway and close to what was then a fresh water source in the creek or river. However, the widespread clearing of surrounding native vegetation has placed these towns dangerously close to the rising water table. Worsening their plight have been decisions taken decades ago to make available an abundant town water supply, replacing the lesser supplies dependent on either windmills or rainwater collection systems. Excess town water now seeps into the water table.

If too little is done to protect Wheatbelt towns from a rising water table, some will not survive; they will be further ravaged by the corrosive effects of salination. The first efforts to address these problems have only recently been taken by Agriculture WA through the Rural Towns Program which has undertaken an audit of the problem in twenty-nine Wheatbelt towns, with the expectation of working with local communities to devise feasible solutions. The CSIRO is conducting similar trials in other towns. Information from these studies will raise sensitive

issues about the towns most at risk. Disclosure of findings from this research will likely have a major impact on the values of many properties. Desperate measures are already being taken in some towns: water is being pumped out from the water table to buy a breathing space while longer term solutions are found; other communities have raised the

level of their recreational facilities to stave off their destruction.

Preliminary estimates suggest the cost is likely to run into several million dollars in each community. This, too, raises difficult issues for the State Government. Will it be economically feasible to ensure the survival of all affected towns? By what measures do we value the worth of these towns? Many are already experiencing population decline and increased ageing profiles. Even without the impact of salinity, many people face uncertain futures due to the steady decline in the terms of trade for agriculture and the lack of alternative economic futures. The impact of salinity will intensify discussion about the social viability of some of these rural communities. As studies have shown, the impacts of deregulation of agriculture and new technology have lowered on-farm labour requirements which, combined with the withdrawal of both government and private sector services, have created multiplier effects in many Wheatbelt towns to the point where their sustainability as viable social units is questionable.[72]

In all, the human impacts of salinity have received little public attention. Yet, the potential consequences are profound. Do we want people to populate the regional landscape and, at what price are we prepared to rescue it from salinity to ensure communities remain viable? These issues are taken up in Chapter 5.

Little recognition has been given so far to the impacts on Aboriginal people of the spread of salinity in the Wheatbelt. Yet the impacts are quite extensive and should be acknowledged as the Noongar people are the traditional custodians of this land, still retaining strong cultural links. However, it is beyond the scope of this book to provide a detailed account of these associations and linkages to the land. Aboriginal people's connections to the remote parts of this landscape—disrupted by the process of settlement—are only recently being recovered by Aboriginal people themselves. This reconnection is being facilitated by indigenous elders whose local traditions have recaptured the Wheatbelt as a place of Dreaming, in which their understanding of salinity is a central part. The 'Dreaming' refers to Aboriginal spirituality that emphasises the need to have carers for the environment, who pass their responsibility from one generation to the next.

In 1993, Conservation and Land Management (CALM) employee Noel Nannup led a group of Aboriginal elders (which included Ralph Winmar and Angus Wallum) on a tour to the heart of the Wheatbelt. It was the first time in over forty years that most had been to the area of the Dreaming Trails which, in Aboriginal cosmology, divide the inland saltwater country of the Yamatji and Wongi peoples from the freshwater drainage systems which dominate the country occupied by the Noongar people.

Noel Nannup recalls his conversations with the Elders:

In March 1994 at the request of Mr Angus Wallam, I accompanied him on a journey from Wagin to Jillikin Rock, which is about 20 kilometres east of Kulin. As we travelled, Angus told me how he could remember his grandfather telling him about the Trail. He recalled being told about people travelling up the river; that's the Blackwood from the coast to Puntapin Rock near Wagin, then on to Wave Rock, which is an important meeting place for Noongars and Wongis. I was told that I would see Jarrah trees growing at Jillikin Rock (near Kulin). These trees had grown from seed taken out there by Noongar people in the early days. Angus said that he did not know of any Jarrah trees that grew any further to the east of there. And CALM doesn't know either. On arrival at Jillikin Rock, Angus was upset to find the largest of the Jarrah trees had been cut down … We climbed to the top of the rock and looked north east out over Jillikin Lake. In the distance I could see standing about the horizon what Angus assured me, was Wave Rock … We then looked back towards Wagin. We could see a chain of lakes stretching off into the distance. These lakes no doubt had provided the people with a natural trail through this area before it was cleared.

As Noel Nannup conveyed:

Aboriginal people had an intimate understanding of the natural drainage systems of the region, and the natural divide that exists between fresh-water and saltwater landscapes. Further, they understood the important role that natural vegetation cover played in preventing the movement of saltwater in the landscape, especially during episodic flooding events. When the descendants of the traditional owners, displaced from their traditional country, worked as hands clearing the landscape of mallee roots, some were able to convince farmers to leave tracts of native bush; their knowledge of the environment making an impression on a few farmers.

The spread of salinity has disturbing elements for many Noongar people. One of these is the disruption to the belief in caring for country. As a recent collection of interviews with Noongar people testified, their belief in this important principle still remains strong. As Richard Wilkes explains: 'The land … the trees are part of the land and therefore it's part of our spiritual Dreaming … too much of our forest and our land has been cleared and this is why we have the water level rising like it is all throughout, and the salinity is set in.'[73] Aden Eades expresses a similar sadness: 'We have been taught that we are part of the land ... To me I have a right to express my concerns for the future of our kids who are losing our culture—our heritage and our whole existence, it all just passes away with progress ... I mean they're clearing the farms, many of the farms have been cleared too much. The country has been destroyed.'[74]

A further disturbing element arising from the spread of salinity is the direct impact on Aboriginal cultural heritage sites. As Noel Nannup explains:

The Dreaming Trails follow natural drainage lines which occupy the lowest parts of the landscape, such as those valley floors that are highly susceptible to rising ground water tables. These Dreaming Trails were also the places burial sites were located. Therefore, both Dreaming Trails and the burial sites along their edges are at risk from salinisation. If a site turns to salt, its significance is lost or changed. The tragedy is that it is only in recent times that youth from Wheatbelt towns are being shown this cultural heritage.

POLITICAL IMPACTS

A disaster on the scale of Wheatbelt salinity deserves some close examination of the system of government which has overseen its spread. How much did governments know about what would happen? Why haven't they been more decisive in finding and funding solutions? As awareness of the extent of the potential crisis has slowly spread, the shortcomings of political responses have become more apparent. There has been informed understanding of the extent and causes of salinity since the mid-1920s, and especially since the 1950s. However, governments have appeared unwilling to take the problem seriously. In 1970, a Senate Select Committee on Water Pollution heard evidence from numerous Western Australian witnesses testifying to the existence of salinity but it was unable to come to terms with the scale of the problem: 'There can be no doubt that salinity is one of the most serious water problems facing Western Australia today but just how serious was impossible for us to determine.'[75] In the late 1980s a Western Australian Parliamentary Select Committee called for urgent action, but none followed. Everywhere there was denial: 'farming interests, politicians and the community at large did not want to accept that there could be major environmental problems. As a consequence, virtually no research effort was put into understanding the true nature and pattern of dryland salinity ... until it was virtually too late.'[76]

Explaining this inaction is not an easy task. The lack of political will that has existed on the salinity problem is certainly tied to the perpetuation of ideas about economic development. Australian governments, and especially state governments, have traditionally had strong ideological ties to the positive benefits of development, through the exploitation of natural resources. As Chapters Two and Three show, strong political expressions of this view continued well into the 1980s. In turn, this created a climate within the State Government and its agencies which minimised real appreciation of the effects of salinity. As late as the 1980s, land was being released without a holistic approach, as Richards observed:

> No broad-scale assessment of land-use needs for the present and the future has been carried out in WA. Each proposal for release of, say 15–20 blocks of 2,000 ha each, is considered as a self-contained unit. The proposal is not related to the broad needs of the State ... In the absence of this analysis and without the benefit of all the concomitant surveys of the land, its natural inhabitants are lost before their existence is even known.[77]

Therefore, no clear voice was present to warn about salinity in agencies whose job it should have been to bring before the State Government the potential for serious problems to arise. Moreover, salinity is a complex issue to explain to the public and not an especially attractive topic for commercial television news which clamours for issues with emotive appeal and very powerful images. For these reasons, salinity was allowed to slip through the cracks of government priorities, especially during the 1970s and '80s when there was a compelling case for action. Given this poor record, some now argue that the case for government action has a moral dimension. Agricultural researcher Ted Lefroy puts the case succinctly: the moral responsibility is 'either to repair the damage done or cease any pretense of commitment to the concepts of sustainability or inter-generational equity contained in the National Strategy for Ecologically Sustainable Development endorsed by state and federal governments'.[78]

However compelling, the 'moral dimension' confronts the political realities of the salinity problem. As a general rule, political parties are reluctant to commit large resources to problems where the electoral gains are uncertain. Salinity certainly fits this rule. It occurs mostly on private land and in rural electorates dominated at the state level by traditional loyalties to the National Party (once known as the Country Party). Thus, the two major parties (Liberal and Labor) have, until very recently, felt no great urgency about it. Current commitments are widely described as inadequate, raising the suggestion that both major parties are reluctant to fully fund salinity by either imposing a special purpose tax or redirecting funds from existing programs in metropolitan electorates.

More profound still, the ability to mount effective measures against salinity may confront the limitations of a democratic political system. Firstly, doubts exist about the capacity of modern liberal democratic states to embrace environmental issues. Crowley argues the case that 'in practice the state's response to ecological demands is very often dictated by economic and strategic demands', leaving it vulnerable 'to political bargaining and trade-offs against human interests'.[79] Salinity presents a compelling case in support of this perspective as the very limited responses initiated during the 1970s and '80s, outlined in Chapter Three, testify. In short, the economic imperatives of agriculture have tended to outweigh consideration of long-term environmental costs, and the intrinsic value of the environment.

The limits of democratic government are faced in other ways. Salinity highlights the tension in Australia's two-tiered system of government. Even though, as pointed out in Chapter Two, the Commonwealth was deeply involved in the approval and funding of the

IMPORTANT

opening up of the Wheatbelt, it has, until recently, left to the State Government the major responsibility for the management of the on-going problems. The reality of Australia's modern federal system is that the states are largely dependent upon the Commonwealth for financial assistance, leaving them with reduced capacity to fund major new initiatives on the scale demanded by the salinity crisis. Thus, in many environmental issues federalism has led to a damaging imbalance in the capacity of government to effect change: the states have the power to deal with environmental problems but lack the funds while the Commonwealth often lacks the constitutional power but retains the greater financial means. These forces can be seen at work in recent debates about funding a salinity rescue as outlined in Chapter Four.

There are still more practical limits to government action on an issue like salinity. Its occurrence on mostly private land raises difficulties imposed by both law and public opinion. Can governments compel farmers to act in certain ways? What legislative controls could governments establish to direct economic activities on private land? Could governments ever gain community consensus for expenditure of the expected massive funds needed to stave off the worst predictions of salinity-induced degradation? Potential problems also arise from the funding of programs to manage dryland salinity. If, as many farmers argue, funds should be passed on directly to individual farmers to manage on-ground works, might this simply constitute a subsidy to individuals who, it could be argued, should have been more responsible for the guardianship of their land in the first place? Agricultural economist David Pannell sums up this view: 'Some would argue that there is no justification for spending public money to preserve what is really a private asset—that salinity treatments intended to conserve agricultural land should be considered by farmers on their economic merits and paid for by farmers if they chose to do so.'[80]

The private versus public issues are but one of the dilemmas facing governments. Showing leadership on effecting solutions to salinity is likely to tax the best of governments. As John Bartle has argued: 'Both the problem and the solution are such big, dispersed, and complex problems that they appear to be beyond resolution.'[81] The call he and others are making to construct a new economic future in the nation's cereal cropping regions will require long-term planning and investment. A CSIRO research paper outlines the scope of this new economy. It is to facilitate the transition from the hydrocarbon economy to the carbohydrate economy using plant material to produce ethanol and methanol as replacements for oil-based fuels and related products. Western Australia could be a significant player in this future with the large-scale planting of deep-rooted perennials, especially Oil Mallee trees, which are highly effective producers of these products.[82] Yet, the scale of action needed to facilitate such a transition is immense and requires high levels of government commitment working in partnership with industry. The work already underway in this area—which is a small pointer to a rejuvenated future for parts of the Wheatbelt—is discussed in Chapter Seven.

All the questions dealing with the problems salinity poses for our political system are not as difficult to define as they are to provide meaningful answers for; the point is that in a democracy—however revered this is as a model for governing—there are limits to government action imposed principally by law and public opinion but, more broadly still, by the economic framework of the free enterprise system. Addressing salinity—in light of these constraints—will therefore be difficult.

Certainly, the lack of a state of readiness, or commitment, among state and national governments is making the inevitability of a crisis all the more real. Despite the substantial commitment of funds to programs such as Landcare and the National Heritage Fund, and despite changes in on-farm land management practices in some areas, the nation is not well prepared to forestall the worst affects of salinity. The scale of the problem overwhelms most affected farmers and rural communities. Yet, until very recently Australian government responses to salinity—and to land degradation in general—were poorly planned and funded and, many argue, remain so. A case for major change in the way in which government addresses land management problems has recently been made by the Industry Commission, which catalogued extensive shortcomings in current approaches.[83] These included a lack of relevant data on the environment from which better management practices can be developed; a lack of clarity about objectives and achievements of many environmental programs; overlapping and poor coordination between government agencies at all three levels of government; and major gaps in the generation and dissemination of information to farmers to enable them to farm in more environmentally sensitive ways. In short, our failure to respond to salinity has been dogged by a lack of political leadership and weaknesses in the institutions of government. In the case of Western Australia, it may not be an exaggeration to claim the existence of salinity on such a threatening level represents a failure of our democratic system. Successive State Governments and bureaucratic administrations have repeatedly ignored expert advice and parliamentary reports and, in so doing, have exacerbated the current crisis.

The massive problems from salinity now facing governments generally serve as an illustration of our conflicting relationship with nature. Exploiting the land for economic purposes can build prosperity—but only in the short term—unless economic activity is constructed on a sustainable basis. Separating economics from the environment as has frequently happened throughout the long history of western development—and which lies at the root of the problems in the Wheatbelt—will eventually create further economic costs as well as strictly environmental ones. The challenge now facing governments—both state and federal—in rectifying this history of damage and neglect is an enormous one. However, they face a dilemma in approaching this task. Prevailing beliefs in economic rationalism—characterised by moves towards 'smaller government', reduced services, and notions of efficiency—stand at odds with the need for the substantial assistance widely seen as necessary to deal with salinity. If government does not provide the needed assistance, who is capable of doing so? Farmers? Local communities? Business enterprises? Critics of economic rationalism have raised concerns about the promotion by government of locally based solutions to land degradation.[84] The rhetoric of local participation can mask a broader government agenda: 'Participatory programs are relatively inexpensive and can legitimise a non-interventionist role

of the state.' In short, governments may no longer have the commitment to the type of government action needed to address the problem.
This issue is taken up in greater detail in Chapter Four.

Parallel to the issue of where major responsibility should lie for the
salinity crisis, is the more difficult issue of whether it will be possible to
repair the damage salinity has caused in large parts of the Wheatbelt.
Much of the rhetoric contained in the State's Salinity Strategy (2000)
is couched in terms of solving the problem.[85] Yet, the scale of the potential damage is so great that some argue the most realistic approach is to
adapt to large-scale salinity in the landscape. Certainly, all the available
mechanisms to deal with salinity—including tree planting, drainage,
and commercial deep-rooted crops—carry scientific, political, and/or
economic costs. These issues are raised in Chapter Seven.

For over a century salinity has been a barometer of our attitudes
towards nature. The aggressive development ethos of earlier generations
has given way to a greater appreciation of the natural environment.
Salinity is now seen as a major environmental threat. What remains
largely unknown is the extent to which this realisation will be transformed into forging a new relationship between people and the landscape in the Wheatbelt.

PART ──⨁──────────────

THE SPREAD OF SALINITY AND RESPONSES TO IT, 1900–1990s

'nearly 4,000 acres of farmland are lost [worldwide] to excess salt every year.'

Source: International Food Policy Research Institute; as quoted in *The West Australian*, 16 February 2001.

CHAPTER 2

The Opening Up of the Wheatbelt, 1917–1970s

Australia's worst case of dryland salinity originated in a bold vision for the social and economic development of the State that was shared by all Western Australian Governments in the decades after the turn of the twentieth century. This vision centred on harnessing the resources of government to turn a vast expanse of the southern part of the State into an agricultural region based around the harvesting and export of wheat. In the feverish release of lands which occurred especially after the First World War, governments hoped that wheat would secure the economic future of the State, become a means to attract settlers to fill its vast empty spaces, and provide a solid base for employment. This vision formed the beginnings in Western Australia of the 'ideology of development', which sustained government involvement in land clearing and agricultural expansion for the next eighty years. Many people took up the opportunity of sharing in one the nation's great land release programs.

Yet, the link between this policy and the current spread of salinity is often overlooked. For example, neither the 1988 Parliamentary inquiry into salinity, nor the Court–Cowan Coalition Government's Salinity Strategy offered any historical explanation for salinity. Where official explanation is offered, the role played by government has been downplayed. For example, one government agency recently wrote:

'Agricultural development involved replacing large expanses of native vegetation with cereal crops and pastures. This brought about a major environmental change largely unforeseen by the settlers.'[1] Missing from this version of history is the extent of governments' knowledge about the salinity problem and its potential impact on farmers. In fact, at the very beginning of the agricultural expansion, experts implored government not to allow the wholesale opening up of the Wheatbelt to farming. Thus, alongside the success of the wheat industry is the parallel story of how successive State Governments permitted the environment of this area to be degraded in the pursuit of unsustainable agricultural practices.

FIRST WAVE OF EXPANSION

In the early 1900s, Western Australia was at an economic crossroads: steadily declining returns from gold mining induced a feeling of gloom about the future; not only were jobs scarce, but also the State could not produce sufficient wheat for its own needs. It was threatened with 'a serious loss of population with all its calamitous effects'.[2] The State's future prosperity rested on its people's ability to develop an alternative export income. The solution was largely seen in an expansion of the State's fledging wheat industry.[3] There was much to recommend it for the scale of rapid agricultural expansion envisaged by State Governments. Firstly, input costs were low: seed and seeding were relatively inexpensive and, unlike sheep farming, wheat did not require expensive fencing. Wheat production also allowed the maximum possible return in the shortest period of time. More attractive still was the boom in worldwide demand and the consequent high prices which marked the first decade of the twentieth century. Sir William Crooks, President of the British Association for the Advancement of Science, embodied the belief in the glowing future awaiting wheat farmers when he

> asserted that all civilised nations stood in deadly peril of not having enough to eat. He declared that the area for wheat was not being increased in proportion to consumption, and that, should

all wheat growing countries add to their areas to the utmost capacity, on the most careful calculation the effort would give only an additional 100,000,000 acres, which with an average of 12 bushels to the acre, would be just sufficient to supply the increase in population amongst bread-eaters till the year 1930.[4]

However buoyant the future of the wheat industry looked at the turn of the century, there was less reason for optimism by the 1920s. In fact, little account was taken by government of past and future trends in world wheat prices when planning the expansion of the Wheatbelt. In fact, prices began to decline during the 1920s when new wheat lands around the world—such as in Canada and the United States—came into production. As Snooks has argued: 'The development of the Wheatbelt in the second half of the 1920s was pursued in the face of numerous indications that further expansion was not economically justified.'[5] The poor planning behind the expansion was indication that economic arguments were only part of the motivation. There was also the prevailing belief in the superiority of rural life; that 'every man should have a chance to be a farmer', and in choosing such a life 'a man showed himself more deserving than the parasites in the city, because he was attempting to add to the real productivity of Western Australia'.[6] The cultural value attached to the ideal of farming made the State Government's land release schemes very popular.

Even with this degree of confidence to support their plans, the expansion of the wheat industry is the stuff of legend. Driving it was the 'vision and dynamic energy' of James Mitchell who, in 1909, was appointed Minister for Lands and Agriculture. Mitchell, a strong man who was 'determined to brook no interference with his plans', pushed the boundaries of the wheat frontier steadily eastwards from Northam. His restless and energetic approach became characteristic of land development in the Wheatbelt over the next seventy years. After locating land thought suitable for agriculture,

the next thing to do was to change the policy of 'selection before survey' to 'survey before selection'. The former was too slow and

wasteful of time for Mitchell. Then came the problem of surveying these millions of acres. The departmental surveyors were too
few and all were required for organisation and administration.
The available contract surveyors in and outside the State were
then engaged, all 37 of them. This number was still insufficient
for the impetuous Minister and so to each was assigned an assis-
tant capable of handling a theodolite [a survey instrument]. Very
soon there were 74 theodolites in the field, mapping out land for
settlement. Work and speed were the watchwords of land settlement. Soon there were millions of acres surveyed into 1,000 acre
blocks.[7]

Within thirty years, wheat production had seen spectacular
growth: from just over 200,000 acres in 1900 to over 4.5 million acres
by 1930.[8] A significant component of the land released in this early
phase came under the Commonwealth/State Soldier Settlement Agreement which purchased land for over 5,000 returned soldiers, many of
whom were rushed onto properties where they were 'compelled year
after year to put wheat in on unproductive wheat lands'.[9]

Achievements on this scale would not have been possible without
the active assistance of government. In fact, Glynn has argued that the
role adopted by successive governments amounted to an 'induced' form
of economic development because the most important decisions were
being taken at the political level as a matter of government policy.[10] The
operation of this policy has been defined as the ideology of developmentalism.[11] It meant that government adopted a powerful position as
a shaper of economic policy—and beyond that, society—as it pursued
interventionist policies to overcome economic disadvantage. Developmentalism, it is argued, best thrives in conservative political cultures
and, in Western Australia, its powerful appeal was used to cultivate feelings of loyalty to the State and to generate 'an inflated rhetoric of
Western Australian greatness'.[12]

The instruments of government policy used as inducements
included the provision of cheap land, and the rapid extension of railways into the wheat districts and, importantly, the ready availability of

developmental capital through the creation of the State Agricultural Bank. It was this last initiative which made Western Australia unique. Whereas as other states were generally content to provide the infrastructure and allow market forces to dictate the results, in Western Australia the provision of a substantial assistance scheme to farmers brought wheat production 'under the wing of the state'.[13] Of particular encouragement to farmers was the advance made by the Agricultural Bank for clearing the land equal to the full value of the work performed. In these generous ways, it has been claimed that many landless people were settled on the land representing 'an achievement not hitherto attempted in any part of the world'.[14] The centenary history of Western Australia also noted the uniqueness of the social experiment in opening up agriculture to working men and women:

> Wheat land is cheaper than elsewhere in the Commonwealth; the land laws are generous; payments for land are spread over long periods; and the Agricultural Bank is the most liberal financial institution to be found in any country. Every facility is afforded to the man with little or no money to obtain a farm of his own.[15]

However, ability and willingness to work were crucial to success. Until the end of the First World War clearing heavily timbered country was often done by axe, and hand-made rollers. Greble describes the process:

> In the forest and woodland areas, the trees are generally chopped down during the autumn, winter and spring—the larger trees axe handle high, and the smaller level with the ground. The term used for this latter operation is 'mullenizing'. The chopping is done so that the trees fall all the one way, for practical felling reasons and in order to assist in securing a running fire when the burning takes place in the succeeding summer. In the lighter timbered country it is customary to pack the stumps of the bigger trees with the undergrowth. On the mallee and other thicket country, as well as on the heavy scrub 'plain', the light timber or scrub is chopped

down or rolled down—usually with farm-made rollers constructed from old steam boilers, huge logs, or with lighter logs bolted to a metal framework.

Even clearing by axe alone, a strong, skillful worker could clear between half and one acre a day, although the process of stacking and burning was a much slower job.[16] But evidence of development could be found all over the expanding wheat frontier. Burning operations after mid-February 'darkened the sky with smoke by day and left myriads of twinkling log-fires at night'.[17]

Under pressure to get the quickest return, the pioneer farmer cut down the largest area possible in the shortest period of time. In fact, the early decades of the wheat industry were characterised by something akin to a speculative boom, notwithstanding the isolation, primitive conditions and hardships endured by most of the early settlers. Men with little or no farming experience were attracted to wheat growing either as a means of avoiding unemployment or as a method of acquiring wealth quickly: 'the land was cheap, and as long as a boom was developing it was possible to clear a farm and sell it for a profit after a few years'.[18]

The scale of assistance to farmers is most easily revealed through the growth in State debt, rising from £12.7 million in 1900 to over $71 million by 1930. Throughout the 1920s, expenditure on railways and agricultural expansion accounted for roughly 60 per cent of total State Government expenditures.[19]

EARLY STUDIES ON SALINITY

The remarkable fact about this early expansionist phase of the Wheatbelt was its occurrence after the link between salinity and land clearing became a widely talked about and established fact. Interestingly, it was railway and water supply engineers who first linked the two. Prominent among these was W.E. Wood, Inspecting Engineer with the Railways Department, whose published paper to the Western Australian Royal Society is often cited as a landmark in understanding the salinity problem. Wood was a resourceful, jack-of-all-trades in his native South Australia before arriving in Western Australia in 1894, where he worked on various surveying projects before joining the Railways Department in 1914.

As his paper to the Royal Society explains, Wood arrived in the West with an interest in salinity having observed it in the agricultural district of Yorke Peninsula (South Australia) in the early 1890s. Not long after he arrived in the West, he 'heard it suggested that destruction of the native vegetation turned the water in the creeks salt'.[20] As he went on to explain, by 1905 a number of railway water supplies had become too salty for commercial use in boilers, necessitating 'a lot of time and thought to the problem' be given by engineers preceding his appointment. Simultaneously, in 1909, N.C. Reynoldson, an engineer with the Country Water Supply, which operated the Kalgoorlie water pipeline and supplied water to railway steam engines, noted a sudden rise in salinity in one coastal reservoir. Comparing the different inflows from the various tributaries he noted that the most saline water came from catchments that had been the most heavily cleared. He recommended that further clearing be stopped and that cleared land be resumed and reafforested.[21] Action was taken to reafforest the area surrounding Mundaring Weir when it was found to have gone salty after the turn of the century.[22]

If the State Government remained uninformed of these findings, the same could not be said of the 1917 Royal Commission on the Mallee Belt and Esperance Lands. The underlying purpose of the Commission had been to create the case for an extension of the railway so as to facilitate the expansion of the wheat industry. But from the outset the Commission was forced to face up to—and dismiss—the problem of salinity. At a crucial early phase of the eastward expansion of the wheat industry, the Commission was told by two soil experts that salinity was a major obstacle to the opening up of this region. However, Commissioners set out to discredit these expert witnesses and to manipulate the findings of the Report which was drawn largely from the evidence of a few recently arrived farmers who had not yet experienced the problem. Without doubt the most prominent witness to appear before the inquiry was the Professor of Agriculture at the University of Western Australia. John Patterson.

Trained in both Edinburgh and Leipzig in agricultural chemistry, Patterson had undertaken extensive testing of the salt content of the soils in the region under review. He had spent fifteen days driving over the lands between Norseman and Esperance in the company of Commissioners, during which time over seventy soil samples were taken. In presenting his report to the Commission on his findings, Patterson arrived at some disturbing conclusions. He found that half of the soil in the area had salt concentrations too high for profitable farming; one-sixth was of doubtful use and only one-third useful. It came as a blow to the plans of Commissioners for a favourable set of findings.

To counter Patterson's evidence, Commissioners continually prodded recently settled farmers in the district into giving glowing accounts of the potential for wheat growing and to downplay any concerns about salinity. James Lewis, for example, told Commissioners:

> I grew crops right down in a lake, and yet I have been unable to scrape up enough salt to cure a bullock's hide. In my opinion we are a little deficient in salt in our country, and if there were a little more salt we would be better. Chairman: do you think there is anything in the statement that there is too much salt down your way to grow wheat? It is a scandalous report, and there is no truth in it. There is hardly enough salt down there.[23]

Interestingly, a dissenting voice was heard from one farmer. Alexander Richardson, pastoralist and Trustee of the Agricultural Bank told Commissioners:

> In the Eastern districts where salt, owing to clearing, is accumulating both the wheat and the grass die. Several salt pans in those districts which were not there originally have come of late years, and when the salt gets beyond the point of tolerance, not only will the wheat not grow, but the grass will not grow.[24]

Richardson's evidence is all the more telling given his official position with the Bank. This institution, after all, was underwriting the expansion of the wheat industry into the very region he claimed to be unsuitable.

The second expert witness, Thomas Mann, faced a torrid encounter at the hands of Commissioners. Mann was employed by the Department of Agriculture as a chemist and he had analysed soil samples supplied to him from the Esperance region in 1912, the findings from which formed the basis of his evidence to the Commission. He informed the Commission that these soil samples contained 'greatly exceeded salt content'. Moreover, he regarded it as a matter 'of ordinary official duty' to draw the Department's attention to this fact: 'I pointed out that agriculture on this land must be considered hazardous.' Mann then revealed he had come under considerable pressure as a result of his findings and recommendations. These had been 'subject to considerable criticism' and 'public interest' which had recently compelled him to review them:

> Realising the importance of the matter, not only to the settlers on the Esperance lands but to the State as a whole, I have again gone most carefully into the whole question … I regret to say that the fullest possible search has resulted not only in confirming my previous opinion, but has shown that even stronger justification exists than I previously supposed.[25]

Following this statement, Mann was questioned by the Commission's Chairman, Charles Dempster, Northam farmer and politician, and fellow Commissioner, Matthew Padbury. Their approach was clearly designed to undermine the credibility of Mann's findings and cast doubt on his professionalism. Dempster asked: 'If some samples came from, say, salt lakes, salt pans, and other parts where farming would be impossible, the value of a report as to the agricultural worth of a district would be discounted if the origin of those samples were not taken into account.' Mann's reply was measured: 'Certainly, but it was reasonable to suppose that the officer who was testing the land for wheat growing would take samples with that objective. In making a survey of the land for wheat growing, it was reasonable to suppose that the samples would not be taken from salt lakes or salt pans.' This was not sufficient explanation for Commissioner Padbury who asked: 'Unless you know the samples have been taken in a proper manner, you are not in a position to report as to the quality of the soil for wheat growing?' All Mann could do was repeat that 'the analyses were carried out in a proper manner'.

Despite their inability to establish any inadequacies in scientific methodology, the Commissioners not only remained unmoved by the expert evidence they heard, but hostile to the very nature of scientific enterprise. In explaining why they were not going to subscribe to scientific findings, the Commissioners included in their report the following statement:

> From personal observation and inquiry, and after lengthy experience in practical farming, we do not hesitate to assert that a very large area of the Mallee Belt will grow wheat and productive crops … In other parts of Australia adverse professional opinion respecting mallee lands has been disregarded with advantages to the State, and the Commission having given the question close consideration strongly urges that scientific prejudice against our mallee lands be not permitted to stand in the way of their being opened up.[26]

Even by the standards of the time, this is an extraordinary statement. To reject scientific evidence might be considered foolhardy enough, but to dismiss this evidence as 'prejudice' clearly indicates a much deeper set of attitudes at work in the Commissioners' deliberations. This determination to discredit and sideline scientific evidence shows the working of developmentalism as a political dogma.

In their reports on the salt concentrations of the soil, there is little to suggest either Patterson or Mann understood the hydrology behind salinity or its association with land clearing. Interestingly, it was non-scientists who continued to stumble on the conceptual breakthroughs. W.E. Wood revisited the problem of saline water when, in the early 1920s, he was assigned the task of inquiring again into the rapid corrosion of the Railway's boilers. He found the clearing of vegetation in the catchment areas had caused an increase in the salinity of railway water supplies which, fourteen years later, were unsuitable for use in steam-driven locomotives. The trouble was remedied by using water only from catchment areas still in the virgin state. Several years later, Wood read a paper about his findings to the Royal Society of Western Australia. Based largely upon his own observations and deductive reasoning, Wood's conclusion was stark as it was simple: 'it will easily be recognised how the increase of salt has followed within a very few years upon the rapid extension of cultivated land in the agricultural portion of the catchment'.[27]

LAND RELEASE CONTINUES

In the early decades of the twentieth century, Western Australian Governments, in cooperation with the Commonwealth and British governments, sponsored nearly a dozen land settlement schemes, including the Soldier Settlement, Group Settlement and various unemployed workers' schemes. As mentioned, funding provided by the Agricultural Bank was pivotal to the realisation of settling the State's vast landscape. In fact, a mindset of developmentalism pervaded parliament, government and the Agricultural Bank in a reinforcing determination to achieve land settlement for agricultural purposes, the centrepiece of which was the expansion of the State's emerging wheat industry. An important statement of this vision was articulated by the 1917 Royal Commission into Agriculture whose deliberations were timed to occur at the crucial take-off point in the land settlement program. Commissioners set the parameters of their Report in their opening lines: 'the future welfare of the Wheatbelt is material to the advancement of the State'. Dispelling any lingering doubts such as those expressed in the recently completed Royal Commission into the Mallee Belt, the Commissioners expressed their assurance 'that every effort to increase production and further development will be amply justified by results'.[28]

Reviewing previous progress to date with the opening up of the Wheatbelt, the Commissioners noted that the 'greatest problem facing the State' was the development of land and achieving closer settlement, a problem made all the more difficult because the various schemes up until the First World War had failed to attract settlers in any number from other parts of the world. Thus,

> the settlers have been recruited largely from within the State. Many of these were inexperienced, and some quite unfitted for the life. Still, they were all the State could muster, and it has been necessary perforce to make the most of the men we have.[29]

Making the most of these men entailed 'special efforts' to

> bring all land under occupation, and probably the best course will be to survey, classify and value all vacant land, working gradually from older settled districts outwards in successive blocks. Such land could then be gazetted as open for selection.[30]

Such was their commitment to the plan before them, the Commissioners had a fall-back position if the public failed to respond with the required enthusiasm: 'The prices could be successively reduced until the land was sold.'[31]

During the 1920s, as additional clearing in the Wheatbelt was being carried out 'with vigour',[32] the next scheme to promote land settlement was being brought to fruition. The Group Settlement Scheme had as its primary objective solving the pre-existing problem of attracting sufficient numbers of British migrants to the immense countryside of Western Australia. In pragmatic terms the scheme tried to match the State's vacant lands with England's unemployed. The terms of settlement were exceedingly generous: each settler was given 160 acres of land to be cleared under the guidance of the Lands and Survey Department, and a sustenance payment of 10 shillings per day. As a later Royal Commission into the scheme observed, it amounted to the settler 'trying out the land at the risk of others'.[33]

Such opened-ended support courted disaster. In 1925 a Royal Commission was established to examine the scheme's failings which, when systematically laid bare, appear to constitute great recklessness motivated by a profound belief in land settlement as an article of faith, a political dogma. Among the Commissioners' findings was the damning conclusion that Group Settlement was launched 'without proper preparation'. The Commissioners were plainly astonished by the realisation that 'for some time the only qualification required of prospective settlers has been that he [sic] should have a wife and family. New arrivals were drafted from the ship without training or selection.'[34] Not surprisingly, many simply abandoned their farms or were left dependent on sustenance payments because they could not make their farms productive.

However unsuited to farming life many of the Group Settlers may have been, there is no doubting the energy they applied to clearing their land. In evidence many gave to the Commission, it is clear that they were not just intent on subduing nature for the purposes of farming, but literally on destroying it. A prominent rural newspaper, reflecting in 1950 on the previous decades of clearing, carried a description of this development as 'an orgy of tree butchery'.[35] Moreover, this practice represented official policy. 'Anything that was big enough to pull up a plough was taken out,' explained one farmer.[36] As a Group Manager explained: 'We have no limit to the size of the trees to be taken out. The rule is to clear so as to get the plough through.'[37] Another farmer supported the claim that farmers were acting on government guidelines in destroying all before them: 'We are supposed to take everything ... out and leave the big stuff for the time being. The guide we were given was that we were to clear sufficient to enable a plough to get between the big trees easily. We had to ring [bark] the big trees.'[38]

All the land settlement schemes were underpinned with the financial largesse of the Agricultural Bank. The Bank acted as the facilitator of wider government settlement and land clearance policy. By the 1930s, the impact of Bank-sponsored developmentalism was impressive. Between 1919–20 and 1930–31 wheat production rose from 11.2 million bushels to 53.5 million bushels.[39] Throughout the State, it was possible to 'pass through many miles of well-developed farming lands, every acre of which has been cleared and improved with the assistance

W. E. Wood, an early commentator on
salinity and the author of the first influential
paper on the subject in Western Australia.
(*Courtesy of West Australian Newspapers Ltd.*)

Early twentieth-century horse-drawn, land-
clearing frame constructed of timber and
used for the purpose of removing scrub.
(*Courtesy of West Australian Newspapers Ltd.*)

Home-made rollers for clearing shrubland, *circa* 1915.
(*Courtesy of the Battye Library, 51223P.*)

Tractor with caterpillar tread and front-end shovel, for pushing down small trees and scrubland. This type of tractor was developed during the Second World War.
(*Courtesy of the Battye Library, 213,183P.*)

Purpose-built tractor with front attachment for pushing over large trees—early post-Second World War. (*Courtesy of Agriculture WA.*)

Typical land-clearing technique using two tractors connected by a ground-level steel cable or chain. This technique was widely used from the 1950s. (*Courtesy of Agriculture WA.*)

HIGH-SPEED CLEARING WITH THE HI-BALL

Speed and low cost are the advantages of clearing with the hi-ball now being tested at Rocky Gully (north-west of Mt. Barker). Modelled on successful North American designs and manufactured at the State Engineering Works, the 8ft. ball is coupled to two 110 h.p. tractors by two 350ft. cables. Proceeding at 1 m.p.h., it can cut a swathe one chain wide in average-size timber. Where two bulldozers working independently with blades can clear 80 acres in a 40-hour week, towing the new hi-ball they can dispose of 500 acres in the same time.

Heavy timber is removed by this outfit to clear the paths for the two bulldozers that tow the ball. The heavy frame at the front of the machine helps to push the tree down. Fallen timber is swept to one side by the angled blade.

Left: The 8ft. ball is being manoeuvred into position before the start of a test run.

The crushed timber in the left foreground is proof of the ball's effectiveness.

The ball leaves vegetation in a crushed condition ideal for firing.

Right: Three minutes before the photograph was taken this was virgin forest. The cleared area is 100yds. long and one chain wide.

This extract from *The Western Mail* shows a 'Hi-Ball' attached by a chain to two tractors, which served to keep the chain off the ground for more rapid and effective clearing of larger timber; it was common after the 1950s.
(*Courtesy of West Australian Newspapers Ltd.*)

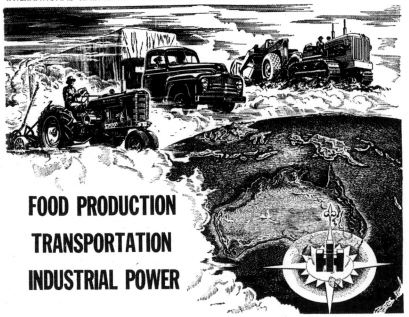

Advertisement for the International Harvester Company promoting the use of earth-moving equipment, and its contribution to national developmental schemes. (*Courtesy of West Australian Newspapers Ltd.*)

Land-clearing bush camp at Kojonup early in the twentieth century, showing the very basic conditions early pioneers had to endure. (*Courtesy of the Battye Library, 4045B/22.*)

A settler burning the fallen timber after clearing. Note the extensiveness of remaining stands still visible in the background. (*Courtesy of the Battye Library, 51888 P.*)

Putting the crop in, *circa* 1920. Note the horizon is completely devoid of any native vegetation. (*Courtesy of the Battye Library, 55053 P.*)

Wheat loading at Wedin, east of Narrogin, *circa* 1930.
(*Courtesy of the Battye Library, 5091B/18.*)

of the Bank'.[40] Yet, appearances were deceptive. The drive for development thrust the Bank into unsustainable—even foolhardy—lending practices which, by the early 1930s and the onset of the Great Depression, could no longer be concealed. By this time the Bank had amassed over £6 million of debts with little prospect of recovering most of the money as falling wheat prices coupled with the high level of indebtedness of many farmers, the rush to settle returned soldiers on farms, and the expansion into unproductive lands, all meant that settlers were 'being carried on from year to year by the Bank in order that the property shall not be abandoned'.[41]

Although the Bank operated independently of the government of the day, the Managing Trustee of the Bank confirmed to the Royal Commission that, in effect, 'it became a Government Department for carrying out the Government's policy of land development'.[42] This policy of land development was conceived on a scale described by the Commission as 'mistaken'. Overall, bigger areas of land were being cleared than it was possible to find men to work,[43] which, in turn, reflected an 'obsession for expansion' by the Bank in the years 1912–29:

> Lands were surveyed, classified, and thrown open for selection carrying a guaranteed Bank advance. So great was the rush of applicants for land that Land Boards were created to deal with and select from the applicants those whom the Bank was of the opinion the blocks should be allotted.[44]

In this way, land became a speculative business. The Royal Commission claimed it was apparent even to the ordinary observer, 'that all the lands being settled through the Bank were not productive wheat lands'.[45] Sustaining these practices was the larger creed of land development for economic and social advance: 'The Trustees by their lax control established among settlers a strong body of opinion that they were doing the State a service by remaining on and working their land'.[46]

The notion that land settlement was a service to the State was, of course, seen exclusively in economic and social terms and even these terms can be questioned given the huge attrition rates involved in settlement. The consequences for the environment arising from such extensive and destructive land settlement did not exercise the minds of those who framed and implemented the policy. This separation of humans from the natural environment in official policy is not only amply demonstrated in the opening up of the Wheatbelt but also in the parallel and compounding activities of forests and forestry.

Concern over the rapid depletion of Western Australia's forests and the lack of an adequate reserve system to protect them gathered pace from the 1920s. No less a figure than the head of the Forests Department issued several assessments critical of the environmental impact of the prevailing ethos of 'development at all costs'. In 1920, the Director wrote: 'The sawmiller, not the forester, has been the man to choose the areas he desired to cut, and he has cut them in such a manner as to reduce them to a state in which practically no growth is taking place.'[47] In 1925 he was equally strident in his comments about the level of destructiveness: he questioned 'to what extent the Department is justified in standing by while timber equivalent to the increment put on by hundreds of thousands of growing trees is being either converted into sawdust or burnt'.[48] He could see these practices were being driven by 'the urgency of developing the land' for soldier settlers and immigrants and that government had sanctioned the depletion of the State's prime timber resources. In 1925 he used his Annual Report to criticise successive governments' failure to make any real progress in the setting aside of State forests to protect the resource, and he registered his concern that the issue was depleting the morale of his departmental officers: 'There is a danger of the matter being treated as an obsession on the part of officers of the Department and having little or no practical importance.'[49]

The urgency shown by government to open up the mallee region for agriculture came to a virtual standstill during the 1930s and '40s, as long-time Western Australian agricultural scientist, G.H. Burvill, later reflected:

> Of course the depression from 1930 until the Second World War had disastrous effects on agriculture in Western Australia. It

stopped all the expansion and it happened also to be a period in which there were several very dry years and there were also the problems of grasshoppers. Wheat prices had been low and there was wholesale abandonment of farms. And of course the war brought quite a number of different aspects to things—shortages of materials and shortages of superphosphate and things of that sort, required all sorts of controls. In addition there were efforts put into growing vegetables for the troops: they wanted dehydrated potatoes and apples and so agricultural people were diverted into that sort of thing.[50]

ROLE OF SCIENCE AND TECHNOLOGY

The expansion of the Wheatbelt was substantially a creation of the interplay between ideology and government policy; the application of politics to the ideal of development. However, the dreams of the State's leaders would not have been realised to anywhere near the same extent but for the facilitating role played by science and engineering. In fact, the steady expansion of the Wheatbelt after the turn of the century mirrors the contribution made by plant science and mechanical engineering.

The crucible of all developments in this area was the ready availability of chemical fertiliser. The poor quality of the soils in most of the Wheatbelt has already been noted. Thus, the tremendous advance in wheat production after the turn of the century would not have been possible without the use of superphosphate. Virtually unknown at the turn of the century, the use of 'super' increased more than six-fold between 1910 and 1949.[51] As the Wheatbelt expanded, demand for the fertiliser spurred a substantial manufacturing industry with up to six production sites in the region by 1950.[52]

The mechanisation of farming after the turn of the century played a major role in making country accessible to clearing and in increasing productivity. The replacement of working horses with tractors occurred at a rapid rate after the 1920s as did the replacement of the stripper harvester with the combine. Writing in the 1950s when this process of mechanisation had become commonplace, Sutton reflected: 'The increase in the size of farm implements has been rendered possible by the very general adoption of mechanical traction. In consequence, the area which can be dealt with per man has been greatly increased, with the result that productivity per man in the wheat areas has also increased and is now of a high order.'[53]

Developments in the use of fertilisers and machinery were practical things to which the Western Australian farmer readily took. Farmers were slower to appreciate the contribution which plant science could make, yet the contribution was a substantial one. In the early decades of the twentieth century, 'the attitude of the farmer towards the scientist or research worker was not very respectful'. Farmers 'looked upon the scientist as an academic theorist of no practical assistance'.[54] However, after the endowment of the Chair of Agriculture at the University of Western Australia, attitudes began to change as common diseases in wheat, such as smut and rust, were eradicated. Later developments, including the application of chemicals to weed and insect control and the introduction of improved varieties of wheat, all sustained the productivity of the industry and the continued faith by governments in agriculture's continued expansion.

MORE CONCERNS ABOUT SALINITY

In the Wheatbelt the consequences of developmentalism were not only manifest in the near-complete destruction of native vegetation, but also in the rise of salinity, about which Patterson and Mann had warned government, but to no avail. When the Royal Commission into the Agricultural Bank inquired into the impact of the Bank's lending policies, they found salinity to be a growing problem in a number of districts. They directed their most savage criticism at the Board's role in allowing the Salmon Gums District to be opened up to wheat growing, the very area Mann and Patterson had cautioned against:

> The evidence of salinity in the soil, given in the Royal Commission on Esperance Settlement, and the presence of many salt lakes in the district, called for a soil survey. No investigations were

made; the area was thrown open for settlement, readily applied for, and clearing and cropping commenced. After two years of crop failure, the Trustees should have realised there was something radically wrong with the soil, have discontinued all further advances for clearing and other improvements, and have conducted a thorough inquiry.[55]

But it was not just the more marginalised country where salinity was found to be on the rise. At Ongerup, the Commissioners reported: 'Salinity is beginning to appear and may become a menace. The settlers … say the land becomes mineralised, that is, it will grow neither crops nor grasses and the patches of mineralised country are expanding year by year.'[56] On one estate in the Northam District, 'the water course to the northwards showed salt badly, and the trees along the bank of the water course are dying.'[57] In the Kununoppin District, settlers were affected by salinity 'to such an extent as to render wheat production unprofitable'.[58] At Kellerberrin, the situation was similar: 'In the Southern part of the area we noticed evidence of salt appearing on many of the farms; these patches are spreading and may become a menace to the district.'[59]

Despite its well-grounded observations, the Commission's Report had no impact in changing land settlement practices: too many settlers had been brought in and too many of these were in dire financial straits once the onset of the Great Depression collapsed the price of wheat. However, one potentially positive outcome arising from the Commission's Report was the appointment of L.J.H. Teakle, advisor to the Agriculture Department on soil matters, to undertake an extensive soil survey in the Salmon Gums District, the site of the single most ambitious post-First World War, land settlement scheme, popularly known as the '3,500 Farms Scheme'. In August 1930, a soil survey party was established which, over the next six years, completed surveys of 1.5 million acres. Such was the awareness of salt among the farmers that the presence of the soil surveyors incited a hostile reaction: 'Some of them threatened to shoot the soil surveyors. They were bobbing up and down in their crops with their guns.'[60]

Teakle's findings, published in a 1939 edition of the *Journal of Agriculture WA*, highlighted the reason behind his investigation: 'It seems that, in many instances in which disappointing returns were being obtained, the first crop [of wheat], often roughly sown on the burn, had been quite good, averaging, perhaps, 5 bags per acre, while subsequent crops … have yielded only half as many bushels.'[61] Teakle had no doubts about the cause: 'On certain soil types salt concentration in the surface layers occurs after clearing and cultivation, and this concentration, associated with a highly saline subsoil, is responsible for a considerable portion of the crop failures'.[62] Teakle also began to shape his understanding of the hydrology of salinity. He wrote that, after clearing,

> percolation is greatly enhanced and much more water reaches the groundwater annually. Small underground streams make their way towards the valleys and the water table rises generally but more particularly in the valleys.[63]

These findings led Teakle to the conclusion that 37 per cent of the Salmon Gums District was unsuitable for wheat growing, although he was optimistic about the remainder of the land.

Teakle's early findings became embroiled in the 1930 State election campaign fought out for the fourth occasion between long-time rivals, Labor incumbent, Philip Collier and Nationalist–Country Party Leader, Sir James Mitchell. Campaigning strongly on the theme of agricultural development, Mitchell told one audience that the strength of his party's approach was 'to get the last acre selected and the whole of the cultivable land put to the fullest use'.[64] Mitchell took a swipe at the Collier Government for shelving the 3,500 Farms Scheme, a decision which it took after Teakle delivered his findings. Mitchell went on the attack: 'The salt bogey is convenient just now because it enables the Government to put off further consideration of the work of settling this area.' Just how deeply felt the prevailing belief in agricultural development was shown when he raised the familiar theme of governments standing firm against the pernicious influence of scientists: 'I am afraid that if the good Lord had provided scientists when Adam and Eve were created, no useful work would have been done … If Dr Teakle's report is taken literally, it will knock the bottom out of wheat land development and create a deal of pessimism among land holders.'[65] Historian Geoffrey Bolton sums up the significance of Mitchell's approach to the election which he went on to win: 'Having thus disposed of the agricultural scientist, Mitchell and his party continued to campaign on the assumption that the limits of profitable growth in the Wheatbelt were still a long way off.'[66]

Interestingly, Teakle's report became the basis upon which the Agricultural Bank stopped advances to settlers involved in the 3,500 Farms Scheme, forcing many into 'battling along as best they can'.[67] Moreover, Teakle's work became the accepted wisdom within the scientific community. G.H. Burvill, who began his career working with Teakle in the early 1930s after completing university studies, has said: 'In the early part of my career it was established and well known then that after you clear country, particularly in the 15–25″ rainfall belt, that you get soaks and springs developing. It was also common knowledge that after they had been fresh for a number of years they often went salty.'[68]

One contemporary letter-writer to *The West Australian* more than strongly hinted at the ethical issues which lay at the heart of the scheme's mis-management by government:

> It is impossible not to feel very deep sympathy for the settlers who went out into those remote parts east of Newdegate seven or eight years ago believing the soil and the rainfall to be good and a railway assured. … They went there and were allowed to go there in good faith, but research and experience have revealed serious soil problems and the collapse of the 3,500 farms scheme has killed any hope they ever entertained of a railway.[69]

With the onset of the Depression, there was no reason to enthuse over the prospects for the wheat industry. The price of wheat fell steadily and many farmers faced disaster. It was only during the Second

World War that the outlook brightened: prices rose faster than costs in a system which guaranteed prices in advance of harvesting. Consequently, farmers' earnings rose appreciably.[70] After the cessation of conflict, the State Government, in cooperation with the Commonwealth, again embarked on a massive land clearance program motivated by the twin needs of repatriating returned soldiers and laying the foundations for post-war economic expansion though the wheat and wool industries.

POST-SECOND WORLD WAR LAND RELEASE SCHEMES

The end of the Second World War was accompanied by an overwhelming sense of the 'ever lasting debt of gratitude', which all sections of the community felt towards those who had served in the armed forces.[71] It was soon realised that repaying this debt could fuse other powerful elements in the State's political culture: the passion for government-sponsored development and the idealisation of farming life. A letter-writer to *The Western Mail* newspaper expressed the broader community view when he wrote:

> Where land settlement is concerned, I feel that every acre cleared and brought into production confers a benefit upon the community as a whole. Irrespective of whether the new settler is an exserviceman or not, I am wholly in favour of any initial costs of settlement being borne by the community—at least to an extent which will give the settler a chance to make good and reap an adequate reward for his labours.[72]

Matching these ideals was the Commonwealth Government, whose involvement in funding the release of land was crucial and had been planned before the end of the war by the Rural Reconstruction Commission. Its 1944 Report into Soldier Settlement noted that the involvement of the Commonwealth was inevitable because the financial burden of implementing the scheme and assessing production requirements for overseas markets was beyond the resources of the states. Accordingly, the states had the responsibility for the original selection of both land and settlers while the Commonwealth 'must decide which plans for settlement of ex-servicemen are to be accepted'.[73]

However, the Commission was at pains to establish that such involvement should only come after the weaknesses and failures of the First World War scheme were thoroughly understood and addressed: 'The Commission emphasises that in 1944 the stage is set for a repetition of the post-war settlement disasters of the previous period, and such repetition will occur unless adequate precautions are taken and, above all, unless the returned men and the public understand the real nature of the problem.'[74] The 'real problem', as the Commission saw it, was the tendency for authorities to succumb to the combined effects of vested interests and an excited public such that projects could not stand objective analysis: 'It will be essential in all future land settlement to approach the subject with the conviction that land selection and settlement is not a job exclusively for the land surveyor, but is one calling for the combined knowledge of the soil expert, the agriculturist and the farm finance authority.'[75] The Commission explicitly cautioned against settlement for wheat growing in marginal country 'except perhaps on specially favourable soils'.[76] Moreover, it stipulated that where 'large areas of land are to be subdivided … it should be a pre-requisite that at least a large scale soil survey is obtained'.[77]

However, pressures were on to circumvent the full application of these principles. Foremost among these was the pressure by governments to grow more wheat. In 1946, for example, the Under Secretary for the Department of Agriculture acknowledged Western Australia's 'reliance on agriculture and the importance of wheat growing', in his annual summation of the sector.[78] Moreover, by the early 1950s, Australia's newly emerging balance-of-payments problems had convinced the Federal Government to view agricultural expansion as the solution.[79]

In pursuit of this objective, the War Service Settlement Scheme in Western Australia was developed to become the largest land clearance program in Australia to that time.[80] It was certainly undertaken on a scale which dwarfed the efforts of other State schemes. By May 1954,

60 per cent of qualified ex-servicemen applicants had been allotted farms, whereas the figure for other states was only 10 per cent.[81] Each farm block was cleared of up to two-thirds of the bush. Government support for farmers was extensive, including the provision of house, shed, dams, water tanks, and fencing. Pasture was sown. In this way, government showed awareness of the difficulties involved in establishing farms, Lavine learnt from past tragedies. Between 1945 and 1961 land under cultivation in the State nearly doubled: it went from 14 million acres to 25 million acres.[82] Development continued at a rapid rate under subsequent schemes throughout the early 1960s when more than 1 million acres were opened up each year. Whereas between 1959 and 1960, all other states allocated just over 2 million acres, in Western Australia the figure was nearly 6.5 million acres.[83] The sheer size of this latest scheme contributed massively to the further stripping of the southern part of the State—and especially the Wheatbelt—of its native vegetation, while bolstering one of the State's main exports.

Underpinning the faith in the post-war land release schemes was the boom in the wool and wheat industries. G.H. Burvill remembered the conditions well:

> Just when they got a lot of these schemes going, wool prices sky-rocketed with the Korean War and wool went up to a pound a pound. All of a sudden these fellows had tremendous incomes … Well of course they all wrote off their debts and they were all in credit with the bank so what they did was freeholded with the Lands Department the 4,000 acres they had under conditional purchase and took up another three or four thousand acres so they then had up to 10,000 acres running sheep, and of course there were some good wheat prices just after the war, and the seasons weren't too bad and they also got into wheat growing.[84]

To facilitate the task, the Land Settlement Board was established to oversee the initial intention to purchase developed and partly developed properties. However, demand from returned soldiers and others, together with the rising farm prices, meant the scheme was forced to rely on alienation and clearing of Crown Land to meet its objectives. A sense of urgency underpinned the whole enterprise: 'a stimulus to the necessity of urgently developing the Crown Lands', wrote the Board in its first Annual Report, 'has become momentous, in view of the demand from Great Britain for additional supplies of foodstuffs'.[85] Not surprisingly, the enthusiasm was shared by the Land Settlement Board which explained in 1950: 'The initiation of large developmental schemes results from the interplay of social and economic factors, which seldom seem to repeat themselves and, unless the favourable conditions are seized, the urge for development may pass and the opportunity missed.'[86]

The War Service Settlement Scheme merged into the New Farm Lands Scheme which operated from 1959 to the late 1960s and which saw a further 5,000 leases covering 3.5 million hectares brought into agricultural production. The new scheme suffered from many of the same defects as previous government-induced land settlement projects. A Commonwealth Government inquiry in 1975 found that:

New land releases were widely advertised, but it appears little attention was given to applicants' prospects for success. The Commission has no evidence that the State Government planned comprehensively for the financial needs of the settlers, and land was released in some areas where development and farming alternatives were unproven … There is no evidence to suggest that early failures were a consequence of the size of the farms. Rather, it appears that inadequate farming experience and low levels of starting assets were the main causes. There do not appear to have been any guidelines set by the Western Australian Government to the Land Board with respect of these matters.[87]

The opening up of such large tracts of land in a climate of buoyant prices for wheat and wool excited a boom in land speculation with claims of hundreds of applicants for each block, trafficking in land, multiple purchases within the one family and absentee owners.[88] Throughout the period of these schemes, grandiose claims about the virtues of development sustained the momentum of the schemes. In 1965, for example, the Minister for Lands, Mr Bovell, told Parliament that land development was the State's 'greatest venture'. Not only did he want people to populate the country districts, but he also believed 'that in the great open spaces there is adventure and opportunity everywhere'.[89]

Within its first year,1950, the Land Settlement Board had drawn up a five-year plan which it submitted to the Commonwealth Government for the development of 1 million acres in the southern areas of the State. Bulldozers moved in and, on already repurchased land, thousands of acres were cleared in the first months, ready for burning that summer. Private contractors quickly sized up the opportunities and showed 'an increasing interest in clearing required by the Government, in view of the comparatively large areas being handled'.[90]

Camps were erected in areas where Crown Land was being cleared. Accommodation consisted of floored tents with central ablution buildings and arrangements for washing. However, faced with a steadily rising basic wage and labour shortages, the Land Settlement Board adopted a policy of mechanising as much as possible the work of clearing.[91]

In fact, steady advances in the mechanisation of land clearing were pivotal to the expansionist plans of post-Second World War governments. The Land Settlement Board enthused about the development of a heavy rake and a ripper for removing mallee roots and the raking up of debris—'without costly hand labour—[it] may enable large areas of mallee and sparsely timbered land in a sound rainfall area to be developed economically'.[92]

Bigger developments followed. In May 1950, the rural press announced, with much fanfare, 'the most revolutionary contribution' to date in the history of land clearing in the State: the conversion of a General Grant tank from 'a war machine to valuable peace-time implement'.[93] The conversion consisted of removing the turret, fitting up tree pushing gear and the 'intricate installation' of an hydraulic lifting mechanism for the raising of the bulldozer blade. Its prowess in removing the bush was extolled in the most colourful language which, in itself, is revealing of contemporary attitudes towards the conquest over nature:

> There is nothing apologetic about this monster as it moves through the bush cracking nine-inch saplings under its tracks like so much matchwood. In pushing out the trees it barely seems to give more than a playful bunt at the tree, but the 400 odd horse-power leaves nothing to the imagination as the tree goes crashing to the ground, only to be picked up and tossed without effort to the top of a stack which in many cases is already over 18 feet high.

But as the Board went on to explain, even these methods were too inefficient:

> The standard mechanised method of clearing with the use of tractors initially developed during the war consists primarily of various attachments to the tractor to give leverage so that trees can be pushed down individually and, later, pushed into heaps for final disposal. This method is necessarily slow as each tree has to be handled individually … The use of a cable drawn by two powerful tractors to pull down a strip of forest is not new, although this method has only been partially successful because of practical difficulties. The principal difficulty is that—owing to its weight— the cable or chain tends to drag along the ground, and, owing to the lack of leverage, quite small trees can 'pull up' the tractors; this necessitates the cable being slackened and raised by some means up the tree trunk so that machines can obtain leverage. Another difficulty has been that—after a tree is pulled over—the cable rides over the limbs and may slide over smaller trees, leaving these standing in its wake.[94]

To overcome these 'practical difficulties', the Board conducted experimental trials in 1951 of the 'hi-ball', an American-designed steel ball—eight feet in height—coupled to two tractors by two 350-foot cables. This method created a leverage of at least four feet at the point of impact of the ball with the tree, thus preventing the cable riding over small trees and ensuring 'the smashing down and tearing off of limbs from fallen trees, thus leaving a good medium for a successful fire'.[95] The American design carried the distinct advantages of increasing the rate of clearing five-fold and allowing for a better burn by leaving the trunks of trees more or less in the same direction, which made the job of pushing them into piles all the easier.

The stream of mechanised innovations to speed up clearing attracted considerable media and public interest. Newspaper headlines heralded the developments as a new era in farming: 'Revolutionary Clearing Developments',[96] and 'High Speed Clearing with the Hi-Ball'.[97] Accompanying lengthy feature articles explained the workings of the new machines as breakthroughs in the conquest against 'the virgin forest'. In fact, the farm machinery companies became one of the driving forces behind developmentalism during the 1950s and '60s, widely promoting the sale of the big, land clearing tractors.[98]

By 1951, the Board was chafing at the restrictions confronting their operations. Within an 80-mile radius of Albany alone, one and a half million acres were in the process of being cleared but delays in receiving machinery slowed progress:

> The number of heavy crawler-type tractors has doubled during the year, but it is still below that necessary to develop timbered areas fast enough for the requirements of the scheme. A heavy bulldozer equipped with blade and tree-pusher on heavily timbered areas can only be expected to knock down and clean up sufficient land for two farms per year. If development in timbered areas only were considered, the existing equipment would therefore only produce 60 farms per year, which is too slow. The Board, therefore, is awaiting with interest the manufacture of the hi-ball and cable.[99]

Contemporary attitudes towards these massive land clearing schemes in the 1950s can be gauged from the recollections of Colin

Cameron, the officer-in-charge of the Jerramungup War Service Project. Two months after arriving in the district, Cameron arranged for a contractor, 'Johnnie' Walker, to begin 'rolling' acres of mallee country:

> Nothing was allowed to stand in the way including that bugbear to speed and efficiency Red Tape, and slowly the wheels started turning. Walker was a man really anxious to go. Discussing the situation with him, it was decided that logging would be too slow, that chaining might be the answer, and so it turned out. A 250 ft length of anchor chain weighing approx five tons was attached to two tractors and these moved forward dragging the chain between them. The chain pulled the scrub down and quite a lot of the mallee was pulled out by the roots. Walker was rather concerned about his 2000 acres contract but I assured him that if he really got going I would make his contract not under 30,000 acres and possibly more. He needed no second telling, night and day his tractor roared and the rolled area rapidly grew. In a short time thousands of acres lay behind him. So well did he do that by the end of Sept 40,000 acres were on the ground. The Chairman and Secretary [of the local Land Board] paid a visit to view progress and were so delighted with what they saw that they decided to hold a field day to let the public see for themselves just what was happening.[100]

Sustaining Cameron's efforts to oversee this massive clearance was his faith in the social purpose of the enterprise. At the conclusion of his task in the area, Cameron was reported to have said: 'How better can we prove our right and title to this land than by developing it, increasing food production and helping to feed the hungry.'[101]

Rex Edmondson, a local of Jerramungup, took up land in the district. His account, told to a newspaper in the late 1980s, also contains revealing insights into the sheer scale of the land clearing operation: 'The clearing was so fast. They (contractors) would clear 1000 acres (405 hectares) a day. One Sunday afternoon they cleared 900 acres (364 hectares).' Mr Edmondson gave the example of one company which started clearing with bulldozers and chains at Jerramungup and did not pack up their equipment until they had almost reached Ravensthorpe, 180 kilometres away. Burning this immense volume of trees and scrub created virtual fire-storms:

> The heat was so intense it almost created a hurricane. The smoke rose in mushroom clouds, the wind sucked pieces of timber 30 metres in the air and truck windscreens were blown out. We had no idea until we burnt the timber what the country even looked like. A lot of people were surprised to find it undulating. There was no commitment for anyone to practise any kind of soil conservation. That was where it all went off the rails.[102]

Throughout the 1950s, land release projects created great public interest. In 1954, for example, the 500,000-acre Gairdner project, north-east of Albany, was opened. Allocated front page in *The West Australian*, the announcement stirred the paper to extol the virtues of the project in an editorial.[103] The opening up of these lands not only confirmed the State's 'enviable record' of war service land settlement, but also demonstrated Western Australia 'is capable of bold imaginative planning in an effort to provide the increase in food production Australia needs so much'.

Five years after the end of the war, applications for farms continued to be received in the hundreds; there were over 370 new applications in 1951 alone.[104] In fact, between 1946 and 1956 about 4.5 million hectares of land were released, comprising over seven and a half thousand farm units, about a quarter of which were allotted to returned servicemen.[105] By the late 1950s, approximately £32 million had been spent on the scheme, 90 per cent of which was Commonwealth money.[106] Much of the land released under the post-Second World War schemes was done so under Conditional Purchase (CP) agreements which entrenched the practice of clearing native vegetation because half the allocated land was required by law to be pastured or cropped within the first six years.[107] Nearly all new farmers were short of funds, and so decisions on land clearing were taken on purely an economic basis. As

Twigg has written, the 'initial chaining or logging of the bush was by far the cheapest operation and so often more country was "knocked down" than could be properly handled'.[108]

However, a range of other factors drove widespread land clearing. Mr Geoff Grainger, a farmer at Fitzgerald on the South Coast of Western Australia reflected on his experience during the 1960s. He identified three main factors driving land clearing, the results of which, by the early 1980s, were showing up in the rising water table and wind erosion. He mentioned the need to get rid of poisonous native vegetation which thrived on fertiliser; the inexperience of many farmers and their consequent lack of farm planning; and the short-term attitude of the finance industry:

> Lending institutions want to see a return on their money in twelve months. Double fencing and strategic fences to preserve native flora give good results with groundwater control and wind erosion control. Reafforestation of selected areas is essential. These things give excellent returns on money invested but not in the short term. They are 'preventative' farming and cannot be rated in an Annual Cash Flow Budget.

As Geoff Grainger knew only too well, the early optimism of settlers gave way to despair for many:

> Poor living conditions, wheat quotas, the fall of wool, sheep, then cattle prices took their toll. We all had droughts and floods. About one-third of the original settlers are left. Most have doubled their original farm area.[109]

Throughout the period encompassing the New Farm Lands and Million Acres a Year schemes, the optimism of farmers like Geoff Grainger was fed by the Agriculture Department. G.D. Oliver came to Western Australia in 1962 and remembers being 'told by young and not so young agricultural scientists that this was the Holy Land for agriculture'.[110]

RENEWED CONCERNS ABOUT SALINITY

Amid this frenzy of land clearing, authorities were well informed about the concerns of informed observers about the threat from salinity. In fact, very much the same pattern occurred in the post-Second World War schemes as had occurred in the initial stage following the end of the First World War: government was in receipt of explicit scientific information which it chose to ignore in favour of rapid development.

In 1945 the problems farmers in the Lake Grace, Newdegate and Pingrup districts were experiencing with salinisation came to the attention of government because many had approached the Rural Bank seeking 'further writing down of their indebtedness on account of the encroachment of salt on the soils on their properties'. The area had been settled twenty years previously but diminished yields started to occur after four or five years. A Committee headed by G.H. Burvill of the Agriculture Department (and who later went on to become Soil Commissioner) was set up to investigate the problem. While recognising the need for farm management plans to be introduced, the Committee came up with a pragmatic solution which was to guide agricultural practice on salt-affected lands for many decades to come, although the Committee's report appears to be its first official enunciation: simply grab more land:

> In viewing the problems of the Lake Grace, Newdegate and Pingrup districts placed before the Committee, it has been constantly borne in mind that these districts have now been settled for over twenty years and that most farmers have established homes and connections in the districts and wish to stay there. It has been considered unwise, therefore, to suggest any scheme which would interfere in a large way with present homes and existing farms. The best course, in view of the circumstances, appears to be in the direction of building up existing farms into more satisfactory units by the addition, if possible and where necessary, of vacant adjoining lands with reasonable adjustments in capital indebtedness and land rents. In this way, it is felt farmers are likely to have

satisfactory prospects for their future livelihood and should be much less default in financial obligations.[111]

In other words, the Committee judged that farmers' obligations to banks be placed ahead of their obligation to the environment. The application of this policy contributed greatly to the worsening of the salinity problem.

In the early stages of the post-Second World War schemes, several studies had been undertaken of salinity in the Wheatbelt, all reaching the same conclusion. In 1950, the Commissioner of Soil Conservation, G.H. Burvill published his findings, the conclusions of which left little room for doubt: 'This salt problem is so serious in places that single farms or groups of farms have been ruined; wheat growing on them has become unprofitable … salt is, undoubtedly, a widespread Wheatbelt problem.'[112] In fact, Burvill had reiterated the science of the problem in a 1945 article for the *Journal of Agriculture WA* which, interestingly, highlights how little farmers actually understood about the problem: 'it is commonly held by farmers that cultivation of salt liable country promotes the spread of salt in the soil. This is not so. The spread is due to clearing of the higher country adjacent, which is responsible for the rise in the water level.'[113]

In June 1950 the strongest possible expressions of concern about salinity in Western Australia were made by members of the Commonwealth Standing Committee on Soil Erosion, which not only held its sixth meeting in Perth but also engaged in a brief tour of the Wheatbelt accompanied by G.H. Burvill and his second in command, L.C. Lightfoot. A journalist covering the tour later wrote:

> Despite the fact that the tour did not embrace areas where West Australians consider that salt encroachment is assuming the status of a serious menace to agriculture, the visitors were seriously alarmed by the spread of salt-affected lands and were unanimous in asserting that in this problem alone we had a menace of the greatest magnitude and one that shrieked aloud for the prompt inauguration of a large-scale programme of research. They were

amazed at the apathetic attitude shown towards the problem which they consider to be alarming. Told that they had not seen what we regarded as badly salt-affected land, they were almost incredulous and one said, 'Why, we've already embarked on a big programme of research because of salt encroachment on a scale that is not a hundredth part of what I've seen this afternoon.'[114]

The next year, a Principal Research Officer with the CSIRO in New South Wales, Mr R.R. Pennefeather, was invited by the Minister for Agriculture to undertake a study of salinity in the Wheatbelt. Travelling with G.H. Burvill, he covered over 2,000 miles. His full report was subsequently published in *The Western Mail* on 12 July 1951 which, in itself, is indicative of public interest in the issue. Pennefeather found that salt had already destroyed over 100,000 acres; land which was not likely to be reclaimed. Up to one million additional acres was thought by him to be at risk, about which he said: 'The position calls for an immediate start on these investigations and justifies considerable expenditure.'[115] The Department of Agriculture, however, barely mentioned his stark findings. The Director of Agriculture duly noted Pennefeather's concerns in the Department's 1951 Annual Report but in a cursory manner which illustrated a lack of concern about the issue. Despite emphasising Pennefeather's finding that the problem was serious and may extend, the Director wrote but one small paragraph in his report on the subject and moved quickly to the gross value of the State's agricultural and pastoral production which, he enthused, 'were at near record levels'. In other words, development was the real issue, and environmental concerns were regarded as of minor interest.

Amid the rush for development in the early 1950s, a conservation ethic—and one which expressed the lessons of the past—could faintly be heard in public debate. The State's foremost rural newspaper, *The Western Mail*, carried several articles challenging the development ethos in the name of protecting forests. In one article, a broad historical sweep was linked back to recent Western Australian experience. 'History shows', the article confidently began, that throughout the ages and throughout the world, the development of new lands has always followed the same sorry pattern. In every case, the removal of the forest, regarded as an encumbrance, took place first and it was not until later that the value of timber cover came to be appreciated by people who were short of timber and fuel, and all too frequently bereft of the very soil which the forebears had cleared at such cost. Australia is still a new country but has already had time to experience some of the ills arising from reckless deforestation.[116]

A separate article reflected on the attitude of farmers to the excesses of the past.[117] 'Most farmers,' the article began, 'are belatedly realising the aesthetic and utilitarian value of trees on a farm.' However, the task of replanting was 'too big a job for the average farmer to tackle' so it was put off 'until some time in the distant future'.

These commentaries, together with findings from the above studies on salinity, are significant. They reveal the emergence of a competing attitude to developmentalism based on the experience of farming a cleared landscape, and an awareness among authorities of the seriousness of the salinity problem arising from that clearing. These alternative narratives to development occurred at the very time when the largest land release program hitherto undertaken in the Commonwealth had just commenced. Sadly, as it turned out, these alternative views were quickly drowned out in the excitement of continued land release. Ignoring the advice of experts, in particular, seems an extraordinary act. The Land Settlement Board provided insights into the prevailing mindset of authorities. In its 1951 Annual Report, the Board enthused about the challenge of rapid development with which it was charged:

> It may be sound policy under normal conditions to examine every new project most critically and ascertain—if necessary—by experiment the answer to every question of management or soil use, as a prerequisite to settlement. Such information, however, may take years to obtain, during which the vital factor of 'timing' may be lost.[118]

In the Board's mind, 'timing' meant the 'incalculable advantages of public opinion, financial buoyancy, and political approval', necessitating 'a calculated risk in developing certain areas on a large scale where the preliminary trials and accumulated experience indicate that the odds are all for success'.

There are several crucial aspects to these statements. Surely they indicate that the Board was aware of the potential salinity problems but decided to proceed anyway. This is its definition of a 'calculated risk'. It is indicative of a short-term perspective and a disregard of long-term consequences. However, it is entirely unclear what Board members meant by 'preliminary trials' and 'accumulated experience' which, in their minds, justified the taking of this risk. After all, farmers had not been long in the districts being opened up, and it had become accepted knowledge that problems with salinity often took a decade or more after clearing to become manifest. It is therefore difficult to avoid the conclusion, and especially in light of the continuing spread of salinity, that government decisions during these and earlier years were imprudent and reckless to the point of potential negligence.

Certainly, an expedient attitude was taken to the process of ensuring that soils were suitable for agriculture. In his memoirs, Colin Cameron described the process at Jerramungup:

> As speed was the order of the day, little time was spent on preliminaries. A party of soil classifiers arrived on the job and proceeded to make a quick classification of the area. Their method was to cover the country at intervals of twenty chains. Although this method gave a general idea of the soils, it was not considered as a thorough classification.[119]

G.H. Burvill also confirmed the absence of systematic soil analysis. When interviewed in 1981, he said that the CSIRO Soils Division did examine a number of the post-war land release schemes but 'when war service land settlement got going I don't think the CSIRO Soils Division could cope with the amount of it, so they went back to just using Land Department, land inspector general classification of the land'.[120]

In fact, steps were taken to ensure that any problems with salinisation did not interfere with the national marketing of the Wheatbelt as a place to settle and farm. Throughout the 1950s, the Agriculture Department, in cooperation with the Government Tourist and Publicity Bureau, issued a promotional pamphlet titled 'Agriculture in the Western Australian Wheat Belt'. The 1949 edition of the publication described the soils, in part of the region, as consisting of 'sandy or gravelly soils, interspersed with broken rocks and salt lakes'.[121] Yet, in the revised 1956 edition of the same publication, the reference to salt lakes was removed from the section on soils.[122] Was this merely coincidence? Or, was it a conscious attempt to remove reference to salinity and so ensure the success of the post-war land release schemes?

LOST OPPORTUNITIES

During the course of the post-war land schemes, governments were presented with several opportunities to review their expansionist agricultural policies. In 1954, for example, Legislative Councillor (and wheat farmer) L.C. Diver, made an impassioned speech in Parliament about salinity; one of the very few occasions the subject was raised. There were several noteworthy features to Diver's approach to the subject. Firstly, he characterised the problem in economic terms; that is, the losses to salinity were so great as to constitute 'a tremendous economic loss to our State'. Secondly, he criticised the Department of Agriculture, one of very few in government circles to publicly do so: 'While the department is carrying out some research into this problem it is not doing it to as great an extent as the position warrants.' Thirdly, Diver called for the expenditure of 'a huge sum of money' to find the best way to reclaim salt-affected land.[123] He nominated £40,000 as a starting figure to deal with 'scores of thousands of acres affected in the wheatbelt', and a mere 'fleabite' if the land could be reclaimed. Diver's analysis, although framed in an economic paradigm, was a cogent dissection of the problem of salinity. Yet, it elicited no response from government. In fact, Diver's criticism of the Agriculture Department was shared by others, although the reasons differed.

In 1954, a member of the Legislative Council, L.A. Logan, who was also a farmer from Northampton, criticised the lack of resources: 'The problem of salt encroachment is one that has been placed before the public and Governments over the last five or six years. There again the Department is so small and we have so few experts that they are unable to get around and advise farmers of the best methods to adopt.'[124] However, in the same year the General Secretary of the Farmers' Union, Mr A.G. Thaine, claimed the problem with the Department was one of priorities; that 'the rapidly increasing salinity of the soils in some areas was not viewed seriously enough by the Department of Agriculture'.[125] This latter view was endorsed by one of the historians of the wheat industry who, writing in 1955, claimed 'the emphasis in agriculture was almost entirely on production. Scientists, Governments and Departments of Agriculture in Australia concentrated all their work on increasing production.'[126] Consequently, governments did not want to hear concerns about salinity. This is confirmed by C.V. Malcolm, an agricultural scientist with the Department, who has claimed that an Agriculture Department soil scientist 'did studies on the cleared and uncleared streams in the Wellington Catchment back in the mid-1950s and showed that clearing was the cause of salting. He tried to tell the government to stop clearing and was ignored.'[127]

Over the next decade, governments periodically revealed the extent of their lack of interest in grappling with the salinity problem. In 1964, for example, the Minister for Agriculture was asked a seemingly innocuous question in Parliament about the then Government's handling of the issue, namely: how many acres of land had become affected by salinity over the past six years. Surprisingly, the Minister, Mr Nader, replied: 'There is no annual collection of data covering salt-affected land.' A year later, that Government defeated a motion calling for a select committee to investigate the allocation of Conditional Purchase land because agriculture was 'the basis of our State's economy',[128] in spite of a string of alleged irregularities, discussed earlier in this chapter.

In fact, Nader came under fierce attack for complacency on the salt problem.[129] His reaction to these criticisms is startling by today's standards:

Scientific evidence had suggested that probably more than 50 per cent of native vegetation would have to be left to prevent the rising water tables. It did not seem logical to lose such a high percentage of land when there was no real guarantee that it would save salt encroachment appreciably.[130]

The Minister's 'logic' is not as garbled as it first appears; it is, in reality, a justification for not interfering with the profitability of the wheat industry: the attitude was 'as too much land would be lost, why do anything'.

Yet, by the early 1950s, salinity problems had become the active concern of the Public Works Department. From that time, the Public Works Department had been investigating and warning about high levels of salinity in the Wellington Dam on the Collie River—Perth's major source of domestic water and a source of irrigation for farming. The Department had a clear view of the causes:

The history of agricultural development of the State shows that where large areas are cleared and cultivated the natural salt balance is upset and a consequent increase in salinity of streams in these areas ensues.[131]

In a 1963 Report, it was pointed out that the water supplies of Western Australia were vital to national development.[132] The Report stated that they would 'eventually limit the population and expansion of the State [Western Australia]'. It was considered essential that the salinity of Mundaring Reservoir be not allowed to increase. This was seen as a likely outcome with further agricultural development. The Report went on (to say) that 'steady progress must be made with the policy already laid down to acquire those alienated lands already in existence'. If this was not done, the holdings would become 'a source of embarrassment'; it would be 'extremely difficult' for future State Governments to resist pressure which would be 'undoubtedly exercised' for further alienation of land on all catchments.

In the early 1960s, the Public Works Department also alerted the

Agriculture Department to salinity problems in Wellington Dam. An engineer with the Public Works Department wrote to G.H. Burvill in 1961 complaining about the clearing of native vegetation in the Wellington Catchment, commenting: 'It is submitted that not only must no further land be alienated, but if the present upward trend in salinities persists, some forms of clearing control of land already alienated will assuredly be necessary.'[133] It will be remembered that this cautionary warning was delivered right at the time of the State Government's most ambitious land release scheme: the 'Million Acres (a year)' promotion.

In 1967, the limited extent of government's expenditure on salinity was revealed in a Parliamentary question when the then Minister, the Hon. A.F. Griffith, told Members that in the three years 1965, 1966 and 1967 the amounts spent on salinity were £15,000, £30,000, and £35,000 respectively.[134] These figures confirm what is apparent from a study of the Annual Reports of the Agriculture Department throughout the 1950s and 1960s—that salinity was not only rated as a relatively insignificant issue, it was framed within an economic context. A Departmental Press Bulletin of August 1966 makes this clear: 'Evidence has shown that clearing has accelerated the rise of water tables but it is unlikely that restrictions on clearing would greatly aid the problem ... because of the large areas that would have to be left uncleared.'[135]

Just as this comment shows the prevailing concern with economics over environment, so too does the following comment from Bill Benson, an engineer with the Water Board during the 1960s. He explained, in a 1982 interview, that Ministers relied heavily on selected powerful heads of departments who were committed to developmentalism. Agreements on land clearing were 'bulldozed through and really the full impact was never canvassed around the Water Board'.[136]

Nevertheless, as the 1960s progressed, salinity became a politically sensitive issue within government. The degree of this sensitivity is revealed in an exchange of memos from the Department of Agriculture to the CSIRO in Perth. In the first of the memos, G.H. Burvill wrote to his Director about a meeting he had had with three CSIRO scientists about various salinity investigations the organisation wished to pursue. He explained to the Director:

> It was pointed out [to the scientists] that there are many pressures and agitations from farmers for drainage work and other such works in an endeavour to control soil salinity and that these matters and related matters of flooding in the wheatbelt have caused great concern in recent years. Consequently we were anxious to avoid any embarrassment to us or any political embarrassment to the Government should undue publicity be given to C.S.I.R.O work suggesting that perhaps the results of research indicated ways and means of achieving practical relief from problems. Sometimes C.S.I.R.O. work is published through the 'Countryman' or through 'Rural Research' in C.S.I.R.O. and this has led to embarrassing Parliamentary questions or other questions from farmers … Any experimental work which proposed the digging of drains should be very carefully considered as it might be interpreted to be that drains were considered to be a solution to some of the flooding and salinity problems. This might lead to pressure from farmers for large Government expenditure on drainage, whether the benefits or changes brought about by drainage appeared to be great enough to warrant the cost.[137]

The Director subsequently wrote back to the CSIRO reconfirming the intention behind Burvill's initial conversation:

> I am glad to know that these joint discussions have taken place in order that the point of view of Departmental Officers towards salinity investigations may be clearly known to you. In particular you will be aware that there has been considerable pressure on the Government, and on this Department, in recent years for action to alleviate flooding and salinity. We would be anxious therefore that any of your investigations should be carefully considered before being given any publicity which might lead to embarrassment.[138]

Such correspondence raises clearly disturbing questions. Here were senior State officers clearly acting in a political manner by trying to direct the activities of a federal research body. Moreover, the exchange indicates the State Government's acute awareness of the magnitude of the salinity problem, for which it was not prepared to devote commensurate resources.

With the benefit of hindsight, the State Government's record on salinity is extremely poor. As Bennett and Macpherson have argued, 'official suspension of belief in the theory linking clearing to land and water salinity lasted for over forty years'.[139] It was not until 1976 that the Court Government legislated to control private clearing of land in selected catchments, a measure it could no longer avoid. It was only at this point, as Bennett argues, that the 'long-matured scientific theory had now become the fully acknowledged official theory as well'. Yet, throughout, governments were well informed about salinity and, by the 1950s, well aware of its implications. However, even at this point governments were to set aside their official policies to pursue further land release programs, as outlined in Chapter Three.

The era of the massive land release programs came to an end by the 1960s with the crash of wheat prices in 1969. Although revived on a smaller scale in the early 1980s, the boundaries of the Wheatbelt were largely in place by the 1970s. The sheer scale of the land clearing undertaken in the seventy years since its commencement make the Wheatbelt region unique. One estimate suggests that 15 billion trees were removed over this period.[140] Yet its place in history is now the subject of competing views and revision. Many people—and especially earlier generations—see, in the Wheatbelt, a mighty achievement; a potent symbol of the power of government in bringing land and prosperity to ordinary people and economic development to the State. Yet this view must now compete with the growing realisation of the consequences of that development. Governments must bear a large share of the responsibility for the salinity problems now ravaging the Wheatbelt, especially as successive governments were widely informed about the science of the problem but dismissed and/or ignored such evidence in their plans for agricultural development.

Yet, it is simplistic to blame governments alone, or to pay too much credence to hindsight. Governments were supported by community opinion favouring development and generations of farmers willingly took up the opportunities offered them. This support was a reflection of a set of cultural attitudes towards nature which tolerated its exploitation. Without this exploitation—and in the face of few other economic alternatives—it is worth speculating whether Western Australia could have ever built a foundation for prosperity.

However, it is also true that the responsibility of government is to protect the public interest. A strong case can be made that successive governments failed to do this. Moreover, the vast sums now needed to address the environmental and social problems surrounding salinity, surely raises questions about the optimistic economic assumptions of the original vision for the Wheatbelt.

Dealing with the Environmental Challenge: Politics and the Environment, 1970–90

The first telling sign that the political attachment to developmentalism might be effectively challenged in Western Australia occurred in 1967 with the founding of the Conservation Council of Western Australia. It was formed by the principal conservation groups at the time to provide a clearinghouse for information and to enable more effective co-ordination of political, research and educational strategies. The broad range of groups included the Campaign to Save Native Forests, the South-West Forest Defence Foundation, the King's Park and South River Preservation Society, the Tree Society, the WA Naturalists' Club and the WA Wildflower Society Club.[1,2] Originally named the Nature Conservation Council, the term 'Nature' was dropped several years later as the Council became involved in broader environmental issues. In 1969 the Council began to plan a political lobbying strategy known as the 'Conservation Campaign'. As a measure of the growing popularity of the conservation movement, the Coalition Government headed by Premier David Brand, which had been in office since 1959 and was due to face the polls in early 1971, indicated it was prepared to yield to some of the demands.

The culmination of the Conservation Campaign was a public rally on 17 March 1970 attended by some 250 people in King's Park followed by a torchlight parade on Parliament House, which had begun its 1970 sittings. Here the public presentation of the 'Conservation Bill of Rights' was made, along with a petition reputed to be signed by 15,000 people.[3] Parliamentary *Hansard* does not verify the presentation of the petition, but *The West Australian* gave the rally front page headlines with the photograph of Premier David Brand observing, from a vantage point in Parliament House, the public gathering with its numerous placards.[4] *The West Australian* had given the growing environmental movement its editorial backing,[5] and in due course the government of the day agreed to the formation of a Ministry of Conservation and to many of the points contained in the Conservation Bill of Rights.[6] An open letter to the Premier, which was published in *The West Australian* on 31 July 1970, helped keep the pressure on the State Government as it was signed by many prominent citizens from a wide range of interests.[7]

Although land degradation and salinity did not attract a great deal of attention in the early 1970s, the Conservation Bill of Rights presented to the Coalition Government did encompass land issues. Suggestions made included the establishment of a Land Utilisation Commission within the proposed Ministry of Conservation; a government policy requirement for 5 per cent of a farm's area to be retained under tree cover, or allowed to return to natural vegetation; and the strict supervision of any clearing of virgin land. A reference was also made to ensuring increased aid be available to farmers for reafforestation, water conservation and meeting soil erosion problems.[8] It was true that the term 'salinity' was not specifically mentioned in the Conservation Bill of Rights, but a start had been made with the inclusion of a heading 'Conservation Relating to Agriculture'.

As these developments reflect, 'concern for environmental protection had reached a new height and even if the Government of the day was not convinced of an environmental imperative, it slowly became aware of an electoral one'.[9] It was even claimed there were votes in the environment.[10] The Hon. Graham McKinnon, the Minister who was the main Brand Government spokesperson for environmental responsibilities in the last year of the Brand Government, commented on the political impact of the campaign. As McKinnon said:

Political pressure also was increasing. As Government was becoming aware of the need for environmental protection, so were some sections of the public. This awareness started as part of the 'consumer movement'. Many thought it was a fad which wouldn't last. Many more thought it was timely and would grow. Grow it did—sometimes leading Government and industry thinking, sometimes lagging. Inevitably, the need for greater care and control became a universally accepted dogma.[11]

Yet, the reality of the challenge posed by the environmental movement of the 1970s and 1980s was not the force indicated by McKinnon. Environmentalism made only a limited impact on the State's political culture of developmentalism as governments of all persuasions preferred to ignore, marginalise and even undermine the initial legislative framework for environmental protection passed by Parliament in 1971. In Western Australia, developmentalism proved to be a tough beast to tame. Forrest summed up the extent to which developmentalism had become the defining characteristic of the State's political culture:

> The emotive significance and political appeal of the term 'development' have been recognised by almost every administration in the history of the state, and if the concept is more closely associated with one party than the other, then this is due to better exploitation rather than a radical divergence of views, for the election manifestos from both sides are replete with plans for even greater and more diverse development.[12]

By the late 1970s, political commitment to developmentalism had been translated to an unquestioning allegiance expected from people working in or close to government: 'a regime of fear existed. Bureaucrats who questioned land release were jumped on.'[13] This is the context in which the salinity issue failed to find the necessary political and bureaucratic support to begin an assault on its mounting effects on the environment.

THE ENVIRONMENTAL PROTECTION AUTHORITY (EPA)

In the wake of the Conservation Campaign in early 1970, Premier David Brand moved to reform Western Australia's environmental structures. His response was to pass the *Physical Environment Protection Act 1970* which, according to University of Western Australia Zoology Professor Bert Main, 'was born of public outcry'.[14]

During the debate on the legislation, Premier Brand indicated that while community education on the environment was important,[15] 'it is accepted that the environmental crisis is less acute in this State than in most parts of the world experiencing rapid development'.[16] Significantly, he did acknowledge that one arena where there was much to be done was the 'deterioration of agricultural lands'.[17] It was not a specific reference to salinity but it was recognition of the concerns held by some of his Coalition Party colleagues.

However, Brand's environmental legislation was not proclaimed. Consequently, the proposed Physical Environment Council never met and, soon afterwards, Brand lost the State election to Labor leader John Tonkin, who had been dismissive of his rival's claims that Western Australia 'was to set the lead and the pace for conservation planning in Australia'.[18] In 1971 Tonkin, who had displayed a command of knowledge about the emergence of environmental concerns in the international sphere and in other states of Australia, guided the Environmental Protection Bill through Parliament.

The objects of the *Environmental Protection Act 1971*, which were said 'to set the scene for environmental management over more than a decade',[19] were broadly to:

–   enable positive action to be taken to control environmental degradation;
–   establish environmental protection policies that would set acceptable standards then and for the future;
–   invoke public opinion where necessary; and
–   provide for appeal in appropriate circumstances.

The Act provided for the establishment of an Environmental Protection Authority (EPA) as an independent statutory body, a Department of Environmental Protection—renamed the Department of Conservation and Environment (DCE) in 1975, and an Environment Protection Council—renamed the Conservation and Environment Council (CES) in 1975. There were also provisions for the setting up of an Environmental Appeals Board for appeals against proposed policy, but not against an approved policy.[20] The framework left the management of specific uses of the environment in the hands of existing departments.

However, Tonkin left no doubt that the Bill defined 'environment' as encompassing 'the physical factors prevailing in the State, including the land, water and the atmosphere. It also includes the social factor of the aesthetics and all factors affecting animal and plant life.'[21] Tonkin also proclaimed in his second reading speech: 'Cabinet will retain its constitutional obligations, while the environmental authority becomes a watchdog—and I would even say a watchdog with teeth.' But significantly he added:

> The fundamental and critical factor which must be borne in mind in considering this legislation is that it must be realistic. It must take account of what we are, what we want to have, for our generations to come. Therefore, this legislation must be balanced. It must achieve a balance between technological extremism, and conservation extremism.[22]

The challenges facing the new authority were considerable. Its first Chairman, Dr O'Brien, also later spoke of the vast range of environmental problems that had been 'saved up' for several years awaiting the EPA or some such environmental umbrella body to consider.[23] The Environment Protection Council, an advisory group of 'stakeholders' to the EPA, was described by O'Brien 'as all powerful and vigorous people'.[24]

However, according to Bert Main, who became one of the Authority's three foundation members, it was 'a fairly toothless tiger' in the early years. Although the new authority created the expectation that it would protect the environment, 'it did not have any authority at all'.[25] He gave the following example of salinity:

> Water salinity in the South-West had become a critical issue. The Wellington Dam was going salty and the Collie River catchment was coming under tremendous pressure. At this stage the concerned water authorities wanted us to impose clearing bans to stop vegetation being removed from the South-West's major catchments. While this possibility was being assessed, it was not possible to hire a bulldozer for any money because they were all being used to clear as much land as possible. The Authority had no power to act because salinity caused by clearing land did not fall under the definition of pollution.[26]

Main regarded education as the key function performed in the early years of the EPA. He drew on another example relating to salinity to illustrate the enormousness of the task in changing attitudes towards agricultural practices:

> We relied heavily on educating people. This presented some difficulty because people tended to think in relatively short terms, perhaps nowhere more so than in the agricultural industries. A senior departmental officer in the early days, Norman Orr, was a particularly fine exponent of the education approach. In the mid-1970s the shires on the outermost limits of the agricultural region were proposing further land releases. The land there was particularly marginal and made worse through a succession of droughts. But land released for development had, by that time, been so extensive that further releases almost anywhere were likely to be environmentally risky in the sense of being drought or erosion prone or at risk of making the already severe regional salinity problem much worse. Without any need for legislative backing, Norman, to his credit was able to work with all concerned with land release so that they were able to consciously consider all the

risks involved at the planning stage of the proposed release and anticipate any undesirable consequences of each proposal. Ultimately the Government proceeded to a revised policy on land release.[27]

Although the establishment of the EPA signified that Western Australia was at the national forefront of institutionalising a potentially powerful approach to environmental protection, its role as an advisory body meant its achievements could rarely match its promise. Indeed, when the Liberal–National Party Coalition led by Sir Charles Court regained power in 1974, the stature of the EPA was soon to be tested. Although Court had promised a Ministry of Conservation with wider powers than the existing Environmental Protection Department, the name changes were accompanied by 'a dramatically regressive shift in government attitude to the environment'.[28] Court, it was considered, aimed to minimise impediments to economic development as it was possible for many resource developments to be covered by Agreement Acts, which were not subject to the *Environmental Protection Act*.

One controversy weakening the standing of the EPA was the so-called 'Wagerup dispute'. This had erupted after protests about the mining in Jarrah forests associated with a proposed alumina refinery at Wagerup. The Court Government proceeded to pass legislation enabling the project to proceed independently of input from the EPA although the latter body undertook a review of the proposal. Then in 1980 the State Government separated the roles of the Chairman of the EPA and the Director of the DCE with an amendment to the *Environmental Protection Act*. Moreover, the independence of the EPA was further undermined in 1981 when another amendment curtailed its powers to publish reports independently and compulsorily acquire information from local authorities. It has been contended that these 'reforms' would have been more draconian but for the media speculation and possible electoral backlash.[29] Sir Charles Court later reflected that much of the criticism had been unfair as very effective work had been done for conservation management.[30] Moreover, as mentioned in the section on land release programs (see page 94–102), Court was aware how his government's attempts to curtail such programs in the South-West of the State were fiercely attacked.[31]

After a decade as the environmental ombudsman, the EPA had helped to check developmentalism but it could not confidently claim it had been able to assist environmentalism in gaining ground. In fact, Colin Porter, who become the Chair of the EPA in 1978, acknowledged as much when, in the foreword to the 1977–78 Report, he wrote that the 'task of environmental agencies is harder in such economic circumstances'. Thus, 'inevitably there is pressure from some quarters for relaxation of environmental standards'.[32] Porter also later mentioned that according to some definitions, salt was not necessarily classed as pollution as it happened naturally.[33] Professor Main, who also went on to hold the post of EPA Chair, also contended the EPA was hindered in its approach to salinity as it 'had no power to act because salinity caused by clearing land did not fall under the definition of pollution'.[34] This was later confirmed when in 1991, in the Supreme Court case of *Palos Estates Pty. Ltd. v Carbon*, Chief Justice David Malcolm broadly held that land clearing fell outside the definition of pollution, which in a dictionary sense meant 'to make foul or unclean'.[35]

Apart from the often discussed definitional questions, prominent conservationists also spoke of the broader problems they encountered in the 1970s and 1980s. 'From the beginning,' said Barbara Churchward who held a leading post in the Conservation Council, 'the relationship between the statutory Environment Protection Authority and the non-government voluntary Conservation Council ha[d] been stormy with few calm periods'. The years between 1974 and 1982 when Sir Charles Court and Ray O'Connor were respectively the Coalition Government premiers, were depicted as particularly difficult times. Conservationists actively involved in issues such as open-cut bauxite mining in the Jarrah forest, and the clear-felling of primeval Karri forests for wood chips, were often treated as extremists.[36] Churchwood, even cited a reference in the 1980–81 Conservation Council Annual Report which stated that 'the atmosphere of secrecy, fear and self-interest which pervades our society provides a grim outlook for the future of the conservation movement and survival of our natural heritage'.[37]

Importantly, though, as the EPA noted as early as its first report, it was hampered by 'the absence of precedents accurately applicable to [the] State'.[38] Of necessity it had to provide advice on a range of projects on a case-by-case basis. What became the dominant role of the DCE service to the EPA was the assessment of the environmental impact of proposed new developments. As Chittleborough, once an EPA officer later observed, 'reacting to an escalating stream of development proposals so consumed the attention of [the] EPA/DCE that the policy making provisions of the *Environmental Protection Act 1971* (ss. 28–53) were not used explicitly'.[39]

The formidable role of assessment of specific projects consumed most of the budget of the EPA, limiting its role as 'environmental ombudsman'. Moreover, even though 'public awareness' was documented in every annual report and the creation of a library was an important avenue for those requiring research, critics questioned whether sufficient resources were placed in this direction. As Chittleborough again observed:

> Over the years, a progressively lower proportion of the EPA/DCE budget has been spent on communication. The procedures for public response continue to operate, but often with shortened time frames and a lack of feedback giving the community the impression that their submissions are not seriously considered.[40]

In these ways, the EPA was unable to provide the framework of effective environmental protection envisaged at the beginning of the 1970s. From 1978, with the information of the interdepartmental Working Group on Land Releases, the EPA was involved in formally approving the controversial land release which occurred in the early 1980s. In reality, it faced an uphill battle in any challenge to the power of the resource-based departments whose narrow focus was described by Bill Benson, an engineer with the Water Board, in an interview given in 1982. He explained that 'each Department by its Statute is required to push its own barrow with a minimum regard to others'. He said this especially related to matters of conservation and the environment where nothing in any of the Acts governing the operations of individual departments required them to consider the preservation of the environment. Compounding the problem was the separate structure by which departments operated:

> I think that one of the problems is that Departments give fairly strong mission oriented advice to government. The Government hasn't got enough expertise to test the department. When you have got all engineers in one Department and all the foresters in another, how can a minister test the advice he is given?[41]

SALINITY AND WATER SUPPLIES

One manifestation of salinity in which the EPA did not become directly involved was the rise in public concern during the 1970s about the high saline levels in Perth's water supply. The issue evolved into a major health scare in 1978 forcing salinity onto the political agenda, where the accompanying media interest served as a vehicle for the first major public education campaign about the causes and consequences of the problem.

As mentioned in Chapter Two, concern about rising salt levels in Perth's water supply were repeatedly raised in reports written by the Public Works Department. However, the issue did not reach public prominence until newspaper reports in the early 1970s drew attention to the release of findings from a long-term survey of the Wellington Catchment which showed a rise in salt levels with the potential to adversely affect plant growth.[42]

Several years later the situation was described as 'serious' by the Public Works Department. Moreover, excessive land clearing was the agreed cause of the problem. However, no immediate solution was in sight: 'Because of the nature of the problem, the research [needed] was long range involving years of work.'[43]

By the mid-1970s the warnings issued by the Public Works Department had become more strident: 'Water from the Wellington

Dam could become too saline for irrigation and risky for domestic use if clearing in the catchment continues.'[44] Indeed, by the mid-1970s, a similar problem was showing up throughout South-West catchments. In the Blackwood River, for example, it was reported that 'there had been an increase of 300 per cent in the salinity of the river water at Bridgetown between 1907–17 and 1956–1970. This coincided with the clearing of inland areas for agriculture.'[45]

By the winter of 1978, salinity levels in Perth's water supply erupted into a public health issue. The newly formed conservation group—the 'Campaign to Save Native Forests'—coopted the issue of salinity to publicise the forests issue better.[46]

Verification of the potential health problems arising from the increasingly saline water supply came from a cardiologist, a paediatrician and a kidney specialist from the University of Western Australia's medical school who claimed that Perth's water was already more saline than was desirable for public health.[47] Patients with heart and kidney diseases 'were finding it difficult to restrict their salt intake with the water supply containing so much'.[48] Children were also said to be at risk from developing high blood pressure from their exposure to the water supply.[49] Not surprisingly, the media jumped on the issue and gave it prominence through headlines, including 'Heart Man Hits out at Salinity',[50] 'Salt Level Controversy',[51] and 'Our Salty Water: Should We Worry?'.[52]

By any measure, the response from both the Tonkin and Court governments was less than decisive. In the early to mid-1970s more research was promised, but when the issue became controversial in 1978, the government at the time tried to minimise its impact: the Minister for Water Resources, Mr O'Connor, explained that the salt level in Perth's water supply rose during the drought then in progress, but had fallen to normal levels again following winter rain.[53] It was a view emphatically challenged by a government research scientist, Dr Maurice Mulcahy, who said that the

> salinisation of streams and extension of the area affected by salt is perhaps one of the most widespread and significant effects of

clearing for agriculture in southern Australia generally. [the cause of salinisation] is essentially the clearing of deep-rooting native plant communities and replacing them with annual crops and pastures with shallow root systems.[54]

The lack of an initial response from government was likely underpinned by the prevailing view expressed in a *West Australian* editorial. It said salinity was 'an unfortunate legacy of agricultural clearing years ago and there is little we can do about it'.[55]

However, by the end of the 1970s, the Court Government was compelled to act. In 1979 it introduced 'lightning legislation' banning all further land clearing in the South-West of the State without a licence: the legislation was rushed through Parliament without any talks between government and farmers, a move designed to prevent them quickly clearing land before the Bill became law. Licences were to be granted sparingly and there were harsh penalties for law-breakers.[56] For their part, farmers did not appreciate the reasons behind the move to ban clearing:

Many have been waiting for their financial positions to improve so they can afford to clear more land and increase production. As many again have been planning their future around clearing more land to enable their children to stay on the farm.[57]

The concern over the water supply stimulated public awareness and interest in salinity which had a positive effect in encouraging governments to consider political responses to the problem. Following the passage of legislation to tighten up land clearing, a window of opportunity opened for government to strengthen its efforts to control salinity. In March 1979, the Pastoralists and Graziers Association (PGA) organised a broadly representative seminar on salinity, at which an agreement was reached to set up a committee to monitor, review and advise on salinity research in Western Australia, 'as a matter of urgency'. Surprisingly, given the opposition from farmers to the recently imposed bans on land clearing, the President of the PGA, Mr J.S. Sampson, gave positive support for more efforts to control salinity. He explained that legislation banning South-West catchment clearing without a licence was 'to be a holding rather than long term position'. Participants in the seminar ranged widely over the issues which the proposed committee might have considered. Dr Maurice Mulcahy, Senior Research Scientist with the Environmental Protection Authority, said the solution 'might involve a change in agriculture', although he 'was not sure how this could be done'. Mr K. Webster, a Public Works Department engineer, foreshadowed debate about salinity in the 1990s when he said that 'he did not believe there was one answer to the problem. A final solution could be a mixture of engineering, reforestation, drainage, clearing control and farming techniques.' Mr F. Batini of the Forests Department advised on the potential of agro-forestry, noting that 'there were problems with the system but it would be better than forcing people to leave the land'. Finally, a representative from the National Country Party suggested the use of belts of fast-growing and slow-growing variegated eucalypts to control salinity.[58] However, no committee was ever established to take up the concerns raised at the PGA seminar.

Despite the lack of action, salinity had finally emerged as a political issue. It had been brought to city people through media coverage, and a broad coalition of concern had been fostered between scientists, farmer organisations, political parties, and public servants for more action to be taken. However, not only did the Court Government allow this opportunity to lapse, it departed entirely from the spirit of its own legislation and the goodwill expressed at the PGA seminar, to engage in another round of land clearance.

THE LAND RELEASE PROGRAMS OF THE 1980s

The State Government's decision to proceed with a new wave of land release programs in the early 1980s, testified to the lack of scope and 'teeth' of the *Environmental Protection Act* to influence policy. The release of new land had slowed in the period between the late 1960s and 1980. The combination of low wool prices and the impact of wheat quotas led to a policy of consolidation rather than expansion.

Yet, by the late 1970s, the urge to expand agricultural land stirred yet again. For the next few years, land release became a focal point of political division between the old-style developmentalists of the '50s and '60s, and the newly energised environmental lobby seeking greater institutional recognition of the rights of the environment. In the short term developmentalists won. The build-up of pressure on politicians from country shires seeking the benefits of extra rates, roads and business from further land development filtered to the Rural and Agricultural Industries Commission (RAIC) that was responsible for advising government on land release. Social pressures added to the case for another surge of land release. These had come from 'young aspiring farmers [who wanted] a chance to get into primary production without the need for big capital sums to buy an established property'.[59]

Yet, there was a deeper social conviction behind the aspirations of young farmers: the survival of agrarian idealism which had been a mainstay of agricultural expansion since the turn of the century. As a recently settled farmer explained to *The Western Farmer and Grazier* in 1982: 'You can't put a value on wanting to go farming.'[60] Even in the early 1980s, the ideal of farming was sustained by a set of beliefs around which:

-   Farming was perceived as a fundamental industry on which society in general depends;
-   Farming was not just a business but a way of life;
-   Full ownership and self-reliance are desired goals; and
-   The family farm is the most appropriate institution where each family member is an integral part of the enterprise.[61]

In fact, such values and beliefs were dominant in the land release policies of the early 1980s, and especially in the selection of young farmers to settle on and develop the land. This selection became part of a societal goal to ensure the continuation of the family farm.[62]

With such idealism to sustain land release, it is not surprising commentators spoke of a 'pro-land release lobby'. This lobby was spearheaded by the Esperance Industrial Development Committee which made an extensive submission to government calling for 40,000 hectares of new land to be released each year for five years. Its Chairman, local MLA, Mr Geoff Grewar, explained that 'the regular release of land is vital to the continued growth of the Esperance region'.[63]

Farmers out in the marginal country opened up in the 1960s were also behind the campaign for renewing the release of Crown Land for agriculture. Ravensthorpe farmer, Mike Linto, explained on ABC television in 1982 that:

> Nobody can afford to buy the next-door neighbour's farm at $400.00 an acre, never hope to pay it back, so they put pressure on the government through the shires to farmer bodies to release more land so that we can all get a go at it. And while there are farmers and farmers' sons, and high land prices, there's always going to be the pressure to release more land.[64]

The new land release programs also occurred in the immediate aftermath of a politically bruising encounter with farmers in the South-West of the State (supported by the WA Farmers Union) over the above-mentioned legislation to ban land clearing without a licence. In response, the State Government encountered 'open rebellion' in 'fiery' farmer meetings throughout the South-West. The lines of argument used by farmers said much about the priority many placed on salinity control and their perception of a State Government which lacked credibility on the issue. At one meeting, farmer representatives argued that salinity control took a back seat to farmer concern over 'the bureaucratic interference with the rights of private owners'. At the same meeting farmers were told that 'the government had known about the salinity problem since the 1920s, yet it had waited not only until the horse had bolted, but until it had disappeared over the horizon'.[65] As a result of the farmer protest, government watered down its restrictions in an episode that showed it was prepared to concede some ground to the rights of farmers before salinity control.

Direct pressure on government for further land release culminated in a report written by the RAIC—whose membership consisted entirely of agricultural interests—identifying three million additional hectares thought to be suitable for agriculture in the Ravensthorpe region. The Report remained secret but in 1980, the Minister for Lands announced that, based on RAIC advice, land was to be released in unserviced areas at a faster rate than in recent years. Opposition to the plan was soon mounted. Conservationists led the attack. To these groups it had seemed governments had learnt nothing from past experience. At a meeting arranged by Friends of the Earth at the University of Western Australia, for example, the process by which the Commission arrived at its recommendation was criticised: 'Not one person with important alternative views was invited to sit on the Commission' and, within a twelve-week period, it had finalised 'a shallow report which can only be described as a disgrace'. Moreover, the process was claimed to be shrouded in secrecy: 'Many government officers realise that a lot of the land earmarked for release is unavailable but are now under pressure not to say otherwise.'[66]

Groups formed to build community opposition, including the Land Release Study Group which attacked the Government's policy in the media. Spokesman, Keith Bradby, put the case on many occasions that 'the area had an extremely high potential for salination problems in the future'.[67] In fact, Bradby has written a vivid account of his reaction to the Government's announced resumption of land releases:

> My personal reaction to the Minister's statement was one of stunned disbelief. I could not believe that such rampant expansion was a course Government, even the W.A. Government, would take. Whilst appreciating that agricultural expansion increased our wheat yields, our tractor sales and so on, I was surrounded by other evidence. My neighbours were having a battle, and every year I had fewer neighbours. We hadn't learned to live and work with our landscapes. The legacy of expansion was becoming increasingly evident through rapidly increasing salinity, wind erosion and a host of land degradation problems. The beauty and richness of the W.A. bush was being turned into a bare and ugly landscape … I cried when I saw the surveyor's pegs go around one piece of bush near my home. It was a place of beauty, home to a

host of rare species, one of which had only recently been discovered on that very block.[68]

Imbued with these concerns, Bradby has told how the Land Release Study Group was formed:

> I lived with a woman who was similarly concerned, and we knew of two friends who were also worried. They knew of someone else who was already fighting the proposals. Next week eight of us sat in a room and talked for a day. It was wonderful to get it all off our chests. So wonderful that we had to meet again a couple of weeks later to have time to talk about what we were actually going to do.[69]

The Group's efforts in opposing the land release schemes were later supported by no less than a principal advisor to the Agriculture Department, Mr Kevin Goss, who informed the 53rd ANZAAS Congress in Perth in 1983 about the 'wide agreement' existing over the lack of knowledge supporting land use decisions in the State, and especially the inadequate soil survey data and the implications for wind erosion and salinity. Extraordinarily, in light of this evidence, reports circulated in country newspapers attesting to the work of the Agriculture Department in being able 'to demonstrate that salt problems of this country can be overcome using modern management and other procedures'.[70]

Contrary to this confident assertion, farmers on the South Coast of the State were growing concerned about the viability of their industry. In 1981 they captured local media attention by openly worrying that the region would eventually be turned into a dustbowl because wind erosion and salination showed that farming systems were not sustainable.[71] In a contradiction difficult to understand, local Member of Parliament, Geoff Grewar, who had a BSc in agriculture and held memberships in the Farmers Union and the Pastoralists and Graziers Association, agreed. In 1981, and in spite of his afore-mentioned support for further land release, he said that time was running out to stop the environmental problems of the Wheatbelt. He complained that government gave no incentives to plant more trees: 'The issue was becoming urgent with growing salinity and erosion problems'. It is vital we become more conscious of reafforestation in our Wheatbelt. If we do not, we will lose the whole character of our countryside with the ultimate result being a vast and treeless prairie.'[72]

In response to these concerns came the first organised stirring of a landcare ethic re-emerged, after the initial efforts had been drowned out by the post-Second World War land schemes. In October 1981, Perth-based forestry consultant, Charles Peatty, told a conference of more than 200 agriculturalists that farmers had to plant more trees to control salinity: 'Tree care is in the minority and the present situation is trees versus agriculture … the need for economic viability had overcome the need for trees. [However] we must plant trees now.'[73]

Just as the State Government approved further widespread land clearing, some farmers began acting on the appeal to plant more trees. *The Countryman* reported:

> Time and money is now being invested to undo the mistakes of the past, or avoid creating environmental conditions which put farmland at risk. In the latter category, Mr Barry Rick outlined his strip clearing policy for a CP [Conditional Purchase] block at Lake Magenta near Newdegate. He regards wind as the most erosive force in the east and south east agricultural regions. His hope is that retained vegetation strips will have a buffering effect on winds sweeping over cleared blocks.[74]

As part of the emerging landcare ethic—although this term was not yet in use—interest was shown in the few farmers who had earlier bucked the trend to clear their blocks progressively of trees. They gained a new respect as the following account of Geoff Cugley's work, published in *The Countryman*, showed:

> Fifteen years ago most new land settlers put no value on leaving any substantial areas of land uncleared on their holdings. But Newdegate farmer, Mr Geoff Cugley, was one of the exceptions.

He came in for some good natured ribbing from fellow farmers about the 'parkland' he was developing. But as far as he is concerned time has proved the value of the bush acres left.[75]

The remainder of the article detailed Mr Cugley's visionary work on his farm: the development of a farm plan; the fencing out of sheep from bush areas; the application of crop rotation; and the collection of native seeds for replanting. His commitment and instinct of working with nature had a beneficial effect in lessening the impact of salinity:

Other conservation work has included the fencing out of two small areas affected by salt. One, in a paddock four years in pasture, was planted with gums, tamarisks, and pines. With grazing stopped, plant cover has come back on the salt pan and the problem appears to be under control.

Mr Cugley's approach to farming could have, and indeed, should have, been a beacon for new farming practices. Throughout the Wheatbelt however, it wasn't; new ways of working with the land were slow to spread and were certainly undercut by the rush to new land releases along the old lines of broad-based clearing. The clamour for blocks ensured that nothing much would change.

In 1982, for example, over 300 applications were received even before the Beaumont Blocks, 100 kilometres north-east of Esperance, were officially released (in two stages). Yet, this renewed commitment was taken in the face of escalating opposition from environmentalists to the land release program on the South Coast. Not long before the Burke Government was elected in 1983, conservationists attracted national attention to the issue. Prominent environmentalist Vincent Serventy wrote a letter to *The Australian*, arguing the case that

a major environmental issue of national importance [is] about to occur in Western Australia. This concerns a stepped up development scheme to clear the remaining mallee-heathlands in the south-west of that state for farming ... [The region] supports by far the richest flora and fauna association of any of Australia's remaining areas of mallee-heathland ... Yet, the West Australian government intends to proceed with a high-risk development on a massive scale which will result in the loss of huge areas of our national heritage.[76]

Pressure on the Court Government's land release policy intensified in July 1982 when the ABC's *Nationwide* program revealed the contents of a leaked letter from the Australian Institute for Agricultural Sciences to the Minister for Agriculture, Mr Laurence. According to the journalist covering the story, the letter expressed

grave concern about the Government's land release plans. The Institute numbers among its members hundreds of agricultural scientists in this State, who are painfully aware of the devastation of ongoing land release policies. The Institute argued for a number of conditions to be met in future land releases; the long-term cost and possible survival of new farms should not be borne by the rest of the community. New release should not bring a risk of salinity, erosion or danger to water supplies. Undue damage to flora and fauna should be avoided and areas of special interest preserved. The Institute told the Minister that these conditions cannot be met with present knowledge for much of the land being considered for release. The Institute is a conservative body; its advice to the Minister is a reflection of the concern felt by many State public servants about the Government's land release policy.[77]

Laurence came under further criticism during the program on two fronts. Firstly, he was questioned whether, at $10 an acre, the low prices being charged for land constituted 'almost an enticement'. Secondly, the Minister fended off criticism that too little investigation had been conducted into the viability of the land for farming by revealing that 'every farm that's released has to be approved by a sub-committee of the Cabinet—of the State Cabinet'. In view of the knowledge that farms were already experiencing salinity, wind erosion and drought, such high-level government endorsement appears to have been a brave guarantee to make.

However, it was confidently asserted that 'recent environmental criticism will not delay the release allocation'.[78] The full extent of misplaced confidence about this particular scheme was the subject of later review in which the authors concluded:

> All soils in the Stage 1 [of the Beaumont Blocks] area suffer from salinity at relatively shallow depths and most have structural degradation as a result of clearing and cultivation. Ninety per cent of the soils in the Stage 2 area are not suited to conventional agriculture and would require special management to prevent a rapid decline in productivity following clearing.[79]

By the 1980s, Western Australian government policy on agricultural development had become caught in a time warp. The developmentalist ethos was now being shown in a different light with the gathering momentum of environmental concern. However, governments changed too slowly. The last big land release projects echoed past certainties. In 1981, for example, the Lands Minister, David Wordsworth, evoked the age-old pioneering spirit of the individual conquering the environment when, defending the most recent land release scheme, he said: 'Many farmers with all their worldly possessions on the back of a farm truck, and tradesmen fresh from their apprenticeships with hardly enough money to hire a tin shed were now millionaires. They have new land releases to thank for this. The resulting growth speaks for itself.'[80] There is a tragic irony in the Minister's fulsome praise of agricultural development. Seven years later he found himself Chairman of the Legislative Council's Select Committee on Salinity, which presented the first full political acknowledgment of the seriousness of the problem.

THE AGRICULTURE DEPARTMENT AND SALINITY

The Department of Agriculture, which had been a key agency of the State Government's developmentalism, did not consider salinity to be a major problem during the 1960s and early 1970s. University of Western Australia geographer, Arthur Conacher, one of the earliest academic researchers on the problem, has reflected that the Department believed land rendered unproductive by salinity was limited to one per cent and, therefore, to be an insignificant problem.[81]

Other evidence suggests that the Department was in no position to form such a view in light of the low priority it gave to researching salinity. The departmental view of salinity was outlined in a telling piece of evidence given by Dr Graeme Robertson, Commissioner of Soil Conservation (which is still part of the Agriculture Department) to the 1988 parliamentary Select Committee on Salinity. This evidence indicates a decision was made by the Department during the 1950s not to make salinity a focus of research because, it seemed, it was too politically difficult for it to do so:

> The Department of Agriculture was at one stage arguing very strongly against release of land in the Wellington catchment area back in the early 1950s but apparently the Minister was rolled in Cabinet and the land was released, which led to the Department of Agriculture washing its hands of the problem. We had put up our case yet the State decided it [the land release] was acceptable, so it went completely off the department's agenda.[82]

Not surprisingly perhaps, this information, collected in transcript, was not included in the Committee's Final Report. It is unclear from Robertson's evidence just how long this attitude lasted within the Department. However, he does briefly state that in the late 1970s, the research effort was still very limited and focused on trying to plant Saltbush on already saline land.[83]

Confirmation of the low priority given to salinity by the Agriculture Department appeared to come from the surveys it carried out among farmers. The first survey, conducted by post in 1962, gained a return of 83.3 per cent. Later surveys conducted under the auspices of the Australian Bureau of Statistics, obtained a 100 per cent coverage from all regions of the State. Conacher has reflected on the serious flaws in the self-reported survey method:

There were some interesting responses by farmers to interviewers' questions as to whether they considered salt to be a problem. Some answered 'no' to the question, even though an extensive salt scald was clearly visible from the homestead … The difficulty here was that the farmers anticipated correctly that a follow-up question was designed to determine what remedial actions they were taking. When they had taken no or very minor and ineffective action, for whatever reason, the farmers were understandably reluctant to acknowledge that there was a problem. One of the farmers who denied having a problem was forced to sell his property a few years later, as it had become economically unviable following the loss of one-third of his productive land to secondary salinity.[84]

Shaped by the above results, the Department tended to thwart efforts of concerned farmers who had formulated alternative theories about salinity and how the problem should be confronted. The longest running battle took place over a salt reclamation technique conducted by Harry Whittington, a Wheatbelt farmer. Whittington had called his 1975 publication *A Battle for Survival Against Salt Encroachment at 'Springhill'*, Brookton, Western Australia and in it he described the steady deterioration of his family's farm:

> Very early in life, I came in contact with soil and water, saw the wonders, beauty and power of nature, watched the crystal clear creek which flowed gently throughout the year, change to a muddy, raging torrent in the winter and a dry sand bed in the summer. Saw a flourishing orchard transformed to dry tree stumps, the evergreen verges of native lucerne on the flats change to waterlogged, bare, barren soil which in time was covered with small white crystals shining in the sun. This substance was called Sodium Chloride—just common salt to me.[85]

CSIRO scientists Duncan McPherson and David Bennett, who met Whittington during the late 1970s, have written of the problems he faced:

In the late 1940s, Harry Whittington faced the task of restoring the farm that had been owned by his father, 'Springhill', which lies on the western or high rainfall border of the wheat belt. The property was producing less than it had when first developed at the turn of the century. Creeks were silted up and there were large salt patches in the valleys and erosion gullies in the hillsides. He rejected the option of selling up and moving to new land as many of his neighbours did.[86]

Whittington's initial step was to seek Department of Agriculture advice, which suggested implementing a program of contour cultivation and other erosion countermeasures. But Whittington lost confidence in the advice mainly because he believed it was aimed at tolerating the existence of salinity rather than, as he thought, the need to fully reclaim land and bring it back into full production. He developed a theory about salinity control quite at odds with the one developed by the Agriculture Department. Whittington believed surface or near subsurface run-off from rainwater flowed to valleys where saline areas developed. The Department, on the other hand, maintained the scientific evidence showed salt is forced up into the valley areas from depths below the surface.[87] Based on his theory, Whittington constructed contour banks, known as 'interceptor banks', to trap the rainfall and prevent it from flowing into valleys. For its part, the Agriculture Department believed the banks to be useless. This fundamental difference in understanding the causes of salinity, or acknowledging that it can result from a combination of causes, became the focal point for bitter division between Whittington and his supporters, and the Agriculture Department, a division which lasted for over a decade.

The story of Harry Whittington and his interceptor banks has 'David versus Goliath' undertones. Having rejected the Department's advice and embarked on his own radical solution—which took eight years to show any results—Harry attracted the attention of his neighbours who were impressed with his success in reducing salinity on his land. The first interceptor banks were built in 1953 and by the mid-1970s, few scalds of salt remained on his property which, as the following description from *The Countryman* newspaper showed, had been brought back into full production: 'Crops and pastures are grown successfully on previously unproductive land ... It took 25 years' work, much of it on a trial and error basis, but finally the salt problem was overcome.'[88]

Although dismissed in some quarters as a crank for pushing a theory science thought could not possibly be right, his services were in high demand in other farming districts. By the early 1970s, Harry Whittington was 'revered as a saviour'.[89] In fact, Whittington became something of a media personality with numerous stories written about him. Press photographs show him addressing hundreds of farmers from the back of a truck. In 1974 his supporters gathered to form a group to promote the success of interceptor banks. Launched by the cumbersome name of the Whittington Interceptor Salt-Affected Land Treatment Society, it was universally known by its acronym—WISALTS. Membership climbed to over 1,000 by 1981 and included a former Minister for Agriculture and the afore-mentioned Dr Arthur Conacher, a leading geographer at the University of Western Australia, whose own research into salinity had shown evidence of the 'flow through' movement of salt in parts of the Wheatbelt.[90] Conacher has confirmed the extent of Whittington's support among farmers: 'at the time, this was almost a third of all wheatbelt farmers reporting a salt problem, demonstrating the extent of disillusionment with the State agricultural agency's advice'.[91] As one Kondinin farmer expressed in 1981: 'Advice from the Department of Agriculture was to fence the land and plant blue bush. But the salt kept spreading.'[92]

Others saw Whittington's rise to prominence in more complex, sociological terms. When a journalist from *The Countryman* reflected on the Whittington phenomenon in the late 1970s, he was genuinely perplexed to explain the enthusiastic response from farmers, especially considering that insufficient time had elapsed to concretely prove or disprove all his theories. He said the response could be explained either as Australians' historical distrust of authority figures which, in the case of farmers, was heightened in the post-Second World War years when government officials oversaw land release schemes, or 'evangelistic fervour'.[93] Whittington was certainly depicted by the press in the role of farmers' saviour. *The Daily News*, for example, once wrote of his work: 'Farmers sat on the banks to hear their prophet preach the theory they regard as gospel.'[94]

Whatever lay behind his rise to prominence, Whittington tirelessly advocated his interceptor banks in addition to the cause of salinity generally. He was an influential figure in the farmers' movement and, as a consequence, had the ear of some influential rural politicians.[95] His passionate advocacy also contributed to the heightened media interest in salinity during the 1970s. WISALTS acted as a lobby group to promote acceptance of the interceptor bank method and to strive for tax deductibility for applying it. More broadly, one of the 'platforms' advocated by the WISALTS group was the removal of responsibility for soil conservation from the Department of Agriculture.[96] Whittington himself was extremely critical of the Department for its failure to provide individual farmers with on-going, intensive advice. In June 1985, for example, he wrote to the Minister for Agriculture outlining shortcomings in the Department's approach:

> Over many years farmers have listened to the advice and recommendations of the Department and have meticulously adhered to that advice. For a short period the problem has been slowed and or camouflaged then it continues to develop. Unfortunately, no officer seems to go back to that farm to evaluate what has happened over a long period and try to understand why the work has not been successful. Of course in most instances by the time that the problem has increased dramatically the officer has been transferred or advanced to Head Office. The next officer carries on with what he knows and apparently does not report to Head Office or his senior officer that there is a breakdown in the methods.[97]

The stand-off between the organisation and the Agriculture Department generated considerable media coverage during the late 1970s and early 1980s. The polarisation between the two camps was underpinned by the rising desperation among many farmers for a solution to their growing salt problem and a history of personality clashes between Whittington and senior Agriculture Department officers.[98] Whittington's personal papers carry several pieces of acrimonious correspondence written in the early 1980s between himself and then Director of Agriculture E.N. Fitzpatrick. On one occasion, Whittington wrote to the Director complaining that 'you have enjoyed the past several years misleading farmers and misinforming members of the Western Australian State Government [about his salinity control methods]'. Fitzpatrick shot back a stern reply: 'This is quite untrue. I believe your statement could be the basis of legal action.'[99]

The Agriculture Department appeared to feel its credibility was under threat from Whittington's campaign on behalf of interceptor banks. As *The West Australian* reported in the late 1970s, 'farmers claim the department is not prepared to accept that practising farmers can come up with a solution that scientists have failed to find'.[100] In 1978 Fitzpatrick, wrote a long letter in *The Farmer and Grazier* expressing 'regret that farmers are spending large amounts of money on this system' and reiterating that scientific data did not support Whittington's approach.[101] Some contemporaries believe the Agriculture Department took very seriously the 'threat' from Whittington. Hyden farmer (and currently President of the WA Farmers' Federation) Colin Nicholl, claims Whittington was 'set upon' by the Department.[102] Research officers working in the Agriculture Department during the Whittington 'era' remember the period as a time of terrible conflict. Key officers remained unconvinced of the merits of Whittington's approach. Research Officer Clive Malcolm, wrote to his superior in 1977: 'It should be clearly appreciated that Mr Whittington is not an authority on soil salinity problems. His comments comprise experiences, ideas, opinions, and interpretations and often lack a critical scientific approach. One of the greatest difficulties in designing a trial to test Mr Whittington's methods will be to discover precisely what they are.'[103] In fact, to the extent that the Department acknowledged improvements on Whittington's property, it explained these as factors of improved farm management, rather than being due to his interceptor banks.[104]

Polarisation was exacerbated when an inquiry was commissioned by the Public Works Department into Whittington's theory. Professor J.W. Holmes, a South Australian consultant, who was assigned the task, quickly concluded after a three-day visit to Western Australia that no scientifically sustainable evidence existed for the widespread support of interceptor banks.[105] Arthur Conacher then responded with an extensive critical evaluation of the Holmes Report on the Whittington Drain Trial. In Conacher's view, Holmes did not adequately review the literature and was confused about the actual significance of the trial:

> Above all his report relies on a misleading theoretical modelling of the situation, to the extent that: he has modified facts to fit the theory (in the case of the amount of runoff from cleared versus uncleared land); he dismisses or discounts empirical findings where they do not fit the model, as in the case of benefits claimed by farmers to follow interceptor bank construction; he ignores or discounts other findings, such as the accumulating empirical evidence from a number of independent studies which collectively demonstrate the ubiquitous importance of throughflow in the wheatbelt landscape; and he ignores socio-economic realities, in that nearly 900 farmers, dissatisfied with previous salinity amelioration measures, are now paying substantial sums of money on an alternative approach.[106]

Later, J.S. Duff, a Conservation Officer from the Victorian Soil Conservation Authority, examined the conflict. He judged it had 'resulted in extensive mass media interest, unfortunately resulting in an apparent loss of credibility of the Agriculture Department'. Duff was worried the dispute could spread to Victoria and he felt it necessary to firmly state his findings:

> Whittington's theory appears to be incorrect, but, it does indicate that farmers are prepared to spend money on 'cure all treatments' of salting and that there is a need for scientific agencies to put forward positive solutions to salting problems despite the costs.

Many farmers eventually will probably regret the time, money and inconvenience incurred in installing and living with Whittington banks.[107]

The stand-off with Whittington forced the Agricultural Department to lift its focus on salinity. Publicly, at least, the Department had not announced a policy position on salinity until 1979, when it 'spelt out its stand on the state's salt problem, announcing a farmer education plan'. This move signalled the Department's 'plans to become more involved in the problem'.[108] In reality, it had probably more to do with restoring its image among farmers and trying to counter some of Whittington's influence.

Unfortunately, the scientific debate over the Whittington banks made it clear there were no simple solutions to the salinity problem in the Western Australian Wheatbelt (or elsewhere in Australia). A parliamentary select committee later judged 'the conflict between WISALTS and the research community has polarised many people, and left the remainder sitting on the fence'.[109] Ultimately, though, it was necessary for officers in government departments, particularly the Agriculture Department, to broaden their horizons to recognise that a major environmental problem could not be 'fenced in' and that multiple strategies had to be applied to begin to address the salinity crisis. However, critics of the Agriculture and Lands Departments saw these agencies as 'members of a captive bureaucracy dependent on agricultural expansion for the sustenance of their own departments'.[110]

THE SOIL CONSERVATION SERVICE

The impotence of the Agriculture Department in dealing with salinity during these years was matched by its specialist sub-section, the Soil Conservation Service. This is in spite of the high hopes held for it when its enabling legislation was passed in 1945. In 1948, its first Commissioner explained in a letter to the Director of the Commonwealth Bureau of Soil Sciences in England that the purpose of the *Soil Conservation Act* was to prevent and mitigate soil erosion, 'and generally to promote soil conservation'. However, he also outlined a bolder objective:

> there is also at present considerable opinion in our wheatbelt area ... that control of land clearing by legislation or regulation should take place, and that farmers should be required to notify the soil conservation authority of their intention to clear any area of land of its native timber or scrub vegetation, or that an inspection of the area should be made before the clearing is done.[111]

While there is no mention of salinity, other than in a general sense, the Commissioner's clearly articulated plans to crack down on land clearing would have obvious benefits to both salinity and soil erosion given the common linkage to land clearing. The fate of the Soil Conservation Service is but another example of governmental inertia over the environment in this period. Of course firm action by governments would have probably carried electoral costs as the development ethos was popular. Political parties, operating in a parliament with rural weighting in its representation, could not afford in electoral terms to curtail the expansion of agricultural tracts. As such, over the next few decades the capacity of the Soil Conservation Service to halt the environmental problems in the Wheatbelt were rendered largely impotent by the strength of political commitment to land clearing and a combination of unaddressed legal obstacles within the *Soil Conservation Act 1945* and lack of resources.

From the outset, it appears that the Agriculture Department was well aware of legal problems standing in the way of effective implementation of the Act. Advice it had received from Crown Law indicated the Act conferred on the Department limited jurisdiction over the activities of private farmers. As D.J. Carder, Adviser with the Soil Conservation Service, explained in a 1974 memo to the Director of Agriculture: 'Crown Solicitor's advice obtained in 1947 [indicates] that a public body is not authorised to affect private rights unless compensation is provided.' In fact, a gaping hole had existed in the legislation for decades, as Carder further explained: 'If the legislature had intended to delegate … power to preclude an owner from clearing his land some such provision would have been expressed in the Act.'[112] Whereas, in actual fact, the Act had stated that the agreement of the owner to interfere with his property rights had to be obtained. Earlier, it had been confirmed that farmers did possess common law rights to pursue litigation if 'it was thought likely a farmer suffered income loss under a soil conservation order'.[113]

In this way, the Soil Conservation Act became a toothless tiger, and was recognised as such within the Agriculture Department. In 1977, the Acting Officer in charge of Soil Conservation noted in a hand-written memo to Carder that the Act 'is not used as a punitive Act and there are no regulations to which attention can be drawn.'[114] Later, G.A. Robertson, Chief of the Division of Resource Management in the Department, and a later Director of the Department, wrote: 'The current Act [Soil Conservation 1945] does have "teeth" but they are not used.'[115]

The legal obstacles did not altogether render useless the process of soil conservation. Potentially, much could be gained from working cooperatively with farmers but resources remained tight. In 1965, L.C. Lightfoot, Chief of the Soils Division, wrote to his Director explaining: 'All of our experience shows best results come from voluntary cooperation between soil conservationists and farmers, plus local authorities and other government departments when required. There has always been a big waiting list under voluntary use of soil conserving practices.'[116]

By the beginning of the 1980s, however, the relevant departments of government recognised that disputes about the solutions to salinity and land degradation needed to be resolved. An interdepartmental Soil Conservation/Salinity Coordinating Committee was established under the direction of a Cabinet Sub-Committee which had been created in March 1981.[117] Senior officers from the departments of Public Works, Forests, Agriculture and Conservation and Environment began examining the Soil Conservation Act with the aim of strengthening the legislation. They sought, in the words of Peter Jones, the Minister for Resources Development, as 'a matter of urgency',[118] to 'ensure all research and practical experience is applied' to the problem of salinity and soil conservation.[119]

Practical problems remained in the way of the effective deployment of the legislation. The difficulty in calling together the Soil Conservation Authority Committee to approve a Soil Conservation Order had meant that no such orders had been issued in the previous five years. In some cases by the time the Committee discussed the problem the damage had been done. Moreover, the powers contained in the Act to create soil conservation districts had not been widely implemented; in fact, only two such districts had been declared in the past. Farmers, it was claimed, 'are reluctant to insist on the declaration of a soil conservation district, because by doing so, they admit the existence of a soil conservation problem in the area'.[120]

The purpose behind amending the Act was to widen the definition of the term 'soil conservation' so it would apply more broadly to the concept of land degradation, including wind and water erosion, salinity, flooding, and the removal or deterioration of vegetation. It was also intended to increase compliance among local communities by making it possible to declare a particular area a soil conservation district, whereupon a regionally based soil advisory committee could be established. It was intended that this committee have the power to advise on approaches to salinity.

The need for amended legislation emerged out of the work of a Cabinet sub-committee investigating soil conservation and salinity.[121] The need for such a review had been highlighted by a Federal Government study into land degradation which it conducted between 1975 and 1977 and which showed that 51 per cent of the total area used for agricultural and pastoral purposes in Australia was in need of soil conservation treatment, a finding used by one Legislative Assembly member to support the amendments.[122]

Although the amendments received cross-party support, reservations were expressed as to the ultimate effectiveness of the revamped legislation. Prominent among the criticisms was the lack of resources given to farmers, local communities, and to the work of the proposed Soil Advisory Committee.

Foreshadowing debates nearly two decades later about the public versus private dimensions of salinity, National Party member Mr

Hendy Cowan was critical of the Bill's intention 'to ask land users to practise soil conservation and pay for it'. He thought it quite appropriate 'to match the commitment that land users will be required to give under the legislation'.[123]

The Labor Opposition was also critical of the lack of funding to promote soil conservation and felt, the amendments did not overcome the reluctance of some farmers and districts to admit to land degradation because of a perceived threat of a drop in land values. According to Labor Party spokesperson on the Bill, David Evans, the State Government

> has an obligation to undertake the rectification of land degradation. It needs to atone for some of the follies of the past, particularly the concept of releasing a million acres of land which it embarked upon with such a great blaze of publicity and acclaim back in the 1960s.[124]

The purposes of the revised Act were to ensure better compliance with the concept and to increase the powers and responsibilities of district committees. The reformed Act sparked 'spontaneous demand' by land users to be involved in soil conservation districts and thus it began to play an important role in changing farmers' attitudes and land management practices.[125] But such legislation did not form part of a systematic political commitment towards the rapidly emerging problems of land management. In fact, one particularly controversial aspect was the provision for the imposition of a levy to address land degradation. The Minister was at pains to indicate the levy was not intended to be imposed for general soil conservation works but rather to be a tool for local government to use should it be involved with district conservation programs. However, the response from local government and farmers was negative with the Premier (from January 1982, Ray O'Connor), Minister for Lands, the Commissioner for Soil Conservation and the Head of the Department of Agriculture quickly coming to the realisation that any form of levy for soil conversation projects, such as the eradication of salinity, would be strongly opposed. Yet again, political issues had been placed before action to protect the environment.

LABOR'S ENVIRONMENTAL POLICIES

The election in 1983 of the Burke Labor Government showed it was no more in tune with the environmental ethic than the Court and O'Connor Governments which had been in power since 1974. Even though there was 'a great surge of community support for environmental legislation',[126] the Government showed its preparedness to consolidate the thrust for development characteristic of all Western Australian governments in the past. Keith Bradby, an environmental activist at the time, recalls the perception that the Australian Labor Party were 'culturally locked into the stance of the previous 100 years'.[127]

The first major change was the creation of a 'mega department' dealing with land management. The creation of the Department of Conservation and Land Management (CALM) incorporating the former Forests Department, the Wildlife section of Fisheries and Wildlife, and the National Parks Authority, came about as the main recommendation of a government-appointed Task Force set up to review 'the present uncoordinated and fragmented approach to the administration and management of land releases'.[128] Apparently, a judgement had been made 'that most land resource management up to that time had failed'.[129] However, the Task Force skirted the issue of soil degradation, failing to recognise it as the State's 'most serious and urgent problem'.[130]

Nevertheless, the Task Force's recommendation for better coordination was adopted and CALM was created. According to its critics, CALM has suffered from several shortcomings. Firstly, some have argued the newly created organisation sparked a conflict of interest between its roles in protecting the environment and ensuring its economic utilisation.[131] Secondly, it lacked the funds and staff essential to survey resources and to implement proper management.[132] Lastly, too little thought was given to environmental planning, including guidelines on the direction and scale of human activities.[133]

Further changes to the framework of environmental legislation were introduced by Labor: under 1986 amendments to the *Environmental Protection Act 1971*, the EPA was restructured. Its membership was increased from three to five members with a provision that no member could be a public servant. However, a division of opinion emerged about its standing. Barry Carbon, the EPA Chairman since 1985, believed the new Act provided a new firm basis for its activities.[134] Moreover, he claimed that 'during the formulation of the Bill the Authority gave advice to the Minister for the Environment and was responsible for responding to the active and constructive public input'. However, critic Chittleborough said the EPA had 'lost most of its independence', arguing:

> The functions of the restructured EPA have also become defined more narrowly, being concentrated upon environmental assessment and pollution control. Apart from a brief diversion in the course of preparing a State Conservation Strategy ... no provision was made for reviewing the effectiveness of environmental management as a whole, nor for providing advice on overall environmental policy and planning. Responsibility for different facets of the environment (soil, water, air, flora, fauna, fish) continues to be fragmented.[135]

In short, Chittleborough believed the system was 'overloaded and geared to specific short-term targets'. Importantly, too, he thought a 'careful review of the state of our environment would have revealed that soil degradation, in its various forms, was our most serious and urgent problem'.[136]

Attempts at bold environmental planning ended stillborn. In February 1985, when endorsing the National Conservation Strategy for Australia, the State Cabinet made a commitment to prepare a State Convservation Strategy specific to the needs of Western Australia, developed within the framework of the national strategy. In January 1987 a *State Conservation Strategy for Western Australia: A Sense of Direction* was drawn up by a consultative committee in association with the Department of Conservation and Environment, and was duly distributed. It did provide a sense of the major environmental problems such as flora and fauna protection, native Karri and Jarrah forest commercialisation, and Jarrah dieback devastation. The Strategy recognised that Western Australia's lands are largely salt prone. Moreover, there was a reference to soil degradation as a continuing problem for much of Western Australia. References to salinity indicated it was being officially recognised as a problem to be addressed, but the 'Implementation Section' of the Strategy provided no confidence that formidable remedial action would follow.

Tensions about the substance of the conservation strategy could be found in the determination of a Conservation Strategy Core Group to publish a *Western Australian Environmental Review*. The document had been originally written for the Department of Conservation and Land Management in December 1986. However, it was not initially published for public consumption partly due to the sensitivity of some of the observations made. Indeed, it was claimed this course of events played a part in the subsequent resignation of the principal author, Dr Graham Chittleborough.[137] The Review left no doubt about the scale of salinity and the need for effective steps to be taken. The high degree of expertise and high productivity of Western Australian farmers were recognised but it concluded:

> An overview of the condition of agricultural lands in this State leads to the conclusion that the long-term objective of sustainable utilisation is not being achieved. Extensive restoration of degraded lands together with modified agricultural practices to ensure a sustainable environment in the future is essential. This is an accumulated environmental debt which is inescapable and must be met by the community.[138]

In fact, the Burke Government had come to power without announcing its policy on new land release.[139] It continued with the same bureaucratic structure of land release begun in 1978 with the establishment of the Working Group on Land Releases, an interdepartmental committee which was convened by the Department of Conservation and Environment and consisted of representatives from the Departments of Lands and Surveys, and Agriculture. It advised the Environmental Protection Authority on the environmental aspects of land release. Showing its commitment to consolidating the previous government's policies on land release, the Burke Government built the roads into the Ravensthorpe region to allow settlers to move in.[140]

Not surprisingly, conservationists were particularly disappointed with the lack of commitment shown by the Labor Government. Ron Richards explained how the new State Labor Government, despite reviews, was prone to mistakes of the past with its land release policies.[141] He complained that 'there is still no intention to collect data on biological factors, soils, salinity potential, erosion potential, and the like'. In fact, Richards argued Labor's retention of the Working Group on Land Release (WGLR) perpetuated a system overly biased in favour of land release:

> The bias of the current structure of the land release system is somewhat disguised by the WGLR. As a committee of review responsible directly to the EPA it appears that proposals would be the subject of broad-based assessments by persons of differing disciplines. The agricultural interests would be called to account for their demands and vie for use of the land along with other interests … and broad scale land use would be considered by officers of four separate government departments. Alas, such is not the case. And so what appears to be a watch-dog of the public interest actually undermines those interests by pretending to be what it is not.[142]

This biased system was in turn fed by what Keith Bradby explained was a 'Wheat, Wheat, Wheat' mentality that ignored other industry options over much of inland southern Western Australia such as wildflower, seed and nursery products, bee-keeping, a gene pool of species, together with recreation and tourism.[143]

By the mid-1980s, the Labor Government felt the momentum for change and set up a review committee on land release. Submissions were received from a wide variety of individuals and organisations including the WA Wildflower Society, the Land Release Study Group, the Commonwealth Development Bank and the Conservation Council of Western Australia. The bulk of submissions were critical of the system of land release and opposed to further releases. The Conservation Council of Australia also put in a submission which was among the most critical. A summary of it included in the final report read:

> Serious objective research prior to land release has only rarely been undertaken. In the process of land settlement, people have suffered, the land has been degraded and Governments have had to spend money on rehabilitation projects. The actions and events of the last three years can be seen as a continuation of a much longer history of land release. Need for public involvement in matters dealing with land release. At present there is a "screen" between politicians and public servants on one side and the public other. Reports and studies of assessment should be made available to public viewing and comment. Detailed biological and botanical surveys of areas being considered for release are required
>
> Need to place reserves where they are needed rather than tolerate them where the land is not otherwise required. Little information is known of species of plants and animals in southern areas. Need for large regional reserves and smaller sub-regional reserves. Land price is too low thus providing the asset security for capital borrowings and an immediate potential for capital profit. Capital requirements criteria in releases is a contradiction in policy. Need for cost/benefit analysis of land release. Consideration be given to funding the purchase of existing farms now for sale.
>
> Budget and economic advice to prospective new land farmers is not always correct. In assessing areas for release on economic grounds there is a need to lean to the conservative and highlight the high option value in uncleared bushland. Need for more comprehensive data on soils and rainfall. There are not sufficient data for the areas in the south-east being considered for release. Rainfall data needs to be collected over a period of at least 20 years.
>
> Need to consider whether or not proposed use of land will be a positive benefit. Other land use options need to be considered in assessment of areas for release. Areas in the south of the State require protection because of the diversity and complexity of

plants and animals. There has been a lack of social planning of CP (Conditional Purchase) releases.[144]

In other words, government had not developed any systematic process to take into account the needs of the environment. Nor had it engaged in any serious reflection on its developmentalist framework for decision-making.

The Task Force called for a higher standard of land-use planning and environmental assessment, although it stopped short of calling for an end to land release. It contained a long list of mainly improved administrative functions to achieve better planning. It is not clear what impact these recommendations had on government. Keith Bradby's recollection is that the Report 'was allowed to slide away. They [the government] weren't game to say no to more land clearing so they called for more studies and these continued for a few more years until the heat went off.'

PARLIAMENTARY COMMITTEES

Such was the record of indifference to, and neglect of, the salinity issue by the State Government and its agencies, that Parliament became the last institution of government where its seriousness could be investigated. Even this occurred somewhat by chance. In late December 1983, under the newly elected Burke Government, the Legislative Assembly decided to appoint a Select Committee to inquire into hardship in the rural sector. In a direct challenge to the aggressively pursued policy of developmentalism, the Committee stated that 'the State government must accept some responsibility for the hardship problems faced by farmers in new land release areas, and also take positive steps in situations where agricultural use is threatening severe land degradation'. However, the Committee's investigations prized open the salinity problem:

A direct consequence of the economic crisis among wheat-growers is the degrading effects on the soil of continuous cropping in many situations. Soil conservation measures are being deferred due to lack of funds, the priority for these being used as working capital. The necessary conservation measures are often unknown or very expensive. Secondary salinisation is looming as a major problem in new land farming areas. Although it is understood that both State and Commonwealth governments are now committed to a substantial soil conservation programme, the Select Committee warns that positive results will not be achieved while farmers lack the financial strength to invest in soil conservation.[145]

Given these findings it was not surprising that dryland salinity itself was to be the subject of a Parliamentary investigation. In late 1987 the Legislative Council established a Select Committee on Salinity with terms of reference to investigate the magnitude of the problem and advise on what legislative and administrative incentives to the private sector were necessary or desirable to assist in controlling or eradicating salinity.[146] Indeed, when the first Discussion Paper was published in June 1988 the Chairperson, Liberal David Wordsworth, who had taken up a Conditional Purchase block at Esperance in 1961 and had been Minister for Lands and Forests from 1978 to 1982, confessed 'none of us had appreciated the full consequences of salinity before we started, but all have become shocked at the situation'. In fact, Wordsworth issued the sternest possible warning:

> If we continue to maintain a civilisation here in our State we have to reverse this process, for not only is it destroying the environment in which we live but also the water we need, not only for our sustenance and for industry, but also to grow the food we produce and export. The capital value of our agricultural land is measured in billions of dollars, yet some Shires report that 10% is already rendered useless for crops, and others are losing 1% a year. Yet other communities are expected to be wiped out through agriculture becoming unviable. It is this situation we face in the year of Australia's bicentenary and I trust that Governments and the people of Western Australia will take heed of the warnings and not just live from year to year. The future of our children depends upon it.[147]

In its diagnosis of the problem, the Committee left no doubt that governments had failed in their duty to take the problem seriously. It said a major drawback to salinity control had been the fragmentation of responsibility for it between government agencies, limiting the capacity for a salinity control program. However, it was not just the lack of an institutional structure that reflected the indifference of governments: there were no plans for salinity control to generate activities in government agencies; 'There is currently a lack of State-wide objectives and policies, a State plan for salinity control, an integrated salinity control budget, overall evaluation and review of performance, and of a co-ordinated research strategy.' As the lead agency in salinity, the Agriculture Department was criticised by the Committee for failing to properly allocate resources to inform farmers about the problem and about the results of its various research projects.[148] In his evidence to the Committee, Soil Commissioner Graeme Robertson, admitted the Department was hamstrung for resources, having far fewer than its counterpart in New South Wales. Moreover, industry groups which gave funds to the Department for research 'have been singularly reluctant to put any money at all into the soil conservation area'.[149] The Department was forced into an embarrassing admission in its evidence to the Committee: 'The Department has emphasised to us that there is still a large percentage of farmers who are unaware of the presence of significant salting on their farms.'[150]

Through its report on salinity, Parliament had authored a damning indictment of government inaction; failure on all fronts when the years of accumulated evidence about salinity should have compelled government into action. This was the conclusion which tireless salinity campaigner Harry Whittington came to when in August 1988 he wrote to David Wordsworth commending the Committee for its 'diligent investigation' but castigating prior inaction by politicians on the issue. It was quite evident, he wrote, that

> no member of the Committee had seriously looked at the problem on any previous occasion. The articles on the salinity problem that have been printed in the press, statements by academics

and individuals, must all have been passed off as romantic story, or the members of the Committee had just believed that the official statement of the Department of Agriculture that the area of land affected by salinity encroachment was about two per cent and that a small percentage was of little consequence, and any other statements being made by people living in the area were just alarmist.[151]

The Committee's work constituted a major statement on salinity. Parliament, at least, had clearly stated its extent and the threat it was beginning to pose to agriculture, to the Western Australian economy and to the rural fabric of the Wheatbelt. It was recognised there were no simple solutions to the problem but it did suggest a set of governmental structures and funding arrangements for the future. Foremost among these was the call to establish a Salinity Control Board. The Committee also documented the economic effects of salinity, establishing the presence of economic multiplier effects which spread throughout the community. Significantly, the effect on individual farmers was highlighted:

Salting is often seen as an irreversible threat to the productive base and a reflection of the farmer's ability. Once salinity is present and acknowledged, farmers can suffer stress, despondency, and frustration at not being able to do anything, especially as the cause of the problem may not be on their property. Aesthetic value of rural areas and pride in local areas are also affected by salinity.[152]

Preparation of the Select Committee's Report must have extracted a personal toll on its Chairman, David Wordsworth, who surely could not have failed to relate his own farming activities and his support in promoting further land releases in the early 1980s, with the creation of the problem. One could have understood any effort on his part to downplay the seriousness of salinity; after all, over a long period most other people in government had done so. In fact, the Select Committee's Report was an impressive investigation; parliamentary work at its

finest and a reminder of the crucial role it can play in holding governments to account. It deserved to be debated and its recommendations
implemented. In fact, political silence prevailed yet again. Partly, the
timing of the Committee's Report was unfortunate, occurring just
prior to the February 1989 State election when it was unlikely that the
suggested recommendations would be implemented. However, the
wheels of government moved very slowly. It was not until after the
Court–Cowan Coalition Government was elected in 1993 that a Salinity Council was established as well as a Cabinet Sub-Committee on
Salinity headed by Deputy Premier Hendy Cowan.

Parliament revisited the broader question of land conservation
with the appointment of a Select Committee on Land Conservation
in 1989 and no effort was spared in an exhaustive and lengthy analysis. The literature review included attention to the Report of the
World Commission on Environment and Development titled *Our
Common Future* (known as the Brundtland Report) which defined the
frequently cited international concept of sustainable development as
that which 'meets the needs of the present without compromising the
ability of future generations to meet their needs'.[153] This time Monty
House, a National Party member in the Legislative Assembly and
farmer with an awareness of the salinity problem, was appointed as the
Chairperson.

As the title implied, the Select Committee on Land Conservation
was not specifically concerned with salinity. However, it did make this
observation:

> [D]ryland salinity is by no means the most (or potentially the
> most) severe soil degradation problem affecting agriculture. Sub-
> soil compaction, soil structure decline and water repellence cur-
> rently pose greater cost penalties on agriculture than salinity, but
> essentially being hidden problems have attracted limited attention
> by researchers. As a consequence, there is no economically viable
> means of control available for these problems at present. Subsoil
> acidification is feared by many to become the major soil degrada-
> tion problem in the future.[154]

The theme of the report was to regard dryland salinity as just one of the land conservation issues. In recognition that agricultural land-use systems in Western Australia were 'at a watershed',[155] the Committee recommended a revamping of governmental structures.

Indeed, there were important changes occurring in official explanations of the causes of land degradation. The Committee accepted that agriculture, as practised, and the extensive clearing of fragile ecosystems were the major causes of most land conservation problems across the State.[156] It raised the need to manage land use in a sustainable manner.

To help develop a greater degree of political consensus and raise the standard of parliamentary debate, it was recommended that a Parliamentary Standing Committee on Natural Resources be established. It was to have access to advice from the State Natural Resources Co-ordinating Committee, individual natural resource agencies, peak councils and any other organisations.[157] Moreover, it was recommended that the Western Australian State Cabinet form a Natural Resources Sub-committee to help ensure effective coordination and implementation of land conservation policy across Ministerial portfolios. Arrangements were sought for the Commonwealth and State governments to examine guidelines for financial incentives with a special Premiers' Conference being mooted. In terms of monies it was recommended that all Western Australians should directly contribute to funding land conservation through the raising of an environmental levy for the Western Australian Land Conservation Fund.[158]

A month prior to the tabling of the Final Report of the Select Committee on Land Conservation, another Select Committee, also chaired by Monty House, tabled its recommendations. The Committee had not focused on salinity or land conservation measures but had been established to review a Right to Farm Bill which Monty House himself had introduced in April 1989. The Bill, based on legislation in some American states and Canadian provinces, had sought to establish by statute the principle that a farmer who had followed genuinely accepted practices, and who had acted within local government land-use regulations, could not be prevented from carrying on legitimate farming operations. Farmers were concerned about their legal rights because of the increased demand for land for industrial purposes, small farms and holiday homes, as well as the prospect of more stringent environmental regulations. Tabulations of both the supporting and opposing arguments made reference to the conservation movement. For instance, it was claimed that 'a Right to Farm statute would help to provide for the maintenance of agricultural practices which are under threat from conservation and other green-minded groups'.[159] On the other hand, one of the reservations about the legislation was based on the 'feeling that farmers, despite their own protestations, are not conservation conscious'.[160] Eventually, though, Parliament did not give passage to the recommended *Agricultural Practices Act*. However, the Committee's deliberations and recommendations revealed that sections of the farming community were extremely insecure about their future livelihood.

Some two decades after a public march on the Parliament to present a Conservation Bill of Rights, it was clear environmental issues were receiving greater attention by Parliament and many agencies of government. Indeed, as Desmond O'Connor, the foundation Professor of Environmental Studies at Murdoch University (who had been deputy chairman of the EPA), observed at the time, 'if we were to judge by the amount of media coverage of environmental affairs, we would be excused for thinking that we are living in an age of environmentalism'.[161] A *Westpoll* taken at the time indicated environmental issues would shift electors' voting intentions.[162] But O'Connor warned that 'it is a mistake to assume, in these hard times, that the environment was uppermost in the public mind'.[163] His argument, with supporting polling evidence, emphasised other issues such as unemployment, welfare, the economy, interest rates, migration and general standards of living were usually more important for the elector.

While salinity had risen as priority environmental issue through the parliamentary committee system, neither the Legislative Council Select Committee recommendation for a Soil and Conservation Authority nor the Legislative Assembly Select Committee recommendation for a broader Natural Resources Coordinating Committee had been implemented. Nor had the recommended Cabinet Sub-committees been quickly appointed. Whether the broader land conservation focus temporarily took away a sense of urgency that was being recognised about salinity is difficult to assess. Government had not rejected the need to address the salinity problem but it had not placed in operation governmental structures, or allocated the resources, to make a formidable assault on what had emerged as a threat to the very future of the Wheatbelt in Western Australia.

The Politics of Salinity and the Environment in the 1990s

The record of Australian governments in embracing environmental policies is relatively poor. According to Cowley and Walker, both major political parties have shown a preparedness to exploit environmental issues for electoral gain but experience difficulty in taking them seriously enough, and especially viewing them in an ecological framework.[1] A study of salinity supports such an assessment. Not only have recent governments allowed themselves to 'be cowered by the enormousness of the problem', individual initiatives aimed at addressing salinity— and land degradation more generally—have failed to sufficiently address the scale of the underlying problems.[2] Specific initiatives which failed to live up to their potential include Landcare, land-clearing measures, the State Salinity Strategy and the National Heritage Trust Fund. An analysis of each shows how political forces have continued to dominate, and ultimately limit, commitment to repairing land degradation.

THE LANDCARE PROGRAM

Wheatbelt farmer and salinity consultant, Marty Ladyman, can take a long-term view about changing attitudes in the farming community. He is the third generation on his Katanning property and he has seen the last of clearing, the decades of denial about salinity, the steadily rising concerns during the 1980s and the intensification in the 1990s. He believes the crunch came in the early 1990s when farmers were forced to examine their costs of production:

> How were we going to maintain our farm viability when we could see no potential increase in commodity price? We started to realise that Australia wasn't an island in this world, it was part of a global market. So we started to look at cost of production and say 'OK, how can we keep our profit margins?' We can't do it by raising our prices so we've got to lower our costs of production. And in lowering our costs of production we started to see we were limited by other things … weaknesses in the system and things that started to crack. And one of those cracks was salinity … It started to bite because we were losing trees, losing productive land. But because commodity prices weren't high we couldn't purchase more land. This attitude of stuff it up and we'll go and buy somebody else's land wasn't possible any more because we weren't generating a cash flow to go and buy the neighbour's place so we started to look inward within our own economic unit … I think if you asked any farmer what his major environmental problem was he would say 'salt'.

The Landcare program was part of the process behind these changing attitudes among farmers; it was also designed to address their emerging concerns about sustainability.

Although farmers' interest in landcare slowly gathered momentum from the late 1970s, it was not until the launch of the formal Landcare program that the Commonwealth Government became actively involved in addressing land degradation issues. Devised as a joint initiative of the National Farmers' Federation and the Australian Conservation Foundation, it was launched in 1989 as a 'Decade of Landcare' by Prime Minister Bob Hawke, with the ambitious aim of achieving sustainable land use around Australia by the year 2000. As such, it promised a major assault on salinity and especially because revegetation and replanting programs were key components of the program. More than a decade on, evaluations of actual achievements are mixed.

Some of those with close involvement in the landcare movement distinguish between the formal Commonwealth program and the more extensive and informal community involvement. As a movement, landcare has substantially broadened awareness of the environment among rural communities. About half of Western Australia's farmers are estimated by the year 2000 to have some level of involvement.[3] This represents a substantial achievement given the low levels of environmental awareness among the State's farmers discussed in earlier chapters. However, the formal Landcare program—while an integral part of the broader movement—has been subject to on-going criticisms virtually from its inception, and especially on the grounds that too little has changed on farms. Community Landcare Coordinator for the Shire of Beverley, Mr Harvey Morrell, sums up the twin perspectives: 'If we hadn't become involved 12 years ago [in Landcare] many wouldn't be farming today. We halted existing scalds, but we haven't solved salinity throughout the catchment.'[4]

As an environmental concept, Landcare held irresistible attractions to politicians. It simultaneously met public expectations for greater community involvement in addressing land degradation while complementing views about 'smaller government' embedded in the rapidly prevailing ideology of economic rationalism. Through Landcare, scarce government resources would be transferred to the community, where objectives would be implemented by farmers encouraged to improve their capital asset and by voluntary labour working on community projects. However, government enthusiasm for Landcare was also motivated by a more pragmatic realisation about the limited success which Agriculture Department officers had had in transferring their expertise and technology about sustainable farming to individual farmers. The idea of community partnerships, in which farmers would be a key group, was thought to be a potentially effective way of overcoming these barriers.[5] In Western Australia, the core principle of partnership was given added strength by the requirement that district Landcare groups have an employee of the WA Agriculture Department as a member.[6]

In Western Australia, as elsewhere, local Landcare groups proliferated. In September 1993, 133 gazetted groups were operating, covering 80 per cent of the State's agricultural lands,[7] earning Western Australia the reputation of 'a leading state in Landcare participation'.[8] Within rural Landcare groups, salinity was rated as the highest issue of concern.[9] Despite its visionary appeal of mobilising local communities, formal evaluations and anecdotal evidence had, by the early 1990s, shown significant shortcomings in the ability of the Program to meet its ambitious objectives. In spite of notable achievements which included the planting of millions of trees, the erection of vast lengths of fencing, and the shaping of community values through a variety of education work, Landcare had little hope of achieving sustainable agriculture.

Foremost among its problems was lack of adequate funding for the scale of land degradation Landcare was intended to address. In the early years of the Program claims by conservation groups, Landcare consultants, and farmers and pastoralists indicated little of the monies allocated by the Federal Government supported works on the ground. No-one knew the exact figure, some claiming it was as little as 4 per cent of total monies. Keith Bradby, then working as a Landcare consultant, argued that much of the money was being eaten up by State bureaucracies for tasks which should have been part of their normal duties:

What I hadn't realised is that the State Government can save an awful lot of money if it lets the Federal Government pay the wages of all the people in the public service that are there to help us. I can appreciate that farmers and other businessmen won't be given money to do works that should be part of their normal business activities—like farming in a sustainable manner. But I can't understand how government agencies get heaps of funding to do the things that should be part of their normal business activities— things like agriculture research, mapping the State's landscapes, planning for the future of horticulture, running staff training programs, researching drain management and so on.[10]

Similar sentiments were expressed by the Chairman of the West Arthur Land Conservation District Council, who claimed budget cuts within the Department of Agriculture were resulting in full-time staff being replaced with contract staff paid for out of Landcare money: 'Landcare had become political … Small amounts of money are being handed out to a lot of different groups—which, of course, is politically very acceptable … It shows the national and State land care bodies in a very rosy light, but it's not solving the problem. Ten years of this has not arrested land degradation.'[11]

A large part of the problem was the move towards debt reduction strategies enforced on State agencies by the Court Government which came to power following the financial losses of the 'WA Inc' years from the mid-1980s onwards. Departmental involvement in salinity was encouraged, but within a budget climate of reduced spending. National Landcare funds resolved this conflicting position. The Department of Agriculture used Commonwealth funds to bolster its own budget. As a consequence there was no overall increase in funding to fight salinity and land degradation in general.[12] Indeed, the practice of 'cost shifting' was raised by the founders of the Program in evidence to the recent House of Representatives Standing Committee on Environment and Heritage. Landcare, argued Rick Farley and Phillip Toyne,

> made it easier for State Governments to withdraw from regional Australia and from their traditional role of providing agricultural support. The Federal Government has provided funds for positions such as Landcare Coordinators, allowing State funded agricultural extension officers to be withdrawn. The Commonwealth agriculture department now funds well over 2,000 full time equivalent positions (over 3,400 individuals) to work on Landcare. The States have used this opportunity to 'cost shift' and substitute federal money and positions for State resources.[13]

Farmers were especially incensed about the monopolisation of Landcare resources by the State Government. In 1995, a spokesman for the Pastoralists' and Graziers' Association claimed that less than 10 per cent of Landcare money was reaching landholders, reinforcing concern 'that more and more money appears to be going to staff build-up in Government agencies rather than to landholders'.[14] To many struggling farmers, the issue of resources to implement sustainability was the hard edge of the Landcare process. Hemmed in by rising costs and uncertain world prices, some farmers felt compelled to 'flog' their land to derive greater yields per acre.[15]

Disquiet over the levels of resources was not uppermost in the minds of other critics who argued the Program lacked focus in addressing the core issue of sustainability. Western Australian Soil Commissioner Kevin Goss, put this criticism in context. In 1995, he warned that, despite all efforts, salinity continued to get worse, requiring a long-range vision:

> To manage this change in landscape hydrology is a 30–70 year job. It requires changes at the heart of farm production, higher performing crops, farm forestry and other enterprises which increase productivity, increase income and increase water use. This is not simply a matter of tree planting. To make agriculture more sustainable requires a very close working relationship between farmers and pastoralists, government supported development, and demonstration in the paddock. That is why farmers are concerned that Landcare funding is not 'hitting the ground'. To change their way of producing from the land, they are asking assistance—tax incentives to adopt conservation technologies, more research and development, and local demonstration of good practice.

Some farmers, and especially those in the eastern Wheatbelt where salinity is a problem, saw no direct benefit from Landcare. According to Marty Ladyman:

> Many of these farmers are marginal. They are not aware that they can get supplementary funding to do things. Some have done nothing at all about salinity. The Agricultural adviser would come

around and say, 'Look you do have a problem, there is money available, you need to make a submission'. So, many of these poor people on the south coast did not have a ghost of a chance of making a submission and were never in a position to be helped. The Department [Agriculture WA] was never in a position to go out to him and say, 'Look you have a problem, here is some funding, and we will assist you through the process'. No, the Department went to him and said, 'Look you've got a salinity, water-logging, wind erosion, soil compact problem. Join your Landcare group and we support them.' How did the agency support Landcare groups? Well they covered their administration costs. So that was the only direct benefit they got. And if the farmers wanted money they had to make submissions for it.

Moreover, the voluntary principle at the heart of Landcare emerged as the Program's great strength, and its major weakness. Sustaining long-term commitment among individuals and groups became a critical factor in the operation of the Program. Some believed 'the intensity of involvement or the magnitude of the task overwhelms participants to the extent they become less effective or drop out of Landcare'.[16] A mid-1990s study found that 'farmers who had belonged to a Landcare group for five or more years were significantly more likely than more recent members to have reduced their involvement'.[17] However, a range of complex factors impact on levels of commitment. There are limits on the number of available people in rural communities with the talent and inclination to be Landcare leaders, and social factors in these communities—age and education levels, high debt structure and accompanying stress—act as restraints on participation. Moreover, accountability requirements frustrate many. The Western Australian Minister for Primary Industry, Mr Monty House, acknowledged the unrealistic burdens being carried by rural communities over the Landcare program: 'There is potential for some landcare groups to lose their focus and enthusiasm due to frustration with the complexity of different funding programs, eligibility criteria and increasingly bureaucratic and administration requirements.'[18]

Despite numerous constructive local programs, the sheer scale of the effort required in most communities simply overwhelmed the available human resources. In the tiny Wheatbelt town of Bodallin, for example, a handful of local farmers took on the challenge of addressing the water quality of the Avon River at its headwater catchment. Over the years it had become silted and polluted mainly through widespread clearing for agriculture. Over a two-year period local farmers planted 100,000 trees which, by any estimate, represented a major commitment and achievement. Yet, to fully redress the problems in the region two to three million trees require planting.[19]

At one level, the Landcare program was a victim of its own success. The mobilisation of concerned people to become involved in addressing land degradation served to highlight the extent and seriousness of the problems. Among farmers it served as a powerful awareness raiser. According to one: 'We've learnt that farms aren't individual islands surrounded by a sea of other people's properties. I think that we now realise that our properties form part of a catchment which forms part of a larger environment and needs to be cared for accordingly.'[20] However, in opening the eyes of rural communities to the problem of salinity, the Program was never properly funded to address the underlying issues and especially the complexities involved in moving towards sustainable agriculture. This has left the Program at the crossroads. It has created 'a platform of participation' upon which more sustainable land-use management can be constructed while, simultaneously, 'the fundamental issues related to the sustainability of rural communities continue to be avoided'.[21] In areas such as the Wheatbelt, the spread of salinity during the 'Decade of Landcare' was an ever-present reminder of this dilemma.

THE CONTROVERSY OVER LAND CLEARING

At the same time as the political process struggled to devise and fund an adequate Landcare program, tolerance was shown to the continued clearing of native vegetation in the agricultural and pastoral regions of the State. Despite the Wheatbelt's reputation as one of the most cleared landscapes in Australia, land clearing had not been a major political issue from the mid-1980s through to the mid-1990s. This changed in 1994 when a leaked report conducted for the Department of Agriculture by scientific officer Frans Mollemans showed the extent of clearing going on and the indifference of government agencies. He had spent over two years studying native bush in the South-West of the State covering 8,500 bush remnants in forty-one shires. In his report to the Department Mr Mollemans claimed that less than 1 per cent of the State's native bush on farmlands remained intact. Moreover, he found that 25,000 hectares of bush were being cleared illegally every year to replace agricultural land lost to salinity. His most contentious claim was that the Department was turning a blind eye to this activity. Consequently, about 80 per cent of bush remnants were so badly degraded there was no understorey left.[22] Mollemans' claims were rejected by the Department of Agriculture but they received support from MLA Mr Jim McGinty, Minister for the Environment in the previous Labor Government, who claimed to have been preparing legislation to protect the State's remnant bushland immediately before the Party's defeat at the 1993 election. McGinty claimed the Department of Agriculture was allowing too much land to be cleared in shires where there was less than 10 to 20 per cent farmland with native vegetation.[23]

However, Labor's claim to have been on the brink of introducing tougher legislation has a hollow ring. After all, it arrived at this decision after overseeing an expansion of clearing activity, both legal and illegal, while it was in office. In the decade 1986 to 1996, 1,060 applications were made to Agriculture WA to clear more than 282,000 hectares of land (most in the period 1986 to 1992) in the agricultural region of the State. Moreover, there had been an upward trend in the number of applications over this period.[24] Conservationists and government were at loggerheads over the seriousness of these figures. Whereas the Soil and Land Commissioner, Mr Kevin Goss, maintained clearing was small in area, tightly controlled and subject to broad environmental criteria, others saw flaws in the system: bushland was being cleared without adequate environmental assessment, confusion existed over roles and responsibilities of several government departments, and prosecutions were difficult to achieve principally through lack of resources.[25] According to one South-West Landcare group:

> Illegal clearing was widespread across the State, especially where bluegum plantations or vineyards were being established in the Great Southern [region]. The department [Agriculture WA] inspected areas where clearance applications were made but did not have the resources to follow up complaints about illegal clearing … Farmers who had gone through the proper channels were being penalised because [their] applications were rejected while other farmers were clearing illegally.[26]

In responding to the situation, the Government found itself caught between competing interest groups: conservationists calling for a total ban on clearing, and farmers' groups complaining about the lack of fairness of such a ban for landowners who would be forced to bear the costs themselves. The Government's response was a compromise, comprising 'more carrot than stick'. In May 1995, the Court Government announced funding of nearly $7 million over five years, to encourage farmers to save and fence their remnant vegetation. In addition it proclaimed new procedures restricting clearing bush on farms where less than 20 per cent of the total native vegetation remained. However, only partial benefits flowed from the Government's tightening up on clearing. While rates of legal clearing dropped from 35,000 hectares in the early 1990s to under 1,000 hectares in 1999, the initial response was to generate a significant increase in applications to clear. This increase was being fuelled by a combination of factors including 'panic clearing', that is, a syndrome exhibited by farmers who feared the right to clear may be removed; high wheat prices and good seasons which meant farmers could afford to clear; and a misconstruing of the '20 per cent rule' which, in some shires, was being mis-interpreted as allowing clearing down to that level. The effect of the continuation of clearing was not lost on some officers within the Department of the Environment who recognised that the Government's approach to salinity was being undermined by the failure to deal with land clearing.[27]

However, the State Government continued to reject calls for a total ban on land clearing. The case for banning clearing came in 1999 and was issued by the Chairman of the State's Environmental Protection Authority, Mr Bernard Bowen. In calling upon the State Government to ban all clearing on farmland, he nominated the salinity crisis and the loss of biodiversity as the justifications: 'Clearing in these agricultural areas cannot be supported environmentally.'[28] Responding to the Premier, Mr Richard Court's, rejection of his call, Mr Bowen articulated the political dilemma facing the State Government over the issue: 'While farmers had a legitimate interest in economic viability of land in the short term, the community had a legitimate interest in the long-term condition of the land and biodiversity.'[29] However, in March 1999, the Court Government adjusted its policy on land clearing again by requiring landholders to prove that any proposed clearing would not cause land degradation. This requirement, it was argued, brought agriculture more in line with the environmental responsibilities of other industries.

Land clearing continued to be subjected to political pressure. In July 2000, the Minister for the Environment, Ms Cheryl Edwardes, who usually gave a good audience to environmentalists, nonetheless overruled a recommendation by the Environmental Protection Authority to save 135 hectares of bush on private property in the northern Wheatbelt which, the Authority found, contained native vegetation vital to species richness in the area. It was not the first time the Minister had overruled the recommendations of the EPA. Several similar decisions upheld appeals by private landowners, including the preservation of 870 hectares of land bordering on the Mt Lesueur National Park.[30]

The struggle to resolve the land-clearing issue was symptomatic of the larger, unresolved approach to dealing with salinity. At the heart of the issue are a range of complexities centring on private rights versus public responsibilities: Do farmers have a right to clear land? Should they be compensated for not clearing? Should they be compelled to contribute to the wider public good? Such private versus public issues relate to other aspects of the salinity problem as later discussion will illustrate.

The lack of community consensus on the rights and responsibilities of farmers to clear land was revived again in March 2001 when a study compiled by the Australian Conservation Foundation (ACF) was publicly released. The Report placed Australia as the greatest clearer of native vegetation in the developed world and the sixth-largest overall. To this record, it claimed that 6,000 hectares was still being cleared throughout the Wheatbelt of Western Australia annually; 'still too much for a State with a bad history of land clearing'.[31] Although this figure was substantially less than the 'massive' clearing going on in Queensland (425,000 hectares per year) and New South Wales (100,000 hectares per year), the ACF believes other states should 'learn from WA, which was paying a huge price for problems caused by bush destruction, such as salinity'.[32]

The release of the Report activated pressure groups to again press their claims for a ban on clearing native bushland. A spokesman for the WA Wildflower Society, for example, said the Society was 'still very concerned about the rate of clearing we do now. It's one of the key threats to biodiversity and it exacerbates the dryland salinity problem. It's absolutely crucial that we stop clearing.'[33] It is a message which has resonated with the Federal Opposition Labor Party which, in March 2000, committed itself to a policy of implementing a national legislation to freeze the destruction of native bush within four years. The policy also promised a ban on clearing in vulnerable areas, unspecified compensation for landholders and an audit system to monitor compliance.[34] This announcement signalled a difference in approach to that of the Federal Liberal–National Government, which has relied on the states to cooperate in reversing the decline in the extent of native vegetation. As the ACF's Report highlighted, such cooperation has not been forthcoming from several states, and in particular Queensland. In the Western Australian context, Labor's policy complements the work done by the Court Government to tighten up on land clearing, but which always stopped short of an outright ban on the clearing of native vegetation. While it could be argued Federal Labor's policy does not go far enough in bringing an end to clearing—given the amount of clearing that could occur within its four-year timetable, its principal effect might be to ensure that land clearing, and the complex issues surrounding it, are given the prominence they deserve in political debate.

THE SALINITY STRATEGY (2000)

After decades of inaction by successive State Governments, a breakthrough occurred in the early 1990s when the Liberal–National Party Coalition committed itself to formulating a Salinity Strategy. Being the first Western Australian Government to devise a long-term plan to deal with salinity was a noteworthy achievement. However, the incoming State Labor Government decided, in February 2001, to establish a Task Force to review the previous government's Strategy, apparently unconvinced it represented an effective approach to tackling the problem. A revised Strategy has been foreshadowed. It is, therefore, timely in our discussion to pose three, broad questions about policy efforts on salinity: What should be the focus of a government strategy on salinity? To what extent did the Court–Cowan Government embody a strategic approach? Does salinity pose intractable problems for any government? Tracing the Court Government's process of formulating its Salinity Strategy—which took a period of more than seven years—provides insights into these questions.

Commitments to tackle salinity originated within the Liberal Party as part of its pre-election platform which brought it to government— in coalition with the National Party in 1993. *Fightback! Western Australia*—the Liberals' election platform—had stirring words about the Party's commitment to land degradation and salinity: 'The Liberals will make land degradation, which is currently Western Australia's number one economic and environmental disaster, the target of a rehabilitation program unprecedented in Australia's history.'[35] The centrepiece of this commitment was 'a massive $600 million twenty-year program to control and reduce salinity and other forms of land degradation in Western Australia.' Unfortunately, such an ambitious commitment was short lived, succumbing to negotiations with the National Party to produce a Coalition policy on salinity and Phil Pendal's failure to win appointment to Cabinet. Importantly, references to the $600 million were removed.[36]

Once elected, the new State Government's progress on formulating a detailed plan was painfully slow. The initial task was given jointly to the WA Water and Resources Council and the Land Conservation Council, which delivered a strategy to the State Government in mid-1995. However, by the end of that year the Government still had not endorsed or released its contents. Criticism inevitably followed. *The West Australian*, which championed the salinity cause from the early 1990s, editorialised on the Government's poor performance. The need for urgent action, the paper argued, seems to have been lost on the Court Government. The paper criticised the Government for sitting on the draft strategy for the past six months apparently procrastinating about the cost estimates: 'After nearly three years in office, the Court Government has fallen abysmally short of its 1993 election promise to spend unprecedented resources fighting salinity and to inspire all sections of society to take up the cause as a united campaign.'[37]

The core issue was the Government's unwillingness to tackle the issue of funding an effective strategy. The proposal for a levy to fight salinity was canvassed again in 1995 in response to the Environment Minister, Mr Peter Foss's, claim 'that he cannot allocate resources to the land degradation problem in rural Western Australia because city voters don't give it high priority'.[38] In fact, *The West Australian* had been polling on the issue of funding and a levy since 1993. In the newspaper's December 1995 poll, 54 per cent of voters stated that salinity was a serious concern, with an equal number prepared to pay a levy. This response was up from the 1993 figure of 43 per cent who rated it a serious issue.[39] Despite this strong support, Mr Court ruled out the introduction of a levy mindful, no doubt, of the political risks involved: the lukewarm response from the Farmers' Federation whose President thought the money would simply be wasted by the bureaucracy, and the opposition from the Labor Party. An election was little more than a year away.

The levy proposal re-emerged at the beginning of 2000 in the lead-up to the release of the revamped Salinity Strategy. It was speculated that the State Government would include a levy as part of its strategy. On this occasion the proposal received wide support: the Primary Industries Minister, Mr Monty House, stated his belief that 'there would be an environment levy at some time'. Conservation groups including Greening Australia and the Conservation Council backed the proposal. This time the Farmers' Federation was also strongly support- ive, arguing a levy reflected the need for collective responsibility for the salinity crisis: 'State governments had encouraged or required farmers to clear their land for agriculture until about 25 years ago. All West Australians had shared the benefits and all should help pick up the tab.'[40] Championing the levy also was *The West Australian*, which argued: 'Given the size and severity of the problem, a levy seems inevit- able. It would draw some protests. But it is a fair assessment of WA community values that most people would come to realise that it would be in everyone's interests to pay to overcome this problem.'[41] An opinion poll conducted during this phase of the debate had support for a levy at 60 per cent of voters.[42]

However, the Coalition was split on the proposal. At the begin- ning of March, Mr Court stamped his authority on the debate by say- ing no levy would be included in the forthcoming salinity strategy, while the Deputy Premier and Leader of the National Party, Mr Hendy Cowan, publicly supported the calls for a levy.[43] However, it was the Premier's position which prevailed.

The paralysis in government decision-making over the funding of a salinity package, reflected a pragmatic political reading of the prob- lem. *The West Australian* alluded to this when it made an oblique, but nonetheless pointed, reference to the politics behind the paralysis. It argued metropolitan concerns took precedence over country ones: 'The Government's worthwhile efforts to ease metropolitan river pollution through a long-overdue commitment to an $800 million extension of the sewerage system have not been matched by its attitude to the fight against salinity.'[44]

Stung into action, the Coalition Government released a Draft Strategy in November 1996 with promises of $580 million in expendi- ture over ten years and the establishment of a State Salinity Action

Council. This commitment made the Strategy even more ambitious than the earlier commitment of nearly the same amount of money spread over double the time period. The Strategy came with an equally purposeful endorsement from Mr Court: 'We want to be the ones who make the biggest assault to turn this situation around,' he said.[45] Welcoming the announcement, *The West Australian* was nonetheless cynical about the timing which, it claimed, was 'almost certainly' linked to a pre-Christmas election.[46] Following its re-election, it was not long before the Government's Strategy came under attack, principally due to the lack of any consultation with salt-affected farmers and its failure to adequately address the issue of salt-affected towns. An extensive process of gathering submissions was undertaken by the Salinity Action Council which, in turn, fed into a new Draft Strategy, released in November 1998. By this stage, commitment of funds had been drastically downgraded. While identifying the need for an additional $3 billion over thirty years, the Draft Strategy identified recurrent expenditure of $15 million per year with a commitment of an additional $10 million, together with some redistribution of funds from government agencies. This brought government funding of salinity to just over $40 million per year, well short of the $100 million per year required.

In 1999, a fleeting opportunity to secure long-term funding to fight salinity was passed up when the Government opposed a motion moved by Mr Phillip Pendal, Independent and former Liberal spokesperson on the environment, who was supported by another Independent Liberal, Dr Elizabeth Constable. Both had been long-time salinity campaigners. Pendal and Constable had sponsored an amendment to the Bill for the privatisation of Alinta Gas. The amendment proposed that $250 million from the expected sale price of $1 billion be set aside for the creation of a 'degraded lands rehabilitation fund'. As Mr Pendal later explained: 'It was the opportunity of a lifetime to signal to the rural towns and communities that the Parliament, and in turn the Government, recognised the seriousness of the crisis.'[47] It was perhaps no great surprise that the Labor Party opposed the amendment because of its follow-on opposition to the privatisation of the gas utility. To Mr Pendal, the greater disappointment was the dismissive attitude of the Government which was intent on using the proceeds from the sale largely to retire State debt: 'Not one minister with responsibility for land resources, agriculture, or land degradation spoke! Not one.'[48]

As a consequence of its inability to fully fund a salinity rescue package, the Government outlined that the core part in its Strategy to deal with salinity was to shift responsibility back to landholders and selected private companies: 'There will never be enough money to solve the salinity problem.'[49] With its revised undertakings, the document remained in Draft form until its official release in April 2000. This release was an important landmark in the fight against salinity. It represented the first occasion a government was prepared to commit resources and thinking to a long-term approach.

Nevertheless, the Salinity Strategy suffered from major shortcomings which any revised document will surely need to address. Foremost among these was a lack of philosophical direction to guide decision-making. Salinity is a complex political issue because it is unclear whether it should be viewed mainly as a problem for private landholders, or a public problem resulting from the spread of salinity from private land use. To say there are elements of both positions in the current crisis simply confounds the potential confusion for government: salinity is largely a product of private land use, yet this same use has had grave spill-over effects on public assets. These include all forms of infrastructure such as roads, recreation grounds and town buildings, but also on the public's 'ownership' of the wider environment and its biodiversity. The Salinity Strategy did not attempt to work through these complex, but vital, private versus public issues. Yet, they lie at the centre of different policy approaches.

It can be argued that farmers caused salinity in choices they made in farming the land. Therefore, scarce public resources should not be devoted to 'bailing out' these people in the form of subsidies. Marty Ladyman, in his role as Chairman of Salinity Forum Inc., set up as a public pressure group on the issue, poses the dilemma for governments: 'Politically does that mean the Government will compensate those people because they encouraged them to go out there in the first place, or is the urban community going to say "that's bad luck, you stuffed it up". As a farmer I can't say either. But I think we've got to recognise that very issue.' There are very different responses to this issue from the groups involved in salinity. Alex Campbell, Chairman of the State Salinity Council, argues that large-scale subsidies on private land are not feasible because of the costs involved, while Colin Nicholl, President of the Western Australian Farmers' Federation, believes one of the obstacles to controlling salinity is opposition to the allocation of government monies on private lands for the greater public good.[50] Both Campbell and Nicholl had, for decades, sought solutions to the salinity problem.

Two problems flow from a view which says farmers are not deserving of substantial public help. Firstly, and as argued in Chapter 2, it was the exercise of government policy which substantially created the current problems for farmers. Governments opened up the land, compelled farmers to clear it and ignored all advice cautioning them about the potential for salinity problems. In retrospect, governments failed to act ethically in their aggressive promotion of land clearing because they did not uphold appropriate duty-of-care principles when ignoring successive warnings about salinity. This shortcoming now creates the strong case for government action to assist affected farmers to adjust to ecologically sustainable farming or to be phased out altogether. As University of Western Australia agricultural scientist David Pannell argues: 'For farmers, at least, the benefits of salinity prevention are usually not enough to outweigh the large up-front costs that farmers have to bear to establish large areas of perennials, not to mention the on-going income sacrifice from the land on which they have they have been established.'[51]

However, the Government's responses to salinity should extend beyond agricultural losses. Its ethical responsibilities should encompass saving the maximum possible amount of the environment from destruction and dealing with the human costs of salinity in the towns of the region. These non-agricultural losses may well be just as great, or even greater, than the agricultural losses.[52]

While it is possible, therefore, to resolve any distinction between private and public in terms of government responsibility towards salinity, this in itself is an insufficient framework for government decision-making. How should government seek to address the problem? Salinity presents governments with added complexity in developing responses because of its effects on both private and public assets. Policies may need to differentiate these two spheres of impact. Addressing the private impacts of salinity fundamentally involves inducing farmers to change their behaviour. In terms of policy tools such change of behaviour can occur in the following ways: by educating farmers to change land-use practices; by public spending such as the acquisition of environmentally critical lands or by subsidising farmers to move out of cereal growing and sheep farming; by offering incentives through the taxation system to do the same; or by enacting legislation to restrict or prohibit certain activities causing salinity. These policy tools require careful evaluation for the contribution each can play in reducing salinity. However, there is no escaping the fundamental question about farming in the Wheatbelt: Should farmers have a choice about the extent to which they engage in remedial measures? Unless all farmers in a catchment are working to reduce salinity, the efforts of those who are can be undermined by those who are not involved.

Private assets affected by salinity not only involve farmers' land but also houses owned by individuals in the many towns that will increasingly be affected over the next few decades. Government's moral responsibility, it can be asserted, surely extends to these private assets as well. Many houses, and indeed some towns, may not warrant being saved. Without compensation to relocate affected people, many will obviously face considerable financial hardship.

Addressing the public assets affected by salinity may well be simpler in terms of the range of policy tools, but is likely to involve complex issues in devising a framework to decide upon priorities. Public assets affected by salinity are unlikely to be dealt with in any way other than subsidies to local government and/or individuals. But are all public assets equally worth saving? The Murray–Darling Commission appears to be further advanced than the State Salinity Council in acknowledging that difficult decisions lie ahead. The Commission's General Manager of Natural Resources, Kevin Goss, previously mentioned as WA Soils Commissioner, has recently explained: 'It will be a matter of applying a sort of triage: some land will be beyond recovery; some, if we act now, will stabilise; and some land, with action, can be recovered. The bottom line will be how valuable the land is, and what recovery will cost.'[53] According to Goss, 'lower value dryland farming' regions of the Murray–Darling 'will be hard to justify expensive remediation'.

Whether public opinion will accept an approach in Western Australia based around 'recover, contain, and adapt' has not been fully tested or debated. It certainly carries significant political sensitivities. If the author of the following letter to *The West Australian* is any guide, there may well be opposition to any attempts by government to 'write-off' areas for largely economic reasons. Challenging the view of those who think the land lost to salinity cannot be economically rehabilitated, the author argued for the consideration of the 'serious social and cultural implications inherent in giving up on the land ... These implications are so serious that the nation as a whole must be informed and consulted.'[54] Although an isolated voice in the current debate, the letter-writer raises an important question: How far is the community prepared to go to save those parts of the Wheatbelt which are salvageable?

The Salinity Strategy did not have a well-developed framework to consider the responses to the loss of landscape to salinity. It states: 'Some lands and waters will need direct government support to protect high priority public assets. However, private landholders and communities have the largest role in managing community and private lands and waters.'[55] Yet, the expected decline in rural population—due to salinity and the precarious economics of farming—leaves open to significant doubt the bland assertions by the Government that local communities have the capacity to be mainly responsible for dealing with the effects of salinity. The Strategy did not subject this objective to any credible analysis. How many farmers can afford to be involved? Will rural communities have sufficient numbers of energetic people in the coming years to take on such an enormous task as this? These questions are simply unanswered, yet upon them rests a key pillar of the

Government's Strategy: reliance on the efforts of local communities. Rural populations are falling at over 2 per cent a year with those under 21 years of age falling at 7 to 10 per cent per year.[56] The experience of Landcare, discussed earlier, shows the limitations of such a strategy. Even the previously mentioned Commonwealth funding which has flowed into positions of local Landcare Coordinators, has not addressed this shortcoming. These positions are limited to three years' duration whereupon responsibility for coordination reverts back to the local community. Evidence indicates that some Coordinators can take up to a year to become familiar with particular local circumstances and, in their third year, be diverted by the need to secure their next appointment. Therefore, over-reliance on individual landowners and local communities to carry the major responsibility of dealing with the salinity problem is likely to create shortcomings in the future fight against salinity.

An equally difficult question to resolve is whether governments can or should compel farmers to adopt salinity remedial measures. Concerted and cooperative action by all farmers in a catchment area can be important because those who may chose not to become involved can limit the impact of remedial measures. This issue has elicited a range of responses from informed commentators. Agricultural economist David Pannell argues the limitations of a democracy 'to directly select a sustainable farming system, because it is not possible to simply order farmers to adopt the chosen system'.[57] On the other hand, the architects of the Landcare program, Mr Phillip Toyne and Mr Rick Farley, argue the case for this problem to be overcome through extension of the concept of mutual obligation for farmers receiving public funding for salinity:

> What obligation will there be on land managers if they are to receive the billions needed for remediation, structural adjustment and other initiatives? Surely the concept of mutual obligation must be extended beyond the welfare system to the much greater personal financial benefits to be received in future by landholders. If land managers are to receive a private benefit from public

expenditure on the scale required, they must accept the goal of sustainable land use and accept independent verification of progress towards it.[58]

Surely, a major public policy dilemma exists over the requirement for farmers to adopt salinity control techniques. Non-adoption by individual farmers, or groups of farmers, for whatever reasons, risks diminished success and, perhaps, loss of public support for funding measures. Enforcement, in whatever way feasible, risks undermining farmer support for salinity control as it threatens the very independence at the heart of the rural ethic. In resolving this dilemma, history can be an important guide. In his survey of the history of soil conservation in Australia, John Bradsen argues the lesson to be learnt is that 'programs that rely on individual action where there is no obligation to act will not be effective'.[59]

Lack of strategic direction is also evident in the Government's consideration of the tools with which salinity can be managed. It identifies the following:

- changing farming practices;
- developing more suitable pastures and crops;
- developing commercial tree crops;
- using salt-affected land more productively; and
- developing engineering options where appropriate.

The contribution each of these options can play in reducing salinity is examined in Chapter 7. However, there was little in the Strategy indicating the extent of the Government's commitment to realise these options. For example, the funding for each mostly came under 'existing programs' with limited new funding identified into the future. As the Salinity Forum Inc. said of the Strategy: 'Most of the programs are not programs at all but merely descriptions of the ordinary business of a Government Department.'[60] Moreover, no targets were set by which these afore-mentioned options would be realised and no assessment was made as to the actual impact on salinity each option could make on its own, or in combination with others. Critically, the Strategy did not establish the extent to which the above options can be brought into operation in order to meet the expected need for the revegetation of the Wheatbelt area. The 1998 Draft of the Strategy clearly articulated the key objective: 'The necessary proportion of woody perennial cover is not known ... but the consensus among scientists is that 20% (or three million hectares) of the agricultural area strategically located in the landscape is the minimum required.'[61]

The obvious question to emerge from such a key statistic is the impact this revegetation will have on the current operations of the wheat and sheep industries. To what extent will they be viable into the future? Little was furnished in the Strategy in the way of action needed by farmers to adapt to new agricultural practices and/or to move off the land. What will happen to families and communities if such assistance is not forthcoming? Yet, the prospect of major social dislocation is a real one. Marty Ladyman's assessment on this point is worth considering:

> There's one hundred per cent of farmers [in the Wheatbelt] affected by salt. To what extent is salinity going to drive them off their farm is the tough one. If it's going to happen it will be in the next generation, the next 25-year period. We're starting to see that now where our sons are not returning ... I think we could probably look at 10–15 per cent of farmers exiting their farms due to overwhelming environmental conditions whether that be through salinity or waterlogging; and they are related. It is going to show up in the low rainfall areas where there are less tools to deal with it. I think you could probably start looking in those areas right now.

Parallel to the failure to provide realistic strategic direction is the issue of inadequate funding. It is likely that no firm figure has been devised regarding the total cost of a credible salinity strategy. Estimates of $3 billion were contained in the 1998 Draft Strategy.[62] Yet, as previously discussed, both State Liberal and Labor parties have rejected the calls for the introduction of a salinity levy. The other source of revenue was the Commonwealth Government. From early on in its planning on salinity, the Court Government had envisaged calling upon Commonwealth money through the establishment of the Natural Heritage Trust (NHT) funded by the sale of one-third of Telstra. The State Government had asked for a special allocation of $30 million a year for ten years claiming that its salinity plan 'could not be successfully implemented without Commonwealth money'.[63] This was a risky strategy. In the first place, NHT guidelines excluded parts of the Salinity Strategy; funding was not secure in the long term; it was designed to build on existing programs rather than create new ones; and it was subject to accusations that it was being used for electoral considerations. By 1999, Western Australia's ambit claim of $30 million a year for ten years especially for salinity had been reduced to $23 million covering all NHT projects in the State.[64] Yet, in its appeal to the Commonwealth, the State Government appeared not to highlight the case for substantial, long-term Commonwealth funding. After all, the Commonwealth approved and funded both First and Second World War land settlement schemes in the Wheatbelt as part of its active promotion of expanding the wheat industry.

Limited funding was not the only shortcoming of the Natural Heritage Trust. An independent review conducted for the Commonwealth Government found serious weaknesses in the design and implementation of the program which cast doubt on its capacity to achieve long-term environmental improvements. Specifically, the review found that programs needed to be based on more thoroughly researched information and funding 'should be directed to longer term, agreed action plans rather than fragmented, 'stop-start projects'.[65] These, it should be reiterated, are a prime cause of landcare burnout.

Among the other critics of NHT were Philip Toyne and Rick Farley, who recently claimed that the $1.5 billion funding for the program has resulted in increased awareness and community action 'rather than substantial on-the-ground improvements on some strategic national priority issues such as land clearing, salinity and water quality'.[66] The Industry Commission has, however, been more specific in its criticism, identifying the lack of detailed objectives and credible measures of what has been achieved, thus limiting the ability to evaluate the program properly.[67]

Recently, in the year 2000, the Commonwealth Government announced the allocation of $700 million to address salinity and water quality nationally but, on the basis of matching state funds (its plan is called *Our Vital Resources: A National Action Plan for Salinity and Water Quality in Australia*). At the time of writing, few details were made available about how and where the money would be spent, although it was reported that Western Australia's share of these funds amounted to $150 million, a figure that might be seen to be surprisingly small given the State's overwhelming share of the nation's dryland salinity problem. In terms of total area, Western Australia has 1.8 of the 2.5 million hectares affected by salt in Australia. Without doubt, the release of the Commonwealth package is likely to involve the expenditure of additional funds by the State Government, possibly even raising again the issue of a State levy. Moreover, the increased commitment of the Commonwealth to the salinity issue will likely focus more critical attention on measures to address the problem. The Commonwealth's funding statement refers to inadequacies of previous Landcare programs and especially 'the lack of agreed on-the-ground outcomes and targets for water quality, salinity and other natural resource management attributes [which have] been a major barrier to guaranteeing a return on the Commonwealth's investment'.[68] Therefore, the Commonwealth envisages a more proactive role in establishing agreed targets between Commonwealth and states, together with the establishment of a single Natural Resources Management Council that can sign off the targets and standards and monitor their achievement.

However, it is not yet clear how cooperatively the State and the Commonwealth can work on salinity. The Commonwealth's recent involvement has only heightened the need to resolve the matter of which tier of government should take prime responsibility for funding and managing the response.

In the light of these difficulties, it is not surprising that growing calls are being made for the Commonwealth to take a more proactive stance on land and water degradation issues. A recent political assessment of the implementation of the national salinity strategy was critical of 'the nation's sclerotic federal system'. The Canberra correspondent for *The Bulletin* magazine confirmed that despite loudly voiced pessimism on salinity in the national statement,

> Canberra and the states still haven't finalised the necessary inter-governmental agreement to cooperate in addressing the problems. While negotiations grind on, only two states have actually signed up, with New South Wales and Western Australia—the two with the biggest problem—yet to agree. Meanwhile no money has been spent on projects. Officials offer various reasons for the stand-off—the states need to find 'new' money for the projects, many of the proposed community catchment management agencies lack essentials such as bank accounts, and state nervousness at Canberra's desire to work through the community groups rather than state agencies.[69]

A recent Federal Government inquiry (by the House of Representatives Standing Committee on Environment and Heritage), argued for the Commonwealth to take a commanding role through the introduction of a new national tax to fund a $60 billion program to rescue Australia's river catchment systems which were claimed by the Committee to be in a state of crisis.[70]

Although salinity was a major focus of the Committee's deliberations, reaction to its recommendations in Western Australia highlighted the lack of a settled policy framework with which to tackle the problem. A spokesman for the WA Farmers' Federation said that

> there was a danger that regulation and punishment would damage the goodwill in WA's successful programs, which were based on cooperation and partnership between local, regional and State bodies … WA was having trouble implementing the national salinity action plan because, unlike some states, it did not have a single major river system.[71]

The opposing view was expressed by a representative of the Australian Conservation Foundation who argued the Report of the Committee 'marks a historical shift in the political debate on the environment and sustainability which has been mired in "states' rights" debates and with the Commonwealth that has declined to take a leading role'.[72]

It is too early to determine whether the Commonwealth Government will adopt an even greater role than already articulated in Prime Minister John Howard's previously mentioned salinity statement and, even, whether the processes for decision-making included in this will translate into effective working relationships between it and the states. It is the case that the gravity of the salinity and water quality issues around Australia are forging new territory in environment policy. However, a key issue will be the provision of effective advice to government on the various options for tackling salinity. Establishing effective bureaucratic structures to handle such a large and complex problem as salinity challenges traditional notions of government by which a single government department is usually assigned responsibility for a particular issue. However, problems ranging across government departments have long presented problems in achieving effective outcomes, and especially when these are based around 'top-down' approaches driven by senior public servants. Recent criticisms of the Murray–Darling Basin Commission illustrate these problems. The Commission was designed to be an advisory body comprised of senior bureaucrats from the Commonwealth and state governments of New South Wales, Victoria, South Australia and Queensland. In July 2000, the Federal Minister for the Environment, Senator Robert Hill, announced an overhaul of the Commission, citing concerns about its framework and relevance. Reports that bureaucrats on the Commission were cautious about making difficult decisions for fear of angering their Ministers appear to be the basis of Commonwealth Government concerns. One strand of thought has it that a bureaucracy-dominated Commission should be replaced with a skills-based group which can make effective decisions and provide 'frank and fearless advice'.[73]

In contrast, Western Australia's Salinity Strategy departed from a 'top-down' approach. It embodied the idea of partnership by establishing a State Salinity Council comprising representatives from interested community organisations and senior public servants from key agencies. In addition, the Council has been linked to the work of regional salinity action groups which, in turn, have feedback into the implementation of the Strategy. There is widespread agreement that this 'hybrid' model is an innovative way to link the specialists in government agencies with the needs and interests of the community. However, at some point decisions will have to be made about which options, in which combinations and in which areas, will be funded. A comprehensive plan for such decisions is not in place. In fact, public forums on salinity can quickly descend into wrangling among the proponents of the various options. The benefits of the hybrid model may dissipate unless some consensus among the various groups on the Council can be reached, assuming it is retained.

The value of the 'hybrid' model has yet to be tested for its ability to grapple with the scale of agricultural restructuring many see as crucial to the future control of salinity. Whether or not a Council composed of disparate interests and built around the search for consensus can deal with the future of the wheat industry, protection of biodiversity and forging ahead with new commercial enterprises has to be in some doubt given the complexity of these tasks.

Despite the active involvement of Commonwealth and state governments in salinity over the past decade, the ability of government to effectively address the problems remains in doubt. This is not surprising: governments have never before faced an environmental crisis on this scale. Like other major crises demanding government and community action, little consensus exists either on the seriousness of the problem, or the necessary control measures. Some people remain optimistic that the necessary adjustments can be made by responsibly farming the remaining 70 per cent of the Wheatbelt which is thought likely to survive. Others are even optimistic about some eventual productive uses being made of large areas of saline land. Yet, there are probably more pessimists and sceptics, especially within the specialist and scientific communities, who tend to highlight the technical limitations of available control mechanisms and to highlight the need to attend to the accompanying social, environmental and sustainable land-use issues. While such differences are to be expected on a complex issue like salinity, the major political parties have shown a reluctance to embrace the full extent of the problem and to devise long-term strategic planning processes which effectively address all the major problem areas. To date, the crisis of salinity has been only partially addressed.

CONTEMPORARY ISSUES
POSED BY SALINITY

'The cost of restoring Australia's landscape
might exceed the $37 billion annual value of
farm production … The cost of doing
nothing is higher still and rising.'

Source: Dr Graham Harris, Chief of CSIRO Land and
Water Division, as quoted in *The Australian*,
18–19 March 2000.

CHAPTER — 5

Katanning: The Salty Heart of the Great Southern

Located in a low, flat part of the landscape, the Wheatbelt town of Katanning is commonly reported to have one of the worst salinity problems in Western Australia. Indeed, given its size and the amount of infrastructure that it provides for the surrounding region some experts believe that it takes an easy first place.

Acknowledgment and acceptance of this situation and its long-term implications vary enormously within the community. At one extreme there are those individuals who are fully aware of the threat, and who work hard to educate others whilst also trying to maintain the morale of the people whose properties are badly affected by celebrating whatever positive steps are taken to save the town and the farmland surrounding it. At the opposite end are the majority of townspeople and the minority of farmers who continue to ignore or deny the problems associated with steadily increasing salinity. Located at other points along this continuum are the people who have some understanding of the situation but respond to it in ambivalent or contradictory ways; the townspeople who get involved in tree-planting projects and encourage the use of native species around the town site while their private gardens are full of shallow-rooted non-native species that require constant watering, for example; or the farmers who plant salt-tolerant species on their own properties but support the use of European vegetation in the town. In order to understand these very different reactions to salinity it is necessary to reflect on the complex interplay of history, politics and cultural attitudes informing all sectors of the community, in Katanning itself and at regional, State and national levels.

One of the major themes running through this book is the importance of recognising the culturally based beliefs and practices that have shaped the approach of successive Western Australian Governments to land management. In the same way, what happens at the local level is influenced by the cultural premises of the farmers and townspeople who have shaped their environment to meet their needs and desires. This case study considers some of the socio-cultural factors that have influenced the district's and the town's responses to the major environmental threat of salinity.

THE HEART OF THE GREAT SOUTHERN

Tourist brochures for the Great Southern Region describe Katanning as a thriving, multicultural, commercial centre that is often referred to, for reasons relating to geography and infrastructure, as the 'Heart of the Great Southern'.

The town site is situated approximately 290 kilometres south-east of Perth on the Great Southern Highway. Katanning has a population of over 5,000 and services approximately 13,000 people throughout the surrounding region.[1] It accommodates five banks and a number of government agencies, including Homeswest, the Water Corporation, Agriculture Western Australia and the Department of Conservation and Land Management. It has a hospital, a TAFE centre, a senior high school, three primary schools, extensive sporting facilities including a new Recreation Centre, a local newspaper and a radio station, along with a number of other community organisations. The region's agricultural production is focused around cereal and legume crops, predominantly wheat, canola, barley and lupins. Sheep are also a major part of the local economy. According to farmers, Katanning is generally perceived as a 'safe' or 'reliable' agricultural area despite the increasing impacts of salinity. Articles in the local newspaper in 1997and 1998, for example, reported that farmers in Katanning and the surrounding region had experienced award-winning, record harvests and were contributing significantly to national exports.[2,3] The town itself is also a major regional centre for the buying and selling of stock with over a million animals passing through its sale yards every year. A large abattoir, located on the edge of the town, provides meat for export and is reportedly the biggest employer in the Great Southern Region. This meat industry is now providing jobs for many of the town's Christmas Islander community.[4]

The Katanning district was initially opened up for sheep grazing in the 1860s, by settlers who followed in the wake of Sandalwood cutters and kangaroo hunters.[5] Katanning, situated close to the mid-point of the Great Southern Railway line,[6] was declared a town site in 1890,[7] and by 1891 had its own flour mill in operation.[8] A year later the State Government made the Katanning agricultural area available for selection and settlement,[9] and local wheat cultivation began to increase, along with the amount of land being cleared.

By the early 1900s natural water sources along the Great Southern Railway were becoming too salty for use in locomotive boilers, a fact that was quickly linked to the clearing of native vegetation. Records suggest that the presence of salt in the landscape also began to concern some farmers in the area around this time, and, although there is evidence that government officials recognised a connection between clearing and increasing soil salinity as early as 1907,[10] they continued to provide encouragement and support for extensive agricultural development in the region.

After 1945 the State/Commonwealth governments' War Service Land Settlement Scheme heralded 'an economic post-war boom, an age of unprecedented growth and change' for Katanning and its surrounding townships.[11] It was during this period, as the Great Southern became more closely settled, that the most extensive clearing of native vegetation in the Katanning Creek Catchment occurred.[12] In 2000, records showed that only 1,000 hectares of remnant vegetation remained, covering a mere 10 per cent of the Catchment.[13] There are now 125 hectares of land 'within or immediately adjacent to the town boundary' that are salt-affected.[14]

AN EMERGING AWARENESS OF SALINITY

Older residents have been aware of the presence of salt in Katanning and its surrounding farmland for many decades. One farmer remembers her aunts talking about saline spots on the family property in the 1890s, just a few decades after the land was first cleared.[15] Another resident reflected on her father's efforts to address salt scalds on his farm in the late 1950s by planting salt-tolerant lucerne and paspalum:

> People noticed that [land] was going to salt, but they didn't know why, they didn't blame the clearing. Dad saw [the salt], he was aware of it and he was worried about it, but the methods they had for combating it weren't radical enough—I suppose he felt that because it had come slowly it didn't need a big [effort] to get rid of it. He didn't think it was a big issue.[16]

By the 1970s salinity was becoming a much bigger issue for farmers in the Katanning Shire. Local tree farmers John and Norma Blythe explained how their business developed in the late 1970s and early 1980s as landholders started to look for ways to limit the spread of salt on their properties. The Blythes were working as fertiliser contractors when they first started to notice increasing levels of salt in the landscape:

> You would drive across one part of a paddock one year and the next year you would get bogged in that same place. The idea came to us that maybe planting trees was going to help, so in 1978 we did a trial, planted nine thousand seedlings in trays, put an advertisement in the paper, and had people coming up to buy them, which was really quite amazing. People were only putting in around forty trees per year, but that was a lot in those days.[17]

Initially, individual seedlings were expensive and planting them was highly time intensive. In an attempt to make tree-planting more affordable for farmers, the Blythes developed a tree-planting machine which could be attached to a tractor. They found that there was a big demand amongst local farmers for contract planting from 1982 up until the end of the 1980s, after which time many landholders became involved in catchment groups and started to take over tree-planting themselves. It was around the same time that the idea of growing tree seedlings for sale took off. According to John Blythe, 'nurseries sprang up all over the place' as the belief in revegetation, as a solution to increasing salinity, began to spread.

KEEPING THE SALT UNDER CONTROL: A VIEW FROM THE TOP OF THE HILL

Bronte and June Rundle had been farming a property east of Katanning for over a decade when they began to notice that their land was becoming increasingly saline. In 1975 they decided to purchase a larger property, higher in the landscape, to the south-west of Katanning. The new property showed only slight signs of salt damage, which they began to address immediately by planting trees. A seminar on tree-planting in Perth in 1980 helped them to develop more efficient planting techniques, which they shared with other farmers in Katanning at a follow-up meeting which was attended by close to ninety people. Like the Blythes, the Rundles also link the timing and extent of this community interest in tree-planting to an obvious increase in salinity in the late 1970s and early 1980s. Bronte Rundle remembered the growing awareness of salt encroachment around this time:

> We started losing trees due to leaf-miners[18] attacking the Flooded Gums. Trees began to die off, and then it just seemed to me that suddenly salinity started popping up all over the place, salt seeps and waterlogging. That was the turning point, I reckon. People really started viewing it fairly seriously.

After attending another seminar in 1988, this time on farm planning, the Rundles chose to implement a long-term strategy that would increase the sustainability and productivity of their property by reducing the potential impact of salinity. Their 12-year plan required an average annual investment of $14,000 in conservation work and involved giving 12 per cent of their farm over to trees.[19] The property is now highly productive and the conservation strategies undertaken have attracted national and international attention. The Rundles have already been able to see the benefits of their work and believe, in the long term, that their whole farm plan 'will overcome the combined problems of wind erosion, waterlogging and salinity'.[20] However, few landholders have had this degree of success.

LOSING THE BATTLE ON THE VALLEY FLOOR

Less than 100 kilometres to the east of the Rundles' property, Gnowangerup farmers Ed and Ros Dixon have had a very different experience of dealing with salt. Ed first noticed evidence of salinity on his property in the mid-1970s. His father, who purchased the partially cleared farm in 1965, chose it believing that its location on the valley floor would mean increased surface water run-off that could be used for watering stock and crops. Ed took over the farm in 1970 and has had to contend with the steady encroachment of salt upon his land ever since. In June 2000 only 1,000 acres of the 2,300 that the Dixons owned was still viable for cropping. Their sheep had already been transferred to a relative's property. Ed spoke of the difficulties he had faced in trying to address the problem:

> About 1975 I started wondering what was going on. I could see something happening. There was nothing really obvious, but you could see pasture diminishing. This farm has always been prone to winter flooding, but I began to notice pools of water being left behind as well.
>
> So I went to a WISALTS school.[21] They talked a lot about contours, interceptor banks, soil types and soil layers. I dug a bit of a hole with the front-end loader [when I got back], but I couldn't make a lot of sense of it. That plan fizzled out because I didn't know exactly what to do and because of the big expenses

involved. Also, I wasn't confident that it would work because at the time the Agriculture Department was a hundred per cent against the WISALTS system, and the WISALTS system was a hundred per cent against the Agriculture Department. [Farmers] became the 'meat in the sandwich', just sitting on the fence watching. There was nowhere to go, no sense of guidance.

In 1988 the Gnowangerup Land Conservation District Committee (LCDC) was formed and began to promote tree-planting as a way of dealing with increasing salinity. Ed became involved in his local Landcare group and eventually accepted the role of Catchment leader. He soon realised, however, that his own conservation efforts at the bottom of the Upper Coblinine Catchment were of minimal benefit as long as farmers higher in the Catchment resisted taking action. In 2000, his property was so degraded that he was forced to work off-farm almost full time in order to earn an income. This meant that he no longer had time to do much Landcare work on his own farm or to continue his volunteer work for the LCDC. At the time of the interview the Dixons were waiting to find out if the Catchment group's application for Commonwealth Government funding (the Natural Heritage Trust—NHT) to help design and implement an Integrated Catchment Management Plan would be successful. Edward believed that this whole catchment plan offered the last hope for their farm. When asked about the prospects for his property without the funding, he said: 'there aren't any. Its not even feasible to sell. It is pretty well that degraded now that it is useless.'

These two accounts are typical of farmers who have taken steps, over the last three decades, to address the increasing salinity on their properties. These stories also highlight the impacts of various environmental, historical and individual factors on the extent of land degradation currently being experienced by landholders in the Katanning Shire and its surrounding districts. It is clearly evident from these accounts that some properties are more severely affected than others as a result of their location in the landscape, and that some individuals are better positioned economically to respond with extensive preventative and remedial actions than others.[22] This inequity presents serious challenges to the ability of the Katanning community to tackle the issue in a unified manner.

LIVING WITH SALINITY: EXPERT OPINIONS AND COMMUNITY VALUES

As for much of the surrounding farmland, the long-term prognosis for the township of Katanning in 2000 was not good. In some places the water table was less than one metre from the surface,[23] and many older buildings were already showing signs of salt-induced decay. In 1999 a Katanning Salinity Management Strategy (KSMS) was prepared for the Katanning Shire Council as a part of its participation in Agriculture WA's Rural Towns Program (RTP).[24] The KSMS states:

> The creek lines above, below and in the town are severely affected by soil salting that has continued [to] spread in the last 20 years. Flooding has occurred in the town with the worst events in 1982. Rising damp and salt affects houses, road pavements, kerbing, creek water quality, recreation ovals and car parks along the length of the town … Water table monitoring and district observations support a conclusion that salinity will continue to spread unless major increases in water use in the catchment, reductions in imported water and, probably, changes to discharge rates,[25] occur.[26]

The Katanning town site is situated at the confluence of the Katanning Creek and the Kojonup Creek, on the 'edge of a broad flat valley floor'.[27] It is positioned low in the Katanning Creek Catchment, on a slope of less than one metre. The surrounding farmland 'drains towards the town, except to the south-east where the Katanning Creek flows away from [it]'.[28] Research shows that the groundwater directly under the town is mainly influenced 'by subsurface flow from catchments above the town',[29] which consist mostly of cleared farmland. Water management must be improved in these catchments in order to prevent the water table under the Katanning town site from rising further.

The other major contributor to the town site's salinity problem is excess surface water, which enters the water table through soak wells, roof drainage, open unlined drains and excessive watering of ovals and gardens.[30] The KSMS lists a number of practical options for reducing the level of the water table under the town.[31] In addition to managing water more effectively higher up in the Catchment, these include collecting and harvesting rainwater; improving the drainage of surface water in the town; reducing the amount of water used on gardens and lawns;[32] recycling effluent and stormwater and planting more trees.[33] The option of pumping groundwater into a large evaporation pond is also being considered,[34] although the initial and on-going costs of such an operation would be high.[35] The KSMS report includes a strategic action plan for 1999 to 2001,[36] which requires the participation of local government, the Land Conservation District Committee, the Water Corporation, Agriculture WA, private landholders, local business and community groups.

As the town attempts to come to terms with the reality and implications of living with salinity, the inevitable tensions and divisions arise. Conflicting priorities and values compete for space, influence and funding grants within the community. Government agencies, the Landcare network and the Shire Council, as well as the individuals who run these organisations and the policies that inform them, jostle against one another in the search for ways to counter the effects of the steadily rising water table and the dissolved salt that rises with it. Lack of co-ordination and communication between individual agencies and other community-based groups has been a major obstacle to achieving a unified approach to salinity in the past, and a core of key people, volunteers and government employees, are now working hard to overcome this.

Perhaps the most obvious division within any rural community exists between landholders who are (or have been) directly involved in agricultural land management, and service providers who live and work within the townsite itself. While some Katanning residents reported a kind of 'us and them' attitude between farmers and townspeople, others emphasised the interdependence and sense of unity they felt was present within the community. There were, however, some obvious differences between farmers and 'townies'. Farmers tended to be much more involved in Landcare than townspeople. Whilst they were frequently characterised as cautious and conservative, it was clearly evident that farmers, along with agency representatives and Landcare workers, were providing essential leadership on the salinity issue within the community. While most of the townspeople who were interviewed were also employed in organisations that required them to address salinity-related issues as part of their work, they did report that they felt other people living in the town tended towards apathy on the issue and often believing that the responsibility for dealing with salinity lay primarily with the farmers.

ON THE FARMS ...

While farmers do tend to be better informed about salinity than townspeople, there are still many who are not fully aware of its implications, or who choose to deny the extent of the problem. Some still do not know how to recognise the early signs of increasing salinity on their properties and the majority of landholders still only start to take action when their businesses begin to experience financial strain. When farmers do become aware of the threat that salinity poses to their land and livelihoods, economic constraints may mean that they are unable to do much about it anyway. Nonetheless, a retired farmer emphasised that those who had 'been around a while and could remember what it was like twenty or thirty years ago, those who were not just ignoring the problem, realised the importance of trying to do something'.

One Landcare Coordinator from a Shire adjoining Katanning explained that many farmers see the situation as being 'out of their hands', too big for them to deal with in addition to meeting daily operational demands and coping with unpredictable seasonal patterns.[37] Margaret Scott, a Landcare technician and the coordinator for Katanning's Rural Towns Program, described the situation in September 2000:

> Farming is going through a period where a lot of people are finding it extremely difficult to make any sort of living at all. People

east of [Katanning] have had three years of terrible frosts and now they are facing a season where there has been insufficient rain. Many farmers can't afford to continue Landcare and environmental work in these situations. It will be done if there is money to do it, but they have to support their families and pay their debts to financial institutions. These priorities come first.

New environmental and economic demands require that landholders alter their farming practices in order to keep their businesses viable. In the past, farmers have been able to seek individual advice and information on new farming practices from Agriculture WA advisors. Recently, however, Agriculture WA has directed its resources into particular focus catchments as part of what its representatives argue is a more strategic and efficient approach to dealing with salinity on a statewide scale. Farmers and Landcare workers in Katanning reported that this approach made it difficult for those whose properties were not located within the designated catchments to get the personalised advice they most needed.[38] Margaret Scott explained how a lot of the one-on-one support that agency employees used to be able to provide to individual farmers had been replaced by large-scale field days, workshops and conferences. She made the following observations:

> The cost for farmers to attend some of these events can be quite prohibitive,[39]... so they have to rely on the information that comes to them. One-on-one extension is always much more effective. The Agriculture Department used to do it very well, but their budgets have been cut. They have tried to address this in different ways, and one of the ways was to deal with focus catchments, hoping that the technical work they did with one catchment would spread to other catchments, but we are not seeing much evidence of that flowing through. There needs to be more interaction with people on the ground, linking farmers together.

Farmer preference for a personalised approach to acquiring knowledge about new farming techniques and technologies was widely recognised amongst Landcare workers and agency employees in Katanning. According to one observer, Agricultural WA's requirement that individual farmers organise themselves into groups if they want an agricultural advisor to come out and talk to them about a particular issue means that farmers no longer use the Department's resources as much as they did in the past.[40] One Landcare worker made the point, for example, that farmers are more likely to ask their stock agents or fertiliser merchants for advice, simply because these people visit their properties and engage in one-to-one conversation. Another Landcare worker made the following observation:

> Farmers are often quite slow [to take up new farming practices].[41] They are reasonably conservative and cautious people. They have to take risks every season. Maybe that is what makes them so cautious. With new advice they seem much more inclined to watch a neighbour down the road to see how he goes with a new project, whether it is contour banks or whatever. The farmer will watch for awhile, maybe talk to his neighbour from time to time, ask how it is going, then he might try it out on one of his small paddocks.[42]

One of the dilemmas for landholders who want to do something to protect their properties from salinity is that none of the strategies being promoted are guaranteed to succeed and many require significant capital input. Conflicting information and opinions contribute to the hesitancy of individual farmers to invest time and money in any particular approach. Farmers have to come to terms with the fact that there is no single simple solution, that what works on one farm may not work on another farm and that, to some extent, all proposed treatments for salinity are still experimental. Most farmers recognise the need for more research, especially in relation to the development of alternative cash crops that are both economically viable and environmentally sustainable. As one retired farmer stated: 'If farmers can make money they will give it a try.'

Farmers and Landcare workers frequently draw attention to the highly independent nature of the people who enter into the business of farming. One Landcare worker pointed out that independence is, in fact, a basic survival skill for all farmers. This quality also meant farmers generally did not want to be told, by anyone, how to run their properties. Working as part of a coordinated catchment group, or organising a group to gather for an Agriculture WA presentation, may be confronting for people who tend to value independence and self-reliance over the ability to work in cooperation with others.

One Landcare worker offered the following insights on what she described as the 'human' aspect of farming, something that decision-makers often appear to overlook when encouraging landholders to adopt new agricultural practices[43]:

> There are a lot of [older] generation farmers around here who say [to their sons] "that's how we did it in my day ... so it should be good enough for you". Change threatens that comfort zone. Farming is very personal, it's a business, but I don't think landholders view it in the same way that they might view, for example, a delicatessen. [A] farm is something much more personal ... The farm is not just a business, you can't just go home at night. The farm is also the life. I suppose getting farmers to change is equivalent of telling someone ... that you don't like their personality and suggesting that they should do things another way. I'm sure it feels like that to landholders. If you tell them "don't do it that way, do it this way", you are really threatening what they have already done, telling them that [their way] wasn't worthwhile, wasn't the right way to do it, you are putting a shadow over what they believed was right. Farmers take a real sense of pride in what they do and how they do it. When you start to tell them that they have to do it differently it is painful, it is like a vote of no confidence, I think that is how they feel.[44]

Long-term changes in agricultural practice are much more likely to be adopted when the cultural beliefs and attitudes of the farmers being asked to implement those changes are actively engaged from the outset. This involves finding ways to encourage people to work with their strengths, to capitalise on their pre-existing expertise and incorporate it into new ways of doing things. Landcare workers and others are clearly aware of the importance of this approach in the context of one-on-one information transfer. Politicians and policy-makers, however, also need to work with a solid understanding and respect for farmer culture as they attempt to promote agricultural change.

Coming to terms with the immediate effects and long-term implications of increasing salinity had already started to have an impact on the health of local farmers. A Katanning medical practitioner, Dr Ralph Chapman, explained that anxiety and stress levels are noticeably higher amongst those people in the community who have a clear understanding of the problems associated with salt encroachment:

> The farmers [who] are sensitive to the problem are making quite significant efforts to do something about it. They are changing the way they do agriculture, [and] obviously at some cost to themselves and their families. They have increasing levels of anxiety and stress, possibly depression and the flow-on consequences of that. Those who don't have an awareness of [the problem] or who can say "well it's too late, my forefathers did this", they probably don't manifest the same sorts of problems because they are willing to say, "well, some other generation has to deal with this"… although ultimately it will affect their income and their wellbeing.

Dr Chapman suggested that the gradual development of salinity meant that the impact was fairly subtle in most cases. Farmers were unlikely to be suddenly overwhelmed by salt encroachment, especially if they had grown up with it. Several of the farmers interviewed, however, believed that the devastation of increasing salt levels on top of other economic and environmental factors, could indeed be overwhelming. They drew attention to the increasing incidence of depression in the farming community, reporting that suicide was a serious problem amongst younger men in the region. One landholder suggested that 'men, and particularly farmers, don't tend to talk about stress or emotive issues', a tendency which reflects the macho image that many

Australian males assume.[45] He said that although farmers are willing to share information about common problems, 'they won't talk about the things that hurt them, the things that are close to the bone, like how they are going to survive next year if money is a bit short'.[46]

IN THE TOWN …

Dr Chapman believed that salinity was not a high-profile topic in the town. He explained:

> We probably aren't as exposed to [salinity] in the town environment as someone involved with agriculture would be, but that is really a failure of education.[47] There is not a great deal of awareness in the schools or in the community at large. You would expect salinity to be higher on the education agenda. It is on the television, and in the agricultural magazines, but it doesn't seem to be pervading the social consciousness of the towns.[48]

One resident, who held several official roles in the Katanning community, estimated that only 5 per cent of the people living in the town of Katanning acknowledged that they were directly affected by salinity whereas, in reality, at least 30 to 40 per cent of properties may have been displaying salt-related damage. He believed that many of the town's residents were still not linking the rising damp in their homes with the water table or the presence of salt and felt that many 'people would see the mortar fretting from the side of house as something that just happens' rather than the result of increasing salinity.[49] Katanning Shire Council's Manager of Works shared this perception in relation to community understandings of the degradation of public buildings.[50] Another Katanning resident pointed out that 're-doing the footings of houses, filling wall gaps and damp courses with silicon treatments, and even just scraping the flaking part out of the wall and rendering it with concrete and painting it' was a big business in Katanning. She said that all these things were 'band-aid' solutions but that people were simply unwilling to accept that their houses were 'falling down' due to the effects of waterlogging and salinity.[51]

One resident who had lived and worked in Katanning for more than a decade reported that he had already had to spend over $30,000 to maintain his home and business premises, both of which were old buildings located in wetter parts of the town. He made the following observations:

> [The people who are aware of the problem] can see the impact of salinity on the town, the degradation of the soil, surface water destroying old houses. We have had to spend a lot of time cutting out damp courses and replacing them and things like that, because the water table is basically above the ground for a third of the year. The ground seeps. A lot of Katanning is like that. Even the car park here, we can't put a solid paved surface on it because in the middle of the year when it has been raining a lot, the water just sort of oozes out of the ground. If you walk around this building in winter time the stumps actually float because the ground water comes up so high that the stumping of the house is actually sitting in salt mud.

Salt-related damage has definitely become more visible in the town over the past few years, although several Landcare workers suggested that townspeople still seemed to think that the problem was limited to parts of the town where salt crusts actually appeared on the ground's surface, such as Prosser Park, the site of the town's war memorial.[52] The Katanning Shire recently instituted an expensive long-term rehabilitation plan for this park in response to community pressure following the 1997 Anzac Day ceremony.[53,54] That the Shire responded so promptly to public concern over this particular site illustrates the ways in which cultural values influence community decisions. Sites such as that of the local war memorial are often ascribed priority status based on their symbolic value rather than on their intrinsic environmental value. In environmental terms, for example, it may well have made better sense for the Shire to invest its money in preventing salinity from increasing in another part of the town instead of attempting to reclaim one of the most badly affected areas; but the historical and sentimental values invested in Prosser Park, and the public pressure exerted on the democratically elected Shire Council as a result, are the likely reasons for its rehabilitation,[55] rather than its hydrological or general environmental significance.

The expressions of concern about the town's war memorial are all the more revealing given that salinity did not generally seem to be a major issue in local Shire politics. Shire representatives reported that concerns about rubbish collections and street sweeping, for example, were of higher priority than lowering the water table and minimising salt damage. Two recent documents prepared for the Shire appear to support this perception. The Katanning Community Charrette (a local community development process undertaken in May 1997),[56] and the current Cultural Policy and Plan for the Shire of Katanning (1999) both make surprisingly few references to salinity. In the Charrette Handbook, for example, salinity appears as third priority on the list of major community issues following the promotion of tourism and the development of streetscapes. It is only briefly mentioned elsewhere in the Handbook.[57] The Katanning Shire Cultural Policy and Plan includes a reference to salinity in its section on 'Local Identity'. It recommends that the Shire Council '[s]upports efforts for Katanning to take the lead in Landcare and salinity research through continuing to support the development of Landcare Catchment groups.'[58] The development and implementation of a townscape strategy, the use of local architectural themes and building materials, and the development of the Piesse Dam are all listed in advance of Landcare and salinity.[59]

These struggles to reconcile the significance of salinity with other community concerns represent a deeper set of conflicts over land use common to all communities. Trigger writes about the contesting ideologies and sentiments of different community groups competing for influence over aspects of natural resource management.[60] He describes how the conflicting value systems of environmentalists and resource developers are part of a complex social struggle over the meanings and uses of land. A similar dynamic can be seen at work in the Katanning community as residents attempt to come to terms with the challenges of salinity, except in many cases the value contests are taking place *within* individuals as well as between identifiable social groups. Gardens, for example, show how deeply entrenched aesthetic values come into conflict with environmental values; many people, including some of those working to address salinity in other contexts, continue to favour European-style gardens and trees over native gardens even when they know the former are maladaptive in terms of water use and salt tolerance.

While improving the Katanning townscape was a priority for a number of the residents interviewed, several people indicated that the form and nature of new public gardens and streetscapes had been a source of conflict within the community. These conflicts include the unwillingness of some community members to have trees planted along the town's main street because of the associated leaf litter. At the same time, however, there was also a lot of community resistance to the removal of some old Sugar Gums and a pine tree (the local Christmas tree) to make way for a 'Heritage Park' in front of the Town Hall. Given the value of large, salt-tolerant trees in reducing the level of the water table, this ambivalence is significant. In addition, when the new Heritage Gardens were planted in 1996 and 1997, the species used to replace the old trees were rose bushes, carefully selected to reflect the Shire's gardening history, deciduous trees, lawn and an assortment of native and non-native grasses and shrubs. Salt tolerance and watering requirements did not appear to have been considered in most of these choices. Instead, the gardens clearly reflect a set of pervasive cultural attitudes that continue to attempt to shape the Australian landscape according to a strongly European aesthetic.[61] Having an aesthetically pleasing town that residents could feel proud of was acknowledged as an important source of community morale.[62]

Towns like Katanning are often noted for their sense of community. Indeed, many residents proudly recall the sense of achievement the community experienced in their efforts to complete the Recreation Centre, the Public Library and the Arts Centre. However, the same community spirit is not yet in evidence in regard to salinity as one resident reflected:

I think the problem we face [in getting the community to act together on Landcare objectives] is that the 'townies' still see [salinity] as a farmers' problem. They haven't yet seen the overall social significance, they don't see that the impact on this town, twenty or thirty years down the track, is that there may not be a town of reasonable size here. They don't have the vision to see that what happens on farms has a significant effect on what happens to Katanning.[63]

Unless an individual's work requires him or her to deal specifically with salinity-related issues, it is still possible for Katanning residents to ignore the environmental crisis which is bearing down upon them. This capacity is, perhaps, part of a much broader cultural attitude that allows many Australians to look past the landscape that surrounds them, to simply not 'see' their environment, except in the most utilitarian of ways. One person who worked in Katanning hinted at this tendency when he commented that 'in the country you just drive through the land, you don't actually see it'.

Although there is minimal Aboriginal involvement in the Katanning Landcare movement, some members of the local Noongar community did express concern about increasing salinity. Eugene Eades, an Aboriginal man who was born in Katanning, said that he became aware of the effects of salinity in the town when he returned in 1982 after an absence of almost two decades. He explained how local environmental changes had affected Noongar people; bush foods had become much harder to find within close range of the town site, and elders were no longer able to teach children about the plants and animals in the area because there was so little left to see. '[What] really puts a lump in our throats now,' Eades reflected, is 'looking at places where we used to get our drinking water, they no longer exist because of the underground saltwater table rising.' He said that local Noongar people were worried about the environmental degradation around Katanning and wanted to have active roles in caring for the natural bushland that remained. Eades himself had been working with Agriculture WA, the Water Corporation, Fisheries WA and the Rural Towns Program to develop a trout farm in Katanning utilising the salty groundwater that the Shire was planning to pump out from under the town site.

RESPONDING TO SALINITY IN KATANNING

Most people attempting to address the issue of salinity in Katanning strongly believe in the need for the community to work together, to pool its resources and skills in an effort to reduce the long-term social and environmental impact. As Margaret Scott said:

> There is always strength in numbers, and in linking projects together. They mesh, they support each other. Since I have been here that is what I have tried to do, to draw people together, to get them involved in projects collectively, to get them to communicate about what is happening and what they need from each other. Together we can do things that, separately, we couldn't.[64]

Along with the Shire, the State government agencies in Katanning, although sometimes constrained by the bureaucratic system, are well positioned to provide leadership and infrastructural support in the local battle against salinity. To what extent they have achieved these goals, however, is disputed.

State government agencies

The State Salinity Strategy (2000) has spearheaded the State Government's response to salinity in Western Australia. Yet, when asked if they thought farmers in Katanning had a good understanding of the Strategy, Agriculture WA employees indicated that the majority of farmers knew very little about it, apart from what they had read in the newspapers. Landcare workers shared this perception and suggested that very few farmers would have even seen the Salinity Strategy documents. Several people in Katanning described the Strategy as primarily political, a document produced for the benefit of urban voters and the media. One government employee commented that the Strategy had, at least, stimulated valuable debate about salinity in Western Australia.

Margaret Scott described some of the responses to the Strategy from within the wider Katanning community:

> There was a lot of disappointment on the Strategy's release that the government hadn't supported it with the funding that was necessary to implement it. In fact, they had reduced their commitment substantially. There was scant [community] consultation [for the first plan which was released in November 1996]. It was very much an agency dominated document and it received an immense amount of criticism and rejection from the community. In the revised Strategy [2000] they endeavoured to improve that situation. There was still criticism that it was a government document with only token community input. There was more that could have been done. But the fact that the State Government wouldn't back [the plan] with the requisite funding was a big disappointment to everyone.

Another government employee volunteered the following reflections on the Strategy and the community's response to it: 'People are looking for a panacea to their problems so a lot of them want to see a document that guarantees [a solution].'

Concerns exist, too, over the effectiveness of individual agencies working to alleviate salinity in the town. The following have a significant presence in the town of Katanning: the Water Corporation, the Department of Conservation and Land Management and Agriculture Western Australia.[65]

The Water Corporation has a central role to play in monitoring and responding to the rising water table beneath the town. It also bears a large part of the responsibility of working to improve general water management in Katanning. The Department of Conservation and Land Management is responsible for 180 nature reserves across the twelve Wheatbelt shires. This agricultural zone contains around 4,000 plant species, the impact of salinity on which has been catastrophic,[66] and, in 2000, the majority of the agency's work in the Katanning Shire involves the protection of the existing remnant vegetation. Agriculture

WA has been comparatively successful in working with the Katanning community to provide support and training in efforts to encourage good farm management and improve general morale.

In addition to running community development programs, Agriculture WA has had extensive involvement in researching and managing salinity. In 1997 it initiated the Rural Towns Program, also part of the Salinity Action Strategy, and by March 2000 there were twenty-seven shires from around Western Australia participating. Katanning was one of the first towns to join the Program in 1997. The Rural Towns Program aims to promote awareness of salinity and salinity management strategies; to provide technical and financial assistance to the Shire and the LCDC in managing the effects of salinity within the town-site; to increase the town's ability to be self-sufficient in the management of its salinity problem; to develop specific strategies for managing salinity; and to carry out 'a cost analysis of various salinity treatments based on a predictive groundwater model'.[67]

Despite these extensive involvements, community cynicism exists about the levels of government commitment to environmental protection in Katanning, as it does throughout Australia. There is a strong suspicion among Landcare workers and landholders that the people with power to make decisions about allocating government funding to community projects are not well informed about the nature of the environmental problem or the kind of community action required to address it. This distrust jeopardises the ability of government agencies to work effectively with individuals and organisations at the local level. Government expectations that the community will eventually be able to solve salinity-related problems itself with a bit of initial financial encouragement appear unrealistic. As one Landcare worker explained:

> The Natural Heritage Trust money that the government provided was described as 'catalytic funding'. The idea was that there would be a few years of funding to start everyone off, to set the ball rolling. [The assumption was] that when that funding was completed there would be sufficient momentum within the community for people to just continue with the work. That is completely

ridiculous. The environmental problem is not that easily resolved. NHT funding lasted for about five years. I heard someone comment that they were trying to explain to one of the people in Canberra that the funding needed to continue, and the response was, 'Well, Why? You have had five years of funding. Haven't you fixed it in that time?'. I don't know if that is true, but you do hear comments like that. It shows a complete lack of understanding of what we are trying to do.

Local government

Involvement in local politics presents some unique challenges, and especially when dealing with an issue as complex as salinity. A Landcare worker made the following comment:

> We have been pushing for years to get local government more involved, and I think, generally, that has happened. But there is a recognition within local government that they are not just dealing with Landcare. They are dealing with everything, from old age issues, to health care, to schooling, all those local things that need to happen. To be a small country town Councillor, you have to be knowledgeable about all of those areas. I think those people are voluntarily stretched beyond their limits. Landcare only gets fifteen or twenty minutes along with all the other issues.

Compromise was the major theme that emerged from interviews with Katanning Shire Councillors. As one Councillor pointed out, the role of local government is to 'walk the middle line, to look at the big picture' and consider the needs of all sectors of the community. He believed that Landcare and salinity were not the responsibilities of local government, which he said had neither the resources nor the expertise to deal with them effectively. Nonetheless, the Shire had become involved in the battle against salinity through its participation in the Rural Towns Program, for which it provided 50 per cent of the funding.

The Shire is responsible for implementing a number of 'strategic actions' aimed at reducing salinity in the town site. These are outlined

Stand of Salmon Gums, once a common species throughout the Wheatbelt.
(*Courtesy of the Department of Conservation and Land Management, WA.*)

Lone Salmon Gum in a field of ripening wheat, between Merredin and Bruce Rock.
(*Courtesy of Wally Edgecombe, Department of Conservation and Land Management, WA.*)

Aerial view of salt-affected farmland in the upper Kent River, west of Mt Barker.
(*Courtesy of Simon Neville and the Water and Rivers Commission.*)

Salinised and eroded creek with remedial plantings and drains, Frankland Catchment. Note that salinity has followed the natural drainage system in the lower parts of the landscape.
(*Courtesy of Simon Neville and the Water and Rivers Commission.*)

Salt-encrusted tree roots. Note that as the tree has died, soil has eroded from its base.
(*Courtesy of West Australian Newspapers Ltd.*)

Farmer on salt-encrusted paddock, Dumbleyung.
(*Courtesy of West Australian Newspapers Ltd.*)

Dry salt lake in the Lake Grace district. Note that such salt lakes are a naturally occurring part of the landscape, particularly in the far eastern Wheatbelt. (*Courtesy of West Australian Newspapers Ltd.*)

Photograph showing the spread of salinity on pastoral lands. (*Courtesy of West Australian Newspapers Ltd.*)

Waterlogged paddock in winter. Note the paddock is waterlogged due to a rising water table. (*Courtesy of Don McFarlane and the Water and Rivers Commission.*)

The same paddock shown above, two months later, depicting crop failure in the water-logged area. (*Courtesy of Don McFarlane and the Water and Rivers Commission.*)

Numbat, a threatened species that is included in a targeted recovery program. (*Courtesy of the Department of Conservation and Land Management, WA.*)

Woillie, a small marsupial driven to near extinction in the eastern Wheatbelt. (*Courtesy of the Department of Conservation and Land Management, WA.*)

Carnaby's Cockatoo. Widespread clearing has reduced its natural breeding habitat to small pockets of the Wheatbelt. (*Courtesy of the Department of Conservation and Land Management, WA.*)

Lake Toolibin (near Narrogin) and other seasonally flooded Wheatbelt wetlands provide important waterbird breeding habitats.
(*Courtesy of the Department of Conservation and Land Management, WA.*)

Sharp-tailed Sandpiper, one of the trans-equatorial migratory birds that are known to frequent Wheatbelt wetlands.
(*Courtesy of the Department of Conservation and Land Management, WA.*)

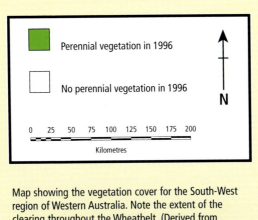

Perennial vegetation in 1996

No perennial vegetation in 1996

N

| 0 | 25 | 50 | 75 | 100 | 125 | 150 | 175 | 200 |

Kilometres

Map showing the vegetation cover for the South-West region of Western Australia. Note the extent of the clearing throughout the Wheatbelt. (Derived from Summer 1996 Landsat thematic mapper satellite imagery. *Courtesy of the Department of Land Administration, WA.*)

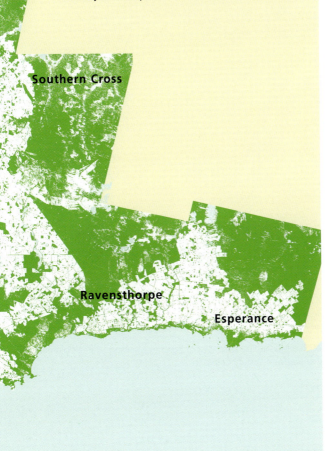

Southern Cross

Ravensthorpe

Esperance

Landcare project on a Morbinning farm, east of Beverley, showing strategic planting of trees. (*Courtesy of the State Salinity Council.*)

Thirteen-year-old spaced Blue Gums for high quality saw logs, located at Dinninup, north-east of Bridgetown. Note that this species is only suited to the higher rainfall areas of the Wheatbelt.
(*Courtesy of Farm Forestry, Department of Conservation and Land Management, WA.*)

Belts of five-year-old Oil Mallees growing amongst wheatfields near Kalannie. (*Courtesy of Farm Forestry, Department of Conservation and Land Management, WA.*)

Oil Mallee resprouting after harvesting. (*Courtesy of Farm Forestry, Department of Conservation and Land Management, WA.*)

Aerial photograph showing shallow drains constructed along the contours of a hill (top left) and along a watercourse.
(*Courtesy of Don McFarlane and the Water and Rivers Commission.*)

Deep drain constructed on a property at Narembeen. Note the problem of disposal of drainage waters when they encounter roads and property boundaries. (*Courtesy of West Australian Newspapers Ltd.*)

Aquaculture in the Wheatbelt. These commercially grown trout were raised in saline water. (*Courtesy of West Australian Newspapers Ltd.*)

Park Street, one of the worst salinity-affected streets. Note the effects on the house mortar and wall, median strip, and road curbing. Note also waterlogging on the road surface in the foreground, from the rising water table. (*Courtesy of Ms Jane Mulcock.*)

Salt-encrusted wall of a public building. (*Courtesy of Ms Jane Mulcock.*)

Piezometer (measuring depth to the water table), installed in the main street to raise community awareness of salinity.
(*Courtesy of Ms Jane Mulcock.*)

Heritage Gardens showing European-style rather than local native species, illustrating cultural attitudes towards the landscape. (*Courtesy of Ms Jane Mulcock.*)

in the Katanning Salinity Management Strategy, developed in 1999 as part of the Rural Towns Program. They include encouraging low water use gardens and raising community awareness of water use; recycling waste water; improving the townscape and lowering the water table by planting deep-rooted trees and encouraging community tree-planting projects; supporting, publicising and rewarding group and individual efforts to reduce salinity in the Katanning Creek Catchment; improving surface water control around the town site by developing an overall drainage plan; developing a master plan for harvesting and utilising rainwater run-off and effluent in the Catchment; applying for grants to provide further financial support for the implementation of the KSMS; encouraging the development of local businesses that are likely to involve high water use, and monitoring the water table and overall water use in the town. While the Shire had pursued some of these actions, many had still not been addressed in March 2001.[68]

Funding is a major dilemma for local governments when it comes to maintaining Landcare projects. The Katanning Shire works with a comparatively small budget based on its annual rates income and has many other community needs to finance at the same time. In 2000, Landcare work only received partial short-term funding through the Natural Heritage Trust. When grant money runs out, local government can rarely afford to step in and keep local projects running. The Shire Council has recently begun to strengthen its relationship with the Land Conservation District Committee, and in 1996 it succumbed to considerable pressure from this committee and its supporters to introduce a voluntary Landcare levy (formerly identified as a soil conservation service charge) of ten dollars into the Shire rate system.

The levy applies to every property in the Katanning Shire and is used to fund the position of the Community Landcare Coordinator—often referred to as the CLC. Reactions to this charge seem to reflect and reinforce a set of divisions within the community. According to several different reports, approximately seventy people attended the initial public meeting held in 1996 to discuss the possibility of applying a Landcare levy. Most voted in favour of the charge and it was pushed through. In 1998, at a second public meeting, the levy was made compulsory, a result of the poor response of the previous year,[69] which, according to LCDC Treasurer at the time, Adrian Richardson, was 'due to community apathy'.[70] One Shire Councillor reflected on this unwillingness, mostly on the part of townspeople, to contribute to Landcare in Katanning:

> [When] someone's house falls down around them, and the cause is identified as being the rising water table and salinity, then maybe their neighbours will have some concern. It is seen as something that the council has to deal with, and [as something that has been] caused by farmers. [Townspeople] see the relationship between knocking over trees and the rising groundwater table, but I suppose they haven't seen that we knocked over trees to build our houses. Looking at the other side, farmers say that they were basically driven by government to knock the trees over to produce wheat products. It was an obligation to actually clear 50 per cent of the land before they got title to it. Whether it is a salinity thing, or just a social thing, there is a 'them and us' sort of attitude. I don't think townspeople see the link between themselves and farmers.

This lack of town-based support for the Landcare levy surprised a number of landholders, especially given complaints from residents about the effects of salinity on Prosser Park. A retired farmer said he was 'absolutely stunned by the reluctance of townspeople to pay the ten-dollar levy', especially since some of the individuals who complained the most lived in parts of the town that were badly affected by salinity. He also believed that some people living in the town resented paying the same amount as farmers who owned much larger tracts of land.

This response to paying a levy in support of Landcare offers a telling commentary on the continued refusal, within the general Katanning community, to accept responsibility for on-going environmental conservation and rehabilitation. It tells the same story as the lack of community response to encouragements from the Shire and the Water

Corporation to reduce the use of scheme water, and the continued insistence, even within the Shire itself, on planting lawn and non-native gardens. Together these things suggest that the community of Katanning has a long way to go before it can achieve a united front against salinity.

Local government is also required to attend to the maintenance of public buildings, parks and roads. One Councillor explained that the Federal funding available for road maintenance and development is allocated to local government according to the size of the population being serviced rather than taking the specific circumstances that each Shire faces into account, increased road degradation due to increasing of salinity for example. Some of the land that was still vacant in Katanning in June 2000 was no longer viable for building and those houses already affected by rising salt were increasingly un-saleable. Manager of Works, Norman Reed, explained that most buildings in the town were initially constructed to suit the drier soil conditions in Perth rather than wet, salty conditions now present in Katanning, a fact which contributes to the extent of degradation in the town site. Another Katanning resident who had worked for local government commented that she was surprised by the lack of pressure that had been exerted on the Shire to address the issue by local business and home owners, given the extent to which increasing salinity levels threatened their investments.

Although the Shire Council was aware of the problem a decade ago, they took very little action until the Rural Towns Program was instituted in the late 1990s. Nonetheless, Shire Councillors and Shire employees indicated that salinity was still not a major issue for the Katanning Shire Council in 2000. The Council, an elected body, is political by nature and has continued to give highest priority to the issues that stimulate residents to make the most phone calls to the Council chambers. These are things that people deal with on a daily basis, and although some of them, like road and drain maintenance, are directly related to salinity, others such as youth crime and unemployment are not. Rob White, President of the Katanning Shire Council in September 2000, believes that there is the potential for local government to become a major player in addressing salinity in the town.

Councillors and Shire employees are well placed to make an impact at the local level but they need to be extensively funded by the State and Federal governments if they are to effectively assume that role.[71]

Community action: Landcare in Katanning

By most measures, Katanning's Landcare program has been a resounding success. Since its establishment in 1990, the Katanning Land Conservation District Committee (LCDC), has been instrumental in developing a local network of concerned individuals and organisations who are now working together to formulate appropriate and practical responses to the environmental problems the town faces. The Committee has provided essential leadership at the local level by raising community awareness, encouraging and assisting farmers to apply for funding, and pushing the Shire Council to get involved in efforts to address salinity. It is comprised of landholders, agency representatives,[72] Shire Councillors and townspeople 'who have come to recognise the importance of a unified front against devastating environmental problems such as salinity'.[73] In combination with local government, the LCDC provides a central focus in the Katanning Shire for individuals and groups who are trying to find ways to reduce the impact of salinity in the town site and the surrounding farmland. The environmental challenges that face Landcare in the area, however, are enormous.

Part of the success of the Landcare movement in Katanning was linked to the community's ability, with the assistance of the Landcare Coordinator, to secure grants and complete projects. Landcare was a big industry in Katanning; by 2000 it had brought over $2.5 million worth of funding into the Shire since the LCDC was established in 1990.[74] In addition to the environmental work that has been done, this income has allowed local businesses, such as nurseries and fencing suppliers, to develop and expand. Community members readily agreed that the commitment and experience of Katanning's Landcare workers had contributed significantly to the town's achievements. In fact, a number of people felt that, despite the extent of the salinity-related problems it faced, the Landcare movement had been more successful in

Katanning than in many other towns. One of the first catchment groups in the Katanning Shire, the Katanning Creek Catchment Group (KCCG), formed in 1990, has been especially effective.

In 1997 the KCCG won the State Landcare BP Catchment Award and in the following year the group was selected, out of 68 finalists, as the winner of the National Landcare Award.[75] The holistic approach employed by the KCCG offers a good example of the role that Landcare groups can play in the community. The group combined town, farm and catchment planning in its attempts to bring government agencies, businesses, local government, other community groups, landholders and the catchment group together to address environmental issues in the Shire. In addition to coordinating activities such as the development of a community nursery, water monitoring and tree-planting, the KCCG provided 'social support in the form of field days, workshops, tours, information exchange and individual contact'.[76]

The Katanning Landcare Centre has also played an important role in raising local awareness of salinity and the work being undertaken to combat it. The Centre opened in April 1997, with street frontage and a large window display area to catch the attention of passers-by.[77] In addition to providing office space, it is also a resource library for the community. One Landcare worker commented that an advantage of the Centre was that it didn't 'feel like a government agency':

> Landholders often feel threatened and intimidated by regulations and requirements imposed by the Shire and the agricultural department. They are definitely happier to come and ask a question here and not be faced by a scientist who might have answers but doesn't necessarily talk on the same level as them. People are welcome in here, no-one who comes in will feel like they have been fobbed off, even if we have to get back to people with an answer. It is valuable to have this room [which is separate from] the Shire and from Agriculture WA. It is more casual, and more neutral.[78]

Yet despite this record of achievement, Landcare has not been embraced by all of the community. Those involved reported that it was often difficult to get support from townspeople, because only those whose houses were damaged by salt had any real interest in the issue. It was also sometimes hard to convince farmers to work with people from the town because the former tended to be wary of 'greenies', whom they perceived as being more concerned about preserving wildlife and native vegetation than in achieving sustainable agriculture.[79]

In sustaining local commitment to Landcare, effective leadership is crucial. Landcare workers have an essential role to play in liaising between each of the groups in the community involved in combating salinity and other forms of environmental degradation. As Lynne Coleman, President of the Katanning LCDC, pointed out, farmers rarely have the time or the expertise to take on these coordinating roles themselves. Many of the people interviewed made a point of acknowledging the leadership and achievements of Jenny Gardner, the first Katanning Landcare Coordinator. According to all accounts, Gardner had an enormous impact on building the momentum of Landcare in the Shire. Within six weeks of taking on the full-time position, Jenny Gardner had mobilised twenty new catchment groups, incorporating 303 farming families, to participate in a major NHT project that focused on the Coblinine Catchment system. In the first three years of this project over 1.2 million trees were planted. During her employment, Gardner produced a regular newspaper column reporting on Landcare activities in the Katanning Shire in an effort to raise community awareness of environmental issues. She also coordinated the town's participation in the Rural Towns Program, on behalf of the Shire, for the first three years of its involvement. This role, in addition to the Community Landcare Coordinator job, gradually became too much for one person, and, in 1999, a part-time RTP Coordinator was employed.[80]

However, leadership alone is insufficient to sustain long-term community commitment. One of the major limitations confronting the Landcare movement is its reliance on the goodwill of volunteers to get things done. This is not sustainable in the long term, especially given the amount of conservation work that needs to be undertaken. Government employees and policy-makers often don't recognise the extent of the costs, both personal and financial, that community volunteers are required to absorb.[81] One Landcare worker described some of the pressures that volunteers face:

> Eventually [volunteers] can't sustain their involvement, so they give up. They are out of pocket a lot, there are phone calls, there are faxes, there is time out from farming work, or time on top of their jobs; they give up a lot of family time, they give up recreation time. They are out sometimes at nights at meetings, which makes for a long day. After years of making these sacrifices, if what you are involved in isn't rewarding, eventually it all becomes a bit hard, it gets a bit depressing, the incentive goes, and you say 'I just can't do this anymore, I have to do something for myself'.

These costs are harder to bear when the same community members feel as though 'they have to fight, tooth and nail for everything, when they have [to] put a lot of time into writing up grant applications, and [get knocked back] because they don't word things correctly or because they are not in tune with what is flavour of the month' with the funding body.[82] Although most farmers and Landcare workers believed that government agency employees were supportive and worked well with them at the local level, many felt that middle managers in those same agencies were removed from, and insensitive to, the needs and limitations of rural communities. The budget cuts imposed by bureaucracies were seen to place unreasonable limitations on what their employees could achieve in cooperation with Landcare workers and the rest of the community. Several individuals expressed the opinion that the agencies had begun to work for their political leaders rather than for the people of Katanning.

It is generally accepted that if farmers were earning more money, they would invest more in Landcare.[83] In 1999 Jenny Gardner calculated that each farming family in the Shire was putting an average of $4,500 per year into Landcare work,[84] with some farmers investing as much as $20,000 a year for several years in order to get a whole farm plan in place. Landholders are required to invest two dollars, in cash or in kind, for every dollar of government funding they receive for Landcare work. One farmer described this situation as a kind of self-taxation. A government employee pointed out that this system ensured that private landholders contributed to work that would have direct benefits for themselves as well as for the Western Australian community as a whole. Another landholder explained that the pressure to apply for funding in groups, rather than as individuals, meant that some farmers would make financial commitments that they couldn't honour, to avoid admitting to their neighbours that they didn't have the money to participate in group-based Landcare projects. The process of applying for funding in the first place has also become problematic for most farmers. Gardner pointed out, for example, that one of the questions on an application form for Federal funding was twenty-three pages long. She said that such unrealistic expectations on the part of the funding bodies dissuaded landholders and Landcare workers form applying for grants:

> In the beginning we wanted one-page applications. You can get a farmer to sign on the dotted line and he is happy. You can sit at the kitchen table and do it with him. There is no way [farmers] are going to wade through pages and pages of stuff. One application required more work than I would do for a report. This has happened because such a small amount of money has to go between hundreds and hundreds of applications. Some people say it is unfair because if you are good at writing applications you tend to get the funding. It is not dependent on an even spread of money so that everybody has a fair go. People become disheartened when they never get funding so they stop applying.[85]

Lack of funding for conservation work was a constant refrain amongst farmers and Landcare workers in Katanning, especially at a time when many landholders were faced with decreasing productivity and increasing overheads.[86] Most people acknowledged that money by itself was not going to create sustainable change, but adequate financial support for those landholders and communities who are committed to making improvements at the ground level is still essential. Many of the individuals who contributed to this case study believed that politics played too much of a part in the way that funds for Landcare work were allocated and divided. They felt that the people in power, the people who should have been providing the community with strong leadership on the issue of environmental management and protection, were not making a serious enough commitment to addressing salinity-related problems. An experienced Landcare worker offered the following reflection:

> Ideally, the Federal Government should be looking at Australia nationally and acknowledging that in two hundred years of White occupation, there has been substantial damage done to this country. [The government] needs a focus on environment that stretches several hundred years into the future, as well as an extensive funding commitment, to remedy all that has gone wrong. Unfortunately, most of it comes back to dollars, but it is also about changing people's attitudes and perceptions. In an ideal world you would be able to get people to see that the environment, clean air, and soil to grow food in, are critical to [the survival] of any society. All of those things need protection.

Several Landcare workers in Katanning argued that government budgets did not seem to reflect a full appreciation of the importance of protecting the natural landscape. One woman attributed this to a lack of understanding about how the environment works, along with an inability to 'see' what is happening to it. A number of people believed that a public outcry on the issue of salinity, similar to the community response to logging in old-growth forests, was necessary in order to mobilise voting power and demand appropriate levels and forms of government funding. As a Landcare worker explained: 'The government should be [providing leadership on this issue], but the government only responds to the community. The community needs more cohesive ways of putting their case in front of [government] so that politicians will listen and learn to understand.'

Despite its many successes, the future of Landcare in Katanning, once NHT funds run out, is uncertain. The Landcare levy reportedly raised between $15,000 and $18,000 per year. This could only support one part-time Landcare Coordinator and cover the basic running costs of the Landcare Centre. Given the central role that Landcare officers have assumed in mobilising and facilitating community involvement in conservation work, especially in the face of Agriculture WA's resistance to engaging in one-to-one consultations, it is difficult to imagine how the momentum of the last few years will be maintained without further funding. Jenny Gardner made the following observation:

> The Landcare Coordinator is a real link into the community, and I don't think Federal Government has really realised that. Funding for Landcare Coordinators, one person in a community, is good, but three years is not long enough. We are looking at a twenty-five to thirty year program to make the sort of changes in landscape that we need to make.

Funding for the position of Rural Towns Program Coordinator was also limited. It lasted for one year only and was not renewed at the end of 2000—again, despite a very positive response from the Katanning community and an impressive list of achievements.

THE FUTURE

In September 2000, one Katanning resident made the following observation:

> There are farm houses in the district that have been built in lovely spots, where they were close to a water supply, a hundred years ago, or eighty years ago, and they are literally sitting in the middle of salt pans. Hope for those houses is not good, but it is just too hard to contemplate building a new farm house. Not that there is a feeling of hopelessness, I think human nature says 'we'll just forget about it, we just have to keep going', and we do. If

everyone could see that the town was sitting on the top of a salty lake then the best solution would be to rebuild the whole thing on a hill somewhere.[87]

This is not the first time that someone has suggested that it would be easier to move the town of Katanning to a new location than it would be to save it in its current position, nor is it likely to be the last. For the people of Katanning, however, this is not an option that has been seriously considered. On the contrary, over the last few years the town has acquired a large sport and recreation facility, a new public library, a community arts centre, a new building complex for Agriculture WA and a trout farm, along with several other developments. Some of the town's parks are being rehabilitated and on-going efforts are being made to preserve and celebrate Katanning's cultural heritage. All of these things are evidence of commitment to the future of the 'Heart of the Great Southern'. But the community is a long way from winning the battle against salinity.

When asked to identify the issues of most concern to the community of Katanning, the things most frequently raised by those interviewed (all of whom did have some awareness of the salinity problem) were the rising water table; the loss of productive agricultural land; low commodity prices and increasing production costs; climatic factors; low morale resulting from (and contributing to) population decline; loss of infrastructure; degradation of roads, buildings and landscape; and loss of biodiversity and a lack of community understanding of salinity [a significant number of individuals also identified street crime as a major concern, although secondary to salinity]. The majority of people interviewed emphasised the need for the whole community to assume a sense of ownership and responsibility for the salinity issue. At the same time many people raised the topic of volunteer burnout. The message is that if responsibility for the problem is more widely shared then it will not be as much of a burden for the committed few. Residents do acknowledge positive developments in the battle against salinity however. These include the establishment of catchment groups and catchment plans and the availability of Commonwealth funding through the NHT; Landcare-initiated tree-planting; attempts to protect remaining vegetation; and efforts to monitor the water table.

Neither hope alone nor denial are going to halt the environmental degradation in the Katanning Creek Catchment. Without considerable government support and intervention, Katanning, like many other Wheatbelt towns, is likely to find itself caught in a downward spiral; farmers whose land is no longer productive will be forced to sell up and move out, local population and infrastructure will decline, more people will leave, and more businesses will fail. Breaking this cycle requires an integrated, well-funded program of action, supported at all levels of government, that acknowledges varying circumstances and responds in constructive and humanitarian ways to the situations in which individuals and communities now find themselves after almost a century and a half of unsustainable agricultural practices.

Redressing the impact of these unsustainable practices will require more than a focus on farming practices alone. Kate Jefferies, a Landcare Coordinator in the Kent Shire, emphasised the importance of focusing on the social structure of rural communities as a necessary part of encouraging new and more sustainable agriculture. She argued that developing a sense of social cohesiveness and pride within a community was necessary in order to get people to work together for the long-term good of that community. There is, after all, little incentive for farmers to invest in conservation if their community infrastructure is falling apart and they cannot see much future in either their economic or social base. These social factors highlight the need for solutions that draw the whole community into a sense of ownership and responsibility for the problem, not just those who live in Katanning and its surrounding regions. The urban population has as crucial a part to play in this process as the farmers who manage the land. A government employee working in Katanning explained:

> As we are getting more and more centralised, more focused on the coast and on Perth, people are becoming a lot less connected with what is happening in rural areas. The big message is that salinity will have an impact on the associated areas, economically,

socially and ecologically. The State assets don't just belong to the rural areas, the whole State owns them, they are a loss to the State. That is hard to get people to connect to. If 30 per cent of the agricultural area degrades you could say that would be, roughly, a 30 per cent drop in economic activity in the State and I'm sure that sort of loss would have some kind of impact on the Western Australian community.

One Landcare worker also talked about the importance of recognising emotional and spiritual connections to the natural environment. She said when such sentiments were expressed they were often met with derision and ridicule, saying that 'you get labelled as a "greenie" and your credibility diminishes. It can really be very frustrating'. She went on to point out however, that 'some people in the farming community [do acknowledge an emotional connection to the land], but it is a minority, and I think that is a big part of the problem, I think we should love the land'.

Overall, those working to address salinity in Katanning expressed an unwillingness to blame anyone directly for the damage already done to the landscape. Many felt that to do so was pointless and distracted attention from the task at hand. They emphasised the importance of moving forward, of working for changes in the future rather than focusing on the mistakes of the past. The importance of changing community-wide attitudes towards land use and agriculture in general was repeatedly highlighted. Many believed it was essential for government and the community to enter into conversation about how much land could be sacrificed, how much needed to be protected and how much funding should be channelled into protecting it. As one agency representative pointed out: 'The big question is where do we want salinity stopped and at what cost?' For the people of Katanning, as for the entire Wheatbelt region, this is the issue that must be resolved.

CHAPTER —(6)———————————————

Environmental Impacts of Salinity

Western Australia's South-West region, of which the Wheatbelt forms a part, has been identified as one of the world's biodiversity 'hotspots' where exceptional concentrations of endemic species are threatened by extinction due to loss of habitat.[1] Each global hotspot features an area which has a separate community of species constituting a biogeographic unit. These biodiversity hotspots, which cover only 1.4 per cent of the planet's land surface, contain up to 35 per cent of all mammals, birds, reptiles and amphibians, and nearly half of all vascular plant (high order) species. In Australia alone around 1,000 species are currently estimated at risk of extinction.[2] Such a mass extinction of species, if allowed to eventuate, would constitute a loss of global significance.[3] Not surprisingly, the State of the Australian Environment Advisory Council reported in 1996 that the continued loss of biological diversity is perhaps Australia's most serious environmental problem. One of the major sites for species decline and loss is the Wheatbelt which sustains a globally significant range of flora and fauna, and is recognised as a staging post for Australian and international migratory birds.

This alarming rate of decline in native species has, as its main cause, destruction of habitat, for which land clearance and salinity are significant contributing factors. Salinity, in particular, has major environmental consequences for Australia as it affects the life and health of plants, animals, and people. In small quantities, salt is essential for life; however, when it reaches greater concentrations in nature it has the capacity to adversely affect many plant and animal species (even causing their death). Bell and Froend noted the existence of different rates of mortality and growth in tree species under stress from increasing salinity.[4] Different animals, like plants, are also able to cope with varying degrees of salinity. In waterbirds, for example, there are some species that can utilise saltwater habitats. Australian Shelduck are well adapted to feeding in the highly saline conditions that exist on Rottnest Island, near Perth. These birds are able to excrete ingested salt by means of enlarged nasal glands.[5] Other animals are less fortunate as they do not have similar adaptations for life in saline environments, particularly when their normal habitats are subject to secondary salinity. Therefore, salinity presents serious problems for many plants and animals alike, and for human settlements and agriculture. Once salinity takes hold in the environment, excess amounts of salt are difficult to combat, as large amounts need to be removed from affected soil or water.

Concentrating a large proportion of conservation support on areas of international importance as biodiversity hotspots, like the South-West region, would go far to stem the mass extinction of species now under way. In conservation planning, the purpose of identifying such hotspots is to concentrate on areas where there is greatest need, and where the pay-off from allocated funds and safeguard measures would be greatest. This systematic strategy is proclaimed as the most cost-efficient way of responding to the current tide of large-scale extinctions. Already Western Australia's *State of the Environment Report 1998* has identified the highest priority environmental issues as being land salinisation, maintenance of biodiversity, and salinisation of inland waters. The need for concerted action has been identified in the recently released *Environmental Action Plan* (1999), which recommends implementation of the *National Strategy for the Conservation of Australia's Biological Diversity* (1996), and development and implementation of a complementary strategy for Western Australia. However, both tasks are yet to be completed and remain significant challenges facing the State.

There is no greater challenge in biodiversity terms than addressing secondary salinisation of the Wheatbelt, which has severely damaged the natural environment and produced an array of specific, and often inter-related problems, such as salinisation of wetlands (including lakes, rivers and streams), destruction of native vegetation and wildlife habitats, and loss of plant and animal species. Similarly, salinity poses a threat to the region's water resources. Major rivers and their catchments not only sustain the natural environment, but are vital for the maintenance of human populations and settlements. Problems of soil and land degradation in farmland adjacent to remnant vegetation may also threaten the integrity of native plant and animal habitats. When driving through the Wheatbelt, Taylor commented that it is 'hard to come to terms with the fact that the land clearance was largely a modern phenomenon, either completed within living memory or still occurring on the fringes'.[6] The memories of Glen Phillips, university academic and poet, further illustrate this phenomenon of a rapidly changing landscape ravaged by over-clearing and associated problems of salinity and loss of biodiversity. The following account of the Wheatbelt environment spans some fifty years from his early childhood to more recent impressions gathered during periodic return visits:

> My mother, whose parents settled a virgin bush block in the East Beverley District at the turn of the century, told us many times how much the Yenyenning Lakes area had changed from her girlhood. I remember myself travelling through the Wheatbelt with the family as we moved from one town to another in the nineteen forties. My father was a headmaster and was sometimes posted to another school hundreds of miles from the previous one. The roads were almost entirely gravel and very corrugated, but the road verges had not been cleared and pushed back as they now have become. In those days you drove in almost perpetual shade in many areas with the tree branches from either side closing overhead. The spring wildflowers we must travel many kilometres to see in abundance [today] carpeted locations much closer to the Avon and Hotham River catchment areas. Clearing was only

partial on many of the newer farms and exotic weeds and grasses had not taken over from the native species. My mother often spoke of the abundant native wildlife which so rapidly disappeared once the rabbit and fox populations exploded after World War One. How often would you see a wallaby these days? Yet they were common, as were tammars, bandicoots, and numbats in earlier days. The salt problem had only barely started to concern people. I recall going to the very first meeting of farmers at Corrigin in 1962 to hear a speaker define the term ecology and cause rumblings among the disbelievers when he spoke of the need to not only stop clearing more land but to actually reverse the process.

When I go back now to the old farm, now deserted of habitation, I can see the remains of the bush block preserved at my grandmother's insistence, at the entry to the farm. Alas! it is much diminished and crops have been grown among the few white gums and salmon gums which have somehow resisted the white man's approach to management of the ecology of this land. Is it a caretakership betrayed?

Now many of the survivors of these original trees are succumbing to salinisation, as well as a number of other human and environmental threats including road-widening, ringbarking by stock, loss from phosphate poisoning or herbicide drift, and continued grazing pressure from stock and rabbits. The region's wetlands have also been significantly diminished in number, areal extent, and environmental quality by agricultural development, mostly drainage and infill, damage by livestock, and salinisation.

IMPORTANCE OF BIODIVERSITY

The prolonged isolation of Australia from other continents has encouraged the evolution of a unique assemblage of plants and animals, which display a high degree of richness and endemism at local, regional and continental scales. Those plants and animals that are confined in their distribution to the areas in which they evolved are said to be endemic to that locality. Seven families of mammals and twelve of flowering plants occur nowhere else in the world, which gives Australia far more endemic families than any other country. At the species level, endemism for land animals and flowering plants is estimated at 80 per cent.[7] Australia is also classified as one of about a dozen mega-diverse countries in the world. It has, for example, just over 50 per cent of the world's species of marsupials, and the second-highest number of reptile species.

The protection of Australia's rich abundance of natural life—its biodiversity—is now acknowledged as one of the cornerstones in achieving ecologically sustainable development. The *National Strategy for the Conservation of Australia's Biological Diversity* (1996) defines 'biodiversity' as 'the variety of all life forms—the different plants, animals and micro-organisms, the genes they contain and the ecosystems of which they form a part'. So, biodiversity is a general term for the extent of variety in nature, and tends to be described in terms of genetic, species, and ecosystem diversity. It is not a fixed entity, but a constantly changing pool that is enlarged by new genetic variation and diminished by extinctions. Estimates of the number of species on earth range from 5 million to 50 million, and perhaps only 1.4 million have been adequately identified and described.[8] Similarly, much of Australia's biodiversity is yet to be described, and there is still a lack of knowledge about almost every major ecosystem.

Some of the existing knowledge gaps may be eliminated through on-going consultation with Australia's indigenous communities. It is well recognised that indigenous people have a unique, practical knowledge of biodiversity, and a continuing cultural and economic interest in, and concern for, the well-being of native species and country. Traditional Aboriginal management of country was not a haphazard process, but well planned and based on as much as a 50,000-year history of experience. These practices had evolved as the most effective means of living off, and caring for, country. As much of the Australian vegetation is fire-adapted, information about Aboriginal burning practices and fire regimes—sometimes referred to as 'fire-stick farming'—may be vital to the future maintenance of plant communities and the populations of animals that depend on them.[9] However, the knowledge held by indigenous people is not 'general' knowledge that everyone and anyone has a right to, but is 'owned' knowledge of the area of country to which they belong. Such traditional knowledge is held by elders to be handed on to their successors. At the same time, there is a global awareness amongst indigenous peoples that their knowledge of the earth and their traditional practices of 'caring for country' can assist policy-makers in developing codes of practice that help to conserve biological diversity and prevent ecological disasters.

Humanity depends on biodiversity for its survival and quality of life. For example, agriculture relies on biodiversity to maintain soil health, absorb nutrients, allow pollination, and help control pests. Some people, however, would not even stop to question the worth of biodiversity in human terms. Instead, they would argue on an ethical basis that people have a moral obligation to conserve other life forms as fellow denizens of this planet. All life forms, like human communities, are considered to have the right to exist. As a result, there is a growing recognition that biodiversity is not only a national asset, but is also of immense global value to present and future generations.[10] At the same time, the threat to species and ecosystems from human activities has never been as great as it is today. The number of species threatened with extinction is unprecedented, and the situation looks set to become rapidly worse.

THREAT TO BIODIVERSITY IN THE WESTERN AUSTRALIAN WHEATBELT

In its original state, the Western Australian Wheatbelt carried some of the heaviest growth of vegetation in the world on some of the poorest soil. It sustained this feat through a natural system of recycled nutrients.[11] The explorer Ernest Giles, when approaching the region from the west, in 1875 found it 'filled to overflowing with the densest of scrubs; nature seemed to have tried how much of it she could possibly jam into the region'.[12] Similarly, Robert Austin, travelling through much of the present Wheatbelt in 1854, reported 'jam and york gum forests', 'dense thickets of cyprus and casuarina scrub', 'a broad expanse of undulating sand plains studded with clumps of gum and thicket', 'white gum forest', 'white gum forest with an undergrowth of prickly scrub', and 'sand plains swarming with kangaroos alternating with gum forests'.[13]

In fact, it is estimated that over 4,000 species of vascular plants occur in the Wheatbelt, and approximately 60 per cent of them are endemic to the region. Of these endemic species, 450 occur in wetlands and low-lying parts of the landscape where they are under threat of extinction from salinisation. Not only does salinity affect the diversity of landscapes that is represented by woodlands and scrubland, but it also affects other associated environments, such as wetlands. Aquatic biodiversity in freshwater wetlands has also been degraded by rising salt levels and prolonged periods of flooding.

Much of the South-West region—encompassing the Wheatbelt— has species numbers commonly in the order of eighty to 100 species per 100 square kilometres.[14] These figures are exceptional in a global context, where thirty species is regarded as high. This rich diversity of life forms survives precariously in some parts of the South-West in very small areas and with low rates of species representation. This is particularly true for much of the Wheatbelt, where land clearance has resulted in the removal of more than 90 per cent of the native vegetation. York Main, for example, describes a stretch of undisturbed bushland, which although surrounded by settlement, provided important Echidna habitat:

> It is only the natural maturity of the wodjil—the dense unburnt growth of sheoaks, tamma and acacias with their twilled matts of fallen branchlets and phyllodes providing unlimited food for the litter-gathering termites—which allows for the maintenance of this local, isolated population of echidnas.[15]

The disappearance of the Wheatbelt wildlife was an event little remarked upon by contemporaries, which is perhaps not surprising given prevailing attitudes towards nature and the environment. Yet, in 1951, at the commencement of the massive post-Second World War land schemes, a series of informative articles titled 'Eastern Wheatbelt Wildlife' appeared in the popular rural newspaper, *The Western Mail*. The author, Bruce W. Leake, who is credited with making many valuable contributions to the study of the State's wildlife, identified twenty animals distributed in the late nineteenth century right through the eastern Wheatbelt, nearly all of them being marsupials. The smaller of these marsupials were mostly gone from the region by around 1900; that is, prior to large-scale clearing and farming. The fate of the Tamar showed the full range of human impacts. The Tamar [Tamma/Tammar], about the size of a Rock Wallaby, dwelt in thick scrub and, at the time Leake wrote about the animal, he noted:

> Tamars have in a few places tried to re-establish themselves, but being obliged to compete against rabbits and with so much of the scrub cleared, they have no chance of doing so. They are still found much farther down in the South West and their skins are sold in the markets.

These smaller marsupials, in particular, were highly dependent on the surrounding vegetation. Leake described the habitat of the Woylie [Woilie], a rat-sized kangaroo:

> The Woilie made a covered nest of rushes on the edges of sand-plains, close to where they joined up with thick scrub. The nest had an opening at one end and when danger threatened, the Woilie would shoot out of the nest and make for the thickets.[16]

Few of the Wheatbelt's native animals were so closely attuned to the environment as the Boodie, like a Woilie in appearance, except the tip of its tail is white. However, its habits were unique. According to Leake, the Boodie was instrumental in the growth of Sandalwood trees by virtue of its habit of carrying the Sandalwood nut in its mouth and burying it in the ground as a future source of food supply. Not all of the nuts were eaten, and when the rains came, the nuts germinated into fully fledged trees.

Boodies were nocturnal, burrow-dwelling animals, whose food source dwindled under the assault of the Sandalwood cutters who grubbed out the prized timber. According to Leake, Boodies 'often ate the young wheat crops just appearing above the ground, and settlers were obliged to lay poisoned baits consisting of pollard and arsenic to destroy them'.[17]

Once larger scale clearing commenced in the eastern Wheatbelt, the bigger marsupials came under threat from loss of habitat. Leake writes of the Brush Kangaroo, the 'rarest and wildest' of the kangaroos, which was forced many kilometres further inland where they were only occasionally seen. In the early 1950s, the status of the Great Grey Kangaroo was similarly precarious. According to Leake, it was still holding its own 'where there is sufficient scrub to harbour in, but nothing like so plentiful as it was before the country began to get cleared, when as many as thirty could be seen in one mob when conditions at that time were favourable for them'.[18]

The remarkable thing about Leake's series of articles—quite apart from the uniqueness of the animals he described—was the timing of their publication at the crucial last stage in the opening up of the Wheatbelt when opportunities still existed to protect some of these species. Leake's writings show that informed observers understood the connection between land clearing, species decline and other adverse impacts of settlement. Interestingly, and despite Leake's own rich knowledge of this relationship, he did not call for balanced development in order to preserve those species that remained. Few others, it seemed, were even remotely concerned about the dwindling fauna of the region, let alone its flora. But, as his articles testify, the information was available for anyone wishing to access it.

As the land was cleared, some wildlife perished and the rest was forced to relocate to remaining bushland that inevitably became over-crowded. In response to limited food supplies animals, like kangaroos, became dependent upon neighbouring crops for food. The consequences of clearing a 100-hectare paddock in terms of loss of biodiversity are the disappearance of an entire bird fauna of perhaps 150 species with 1,000 individuals, as well as the entire ecosystem of millions of plants, insects, mammals, soil, other forms of fauna and microbes.[19] Many of the remaining areas in the Wheatbelt are now small islands of remnant vegetation surrounded by farmed land. Under these circumstances, animals are unable to move between their preferred habitats when barriers are imposed by cultivated land and distances are too great. It is therefore not surprising that the greatest number of extinctions in Western Australia has occurred in the Wheatbelt region.[20]

Today, nature reserves occupy only about 7 per cent of the region, and most reserves are small with an average size of about 114 hectares.[21] Over time such isolated small areas are frequently unable to maintain their full complement of plants and animals. Woodlands and mallee occur on the more fertile soils and have largely been cleared for agriculture, except along the boundary with the Goldfields. Consequently, these vegetation types are poorly represented in conservation reserves, which in turn affects the conservation status of those animals that depend on them. Of the few larger reserves that remain in the Wheatbelt, Boyagin, Tutanning and Dryandra are among the best, supporting important vegetation communities and breeding populations of threatened animals such as Numbats and Woylies.[22]

The process of species decline continues today, with many more species about to become locally extinct. Large flocks of Carnaby's (or White-tailed Black) Cockatoos were one of the features of the Wheatbelt, with their constant loud communications and playful aerobatics. They have nearly disappeared because most of their nest holes in tall trees have gone, as have the banksias and hakeas on which they feed. The existing flocks show little evidence of recruitment as they contain mostly older birds. This, in turn, is having an adverse effect on the remaining banksias, which cannot produce seed without the assistance of cockatoos to break open flowers and remove weevil larvae. Taylor noted that these weevils are now so abundant that nearly every seed head is eaten out, with the result that few set seed.[23] Nectar-feeding birds, such as honeyeaters, also rely on banksias for food. These events demonstrate the complex inter-dependencies that occur in natural ecosystems, so that even minor interference may have far-reaching and unexpected results.

Despite extensive clearing, limited research shows that the Wheat-belt mammals, reptiles and amphibians are more diverse than in the South-West forests, and contain elements of the wetter South Coast as well as the arid interior. However, the remaining areas of bushland are undergoing continued habitat modification and alteration in species composition. These fundamental changes began with the loss of Aboriginal land management practices (for example, burning) and later decline in many of the native mammals. The situation was also worsened by the invasion of exotic species such as cats, foxes, rabbits, and agricultural weeds. Today, biodiversity in the Wheatbelt is represented by an increasing proportion of ageing animals and plants that will not be replaced, causing further links in the original species network to be broken.

Between 1976 and 1981, the Western Australian Museum published a series of monographs on biological surveys of a sample of nature reserves in the Wheatbelt area of Western Australia. While such pioneering research contributed to the overall scientific understanding of biodiversity in this region, little knowledge existed about the condition and value of remnant bushland on farms. It was not until the work of Mollemans in the early 1990s, that any overall picture was developed of the remaining vegetation in the Wheatbelt. Mollemans found the remnant bush to be in poor condition. 'It is not possible now-a-days,' he wrote, 'to identify a bush remnant in its entirety which is not modified in some way.'[24] Poor management by farmers and encroaching salinity were the major causes of the deterioration. Mollemans called for urgent action to be taken, otherwise, 'there will come a time when all areas of remnant bush are beyond redemption'.[25] Mollemans developed a simplified, practical key for the assessment of the ecological significance of these on-farm bush remnants in the Wheatbelt. However, information on biodiversity is still mostly limited to specific localities and selected reserves, with an emphasis on higher order plants and animals.

Most of what is known about Wheatbelt biodiversity on a broad scale comes from the first comprehensive and systematic survey of the agricultural zone by the Biological Survey Group of the Department of

Conservation and Land Management (CALM). This four-year survey of flora and fauna of terrestrial and wetland environments began in 1997 as a State Government initiative announced in the 1996 Salinity Action Strategy. The survey will result in a more accurate understanding of current biodiversity and the species most threatened with extinction. For example, the survey uncovered 'numerous new records and major range extensions of rare and priority flora'.[26] These results will form an important database from which strategic policy can be developed. However, it is important to underline the scale of effort needed to act on this data and the limited achievements to date.

The Wheatbelt is described in the survey as a centre of species diversity for many Western Australian species-rich groups of vascular plants, including *Acacia*, *Dryandra*, *Eucalyptus*, *Grevillea* and *Verticordia*. Furthermore, the biodiversity of the agricultural zone is much higher than previously estimated. For example, detailed surveys of the Lake Muir and Unicup reserves have revealed a vascular flora of almost 1,000 species, and over 500 species (including two previously unknown species) in the small Quairading Shire reserve. A presumed extinct aquatic plant was also rediscovered, and two other previously unknown species have been discovered.

A total of 850 species of vascular plants were found to occur in naturally fresh or low-lying, naturally saline lands which now are directly threatened by rising ground water and salinity. Similarly, several hundred other species found only in woodland sites will be under threat in the longer term. Such areas affected by salinity show major declines in vascular plant diversity, as species-rich, complex communities are replaced by a few succulents and weeds. However, it should be noted that naturally saline areas also have important biodiversity values and may provide a potential source of native plants for future revegetation. These habitats, and the plants and animals they support, are similarly at risk from rising water tables. Overall, the 'Status Report', emanating from the research begun in 1997, warned that salinisation will cause significant loss of plant communities and a major rise in the extinction rate of native species in the Wheatbelt unless significant efforts are taken to reverse current threats.

Even the first year of the survey dramatically increased available data on the distribution, status and habitat of small Wheatbelt vertebrates and ground-dwelling arachnids (spiders, centipedes and scorpions). For example, to date over eighty species of reptiles, mammals and frogs have been recorded, compared with Western Australian Museum records of 125 species for the whole agricultural region. Strong biogeographical patterns in the distribution of species are apparent across the Wheatbelt, and different communities occur on the various soil types, such as sands, clays, loams, and saline valley floors. Those areas affected by salinity display a significant decline in the biodiversity of terrestrial animals, with an average of 30 per cent fewer species. Additional information on the distribution and abundance of bird species on farms and country roads verges has been provided through a project initiated by Birds Australia (formerly Royal Australasian Ornithologists' Union).[27]

As wetlands occupy the lowest parts of the landscape where salinisation is first likely to occur, twenty-five wetlands in five categories (ranging from fresh to saline) were included in the survey to monitor changes in waterbirds, fish, frogs, and micro-invertebrates. Survey work to date in Wheatbelt wetlands has resulted in the identification of more than 560 invertebrate species, with 45 per cent restricted to freshwater with salinity less than 3,000 milligrams per litre (mg /L). If all wetlands in the Wheatbelt become saline (more than 10,000 mg /L), approximately 220 of these aquatic invertebrates will disappear. An important relationship between species richness and increased levels of salinity has emerged from these surveys. Species richness has been shown to decrease with increasing salinity: the average number of invertebrate species found in freshwater wetlands is about fifty; wetlands with salinity of 20,000 mg /L have about twenty-five species; in those with salinity of 50,000 mg /L there are about twelve species; and wetlands with salinity greater than 100,000 mg/L support as few as four species. These results highlight the general principle that with a doubling in the concentration of salinity the number of aquatic invertebrate species is halved. Aquatic invertebrates are highly sensitive to changes in their environment, but are prone to sampling error due to the minute size of some species and the variable distribution of others.

As waterbirds are situated towards the top of the ecological food chain in wetlands, they also serve as an indication of a wetland's total well-being and environmental integrity. Different species also display varying degrees of tolerance to saline water. For example, Blue-billed Ducks, prefer freshwater habitat, while others species like the Chestnut Teal, are commonly found on inland salt lakes. Of the sixty-one more common waterbirds, only sixteen prefer strongly saline (more than 20,000 mg/L) or hypersaline (more than 50,000 mg/L) habitats. An average of five waterbird species used hypersaline wetlands in a 1981–85 survey of nature reserves in the South-West, compared with twenty in saline wetlands, and forty in freshwater habitats with live trees and shrubs. Consequently, the death of trees and shrubs in many Wheatbelt wetlands due to salinity has caused a 50 per cent decrease in the number of waterbird species using them.

Land clearance and associated dryland salinity initiate a sequence of events leading to the death of vegetation and poor water quality in wetland environments. Increased inputs of water and salt from cleared land in the Lake Towerrinning Catchment, south of Darkan, have resulted in a decline in water quality (characterised by a loss of water clarity and an increase in algal blooms) caused by the demise of fringing vegetation. This vegetation formerly stabilised the sediment and intercepted nutrient-rich run-off from agricultural land.[28] A preliminary study of Coomalbidgup Swamp, near Esperance, also served to demonstrate that increased salinity and waterlogging can create favourable conditions for extensive weed invasion in wetlands, which leads to further degradation and change in vegetation communities.

A significant outcome of CALM's biological survey, commenced in 1997, is the planned identification of up to ten Biodiversity Recovery Catchments that will require more detailed surveys after the completion of the current project in 2001.[29] These sites will serve as future strongholds for biodiversity in the Wheatbelt.

The current systematic biological surveys of the Wheatbelt will provide a baseline for monitoring future changes in regional biodiversity. As there have been no systematic surveys of this kind in the past, it is not possible to make accurate judgements about the extent of loss of biodiversity since European settlement. However, some insights can be gained from the examination of data specifically relating to individual sites that have been studied over a period of time. The impacts of prolonged flooding and increased salt levels on vegetation and wetland habitat have been investigated in several Wheatbelt lakes and swamps.

CASE STUDY ON THE EFFECT OF INCREASING SALINITY ON BIODIVERSITY: LAKE TOOLIBIN

An important site where longitudinal trends in salinity and vegetation change can be examined is Lake Toolibin, east of Narrogin. Lake Toolibin is highly significant as a relict example of a wetland type (in this case, a wooded swamp) that was formerly widespread throughout the Wheatbelt. In its natural state, the lake and its surrounding catchment were rich in vegetation consisting of heath and open woodlands of White Gum on the gravelly sands of the higher ridges and Salmon Gums and York Gums on the heavier valley soils. The stream channels were frequently fringed with galleries of Flooded Gum and the wetlands supported dense thickets of *Casuarina* and *Melaleuca* species. Now, only small stands of this vegetation remain.

Despite the lake's degradation, surveys of waterbird populations show that it is the most important inland wetland in the Wheatbelt, with both greater numbers of birds using it for breeding and greater diversity than any other inland lake.[30] It has the highest known number of breeding waterbird species, particularly colonial waterbirds (for example, cormorants, egrets and herons) and the threatened Freckled Duck, of any wetland in south-western Western Australia.[31] One of the factors that makes the lake so suitable for breeding is the relative freshness of the water during spring.[32] While salinity levels vary considerably over an annual filling and drying cycle, the salinity during the critical breeding months is usually below an acceptable 3,000 mg/L. The fresh to brackish status of the water still enables the wetland to retain most of the dense thickets of trees (Swamp Sheoak and paperbarks) that grow over a large part of its basin. For these reasons Lake Toolibin has the status of being one of the most important wetland habitats in the Wheatbelt.

The wetland has a catchment of about 440 square kilometres, of which approximately 90 per cent has been cleared of its native vegetation. Land was first taken up for farming in the late 1890s but little clearing took place before 1905.[33] About one-third of the clearing had occurred by the mid-1930s; by 1962, 85 per cent of the area had been cleared and this had increased to 90 per cent by 1972.[34] Most of the remaining area was cleared in the late 1940s and 1950s. This clearance of native vegetation has caused the water table to rise and saline stream flow to enter the lake's catchment. Due to the increasing salt levels, some of the trees in the lake have died, mainly on the western side. Groundwater levels under the lake have risen about 12 to 15 metres over the past seventy years to within half a metre of that part of the lake bed where all trees are dead, and to within 1 to 2 metres where the vegetation is still healthy.[35] As a consequence, the former freshwater habitat is now becoming brackish, and if this trend continues, it will become saline in the not-too-distant future.

If Lake Toolibin becomes truly saline, the number of resident and breeding species of waterbird are likely to drop by at least 50 per cent.[36] Higher salinity would adversely affect the threatened Freckled Duck, as it only breeds in freshwater wetlands that contain dense tree or scrub vegetation. The lake is not only a major breeding ground, but also a stronghold necessary for the survival of the entire population of the South-West. Possibly five or more pairs breed when the water level is more than 1 metre deep during spring. The nests are placed on top of swan nest mounds or at the base of spreading trunks of living trees, usually under extensive canopy cover. More than fifty of these birds were present from March 1982 to January 1983, and the count of 600 in December 1982 (when the lake was 0.8 metres deep) is the highest number counted in south-western Australia.

Other significant species would also cease to breed if the level of salinity continues to rise, including up to fifty pairs of Little Pied Cormorants, and smaller colonies of Great Cormorants, Great Egrets, Little Black Cormorants, Yellow-billed Spoonbills, and Rufous Night Herons. Some of these colonies are the only regularly used, inland colonies of these species in the South-West. Table 3 on page 210 shows

TABLE 3: Nesting preferences of waterbirds at Lake Toolibin

Nesting habitat	Waterbird species
Floating or anchored nest of rushes, aquatic plants or sticks on water	Great Crested Grebe, Hoary-headed Grebe, Australasian Grebe, Black Swan, Eurasian Coot
Nest of sticks in, or under cover of, tree over water	Great Cormorant, Little Black Cormorant, Little Pied Cormorant, White-necked Heron, White-faced Heron, Great Egret, Rufous Night Heron, Yellow-billed Spoonbill, Freckled Duck, Blue-billed Duck, Musk Duck
Nest in tree hollow	Australian Shelduck, Grey Teal, Pink-eared Duck, Australian Wood Duck
Nest on ground in grass or rushes	Pacific Black Duck, Australasian Shoveler

Source: Adapted from Halse, 1987; English and scientific names according to Marchant and Higgins (1990, 1993), Christidis and Boles (1994), and Higgins and Davies (1996).

the preferred nesting habitat of waterbirds known to breed at Lake Toolibin. The twenty-two species recorded breeding between 1981 and 1985 were divided by Halse into four categories according to the usual location of their nests, even though most species sometimes chose other sites.[37] Nine species nest in trees over water, several using only live trees. Two species build nests under the cover of trees, and a further two species nest in dense rushes or grass, four species nest in tree hollows often some distance from water (Pacific Black Ducks often nest this way instead of on the ground) and five species build open nests that are either floating or built up of sticks from the bottom of the lake. These preferred nesting habitats of waterbirds support the notion that live vegetation in the lake is vital for the future breeding success of these species.

The highest number of waterbirds counted on Lake Toolibin was 1,650 in January 1982, and Grey Teal represented the most abundant species. The need to conserve Lake Toolibin as a freshwater breeding

ENVIRONMENTAL IMPACTS OF SALINITY • 211

habitat goes beyond the protection of Freckled Ducks, as increased
salinisation would have a marked effect on the population sizes of several other species in the South-West. Large numbers of more common
duck species breed there most years, and this contributes to their overall population sizes. Therefore, the breeding habitat of common species
should also be protected to ensure an abundance of birds in the region
and to prevent them becoming rare. It is much easier to conserve
species when they are abundant, and population sizes are large enough
to accommodate natural fluctuations in numbers. If a species is rare,
then a drop in number that is part of a natural population cycle can
lead to extinction.

Lake Toolibin and some of the surrounding environment are
incorporated in public reserves and have been intensively monitored
since the impacts of secondary salinisation were first noticed in the
early 1970s.[38] Early rehabilitation measures included purchase and protection of adjoining vegetated land, as well as small-scale replanting
within the reserve and catchment. In 1994 a recovery plan recommended urgent short-term action (diversion of major saline surface
flows and installation of bores and pumps to lower groundwater
beneath the lake), as well as strategic long-term action (revegetation of
catchment farmland to reduce regional groundwater levels). The Lake
Toolibin Recovery Project has become a major landscape rehabilitation
experiment and there has been a considerable investment of time,
resources, and expenditure by government agencies. A saline surface
water diversion system and bores were installed in early 1995, while
more recent initiatives have included alley farming and eucalyptus oil
plantations in the catchment to reduce regional groundwater levels.[39]
The construction, in particular, of a diversion channel to carry the surface flow around the lake has resulted in 4,000 tonnes of salt being
diverted around the lake.[40] These efforts appear to be paying dividends
as salinity levels in Lake Toolibin are reported to be decreasing in
response to the remedial pumping and drainage.[41]

However, these noteworthy efforts need to be placed in their
wider environmental context. Lake Toolibin is but one of many threatened sites which it is crucial to protect from rising salinity in order to

prevent major species loss. Expenditure on the Recovery Plan is esti-mated to be nearly $5 million over the ten years, 1994 to 2003.[42] Even this level of expenditure will not lead to full recovery and on-going commitment of funds will be necessary. To date, there is no publicly available estimate to inform the community of the resources needed to protect all the region's wetlands and their wildlife from salinity. On the experience of Lake Toolibin, the overall cost is likely to be very high.

AUSTRALIA'S OBLIGATIONS TO CONSERVE BIODIVERSITY

Species loss due to human activity, particularly habitat clearance, is a world-wide problem. Therefore, it is important that Australia as part of the world community fulfils its obligations to seize every available opportunity to protect its remaining biodiversity. To this end, Australia was one of more than 150 nations to sign the International Conven-tion on Biological Diversity, developed in the lead-up to the United Nations Conference on Environment and Development (also known as the Earth Summit), held in Rio de Janeiro in June 1992. This is arguably one of the most important of the international environment agreements.[43] A key document that formed part of the Rio Declaration is *Agenda 21*. It serves as an action plan for the implementation of the Declaration's key principles, and directs countries to develop Ecologi-cally Sustainable Development (ESD) policies and State of the Envi-ronment (SOE) reports.

This means Australia has special obligations to manage and use its biodiversity sustainably, and under the agreement is required to report annually its implementation of *Agenda 21*. These obligations are out-lined in detail in the *National Strategy for the Conservation of Australia's Biological Diversity*.[44] The Strategy provides mechanisms for achieving ecologically sustainable use, and for minimising impacts on biodiver-sity through the integration of biodiversity conservation and natural resource management. One stated objective that has relevance to the maintenance of biodiversity in the Western Australian Wheatbelt is to 'manage biological diversity on a regional basis, using natural boundaries to facilitate the integration of conservation and production orientated management'.[45]

This objective is supported by the following selected principles, which form the basis of the Strategy:

– Biological diversity is best conserved 'in-situ' (on site);
– Although all levels have clear responsibility, the cooperation of conservation groups, resource users (including farmers), indigenous peoples and the community in general is critical to the conservation of biological diversity;
– It is vital to anticipate, prevent and attack at source, the causes of significant reduction or loss of biological diversity (this principle is particularly relevant to the effects of increasing salinisation);
– Lack of full knowledge should not be an excuse for postponing action to conserve biological diversity; and
– Central to the conservation of Australia's biological diversity is the establishment of a comprehensive, representative and adequate system of ecologically viable, protected areas integrated with the sympathetic management of all other areas, including agricultural and other resource production systems.[46]

Benefits arising from conserving biodiversity include not solely species and habitat protection, but also the maintenance of a wider array of ecological 'services', including the protection of water resources and soils from a threatening process like salinity.

Enactment of the new Commonwealth *Environment Protection and Biodiversity Conservation Act 1999* in July 2000 led to the amalgamation of several pieces of Commonwealth legislation on environment protection, conservation and wildlife. It is one of the only comprehensive biodiversity acts in the world and was described by Dr Thomas Lovejoy (Chief Biodiversity Advisor to the President of the World Bank) as among the most innovative in the world, including in the United States and Europe.[47] This Act acknowledges the National Strategy on Biodiversity, and moves to develop a cooperative national framework for meeting the Strategy's six target areas:

- conservation of biological diversity across Australia;
- integrating biological diversity conservation and natural resource management;
- managing threatening processes;
- improving our knowledge;
- involving the community; and
- emphasising Australia's international role.

For example, governments are presented with a range of opportunities to strengthen native vegetation conservation efforts through protection of listed ecological communities, listing native vegetation loss as a matter of national environmental significance, and listing native vegetation loss as a key threatening process. But past experience shows that there has been considerable resistance to such initiatives in Western Australia. The Act now provides mechanisms for the Commonwealth Government to convert the Strategy to on-ground action. However, all levels of government are likely to face considerable difficulties in meeting those targets, particularly in relation to conserving the remnant native vegetation needed to protect existing biodiversity. Overcoming any impediments that may stand in the way of achieving bilateral agreement between governments must be given utmost priority. The urgency for such action is highlighted by a recent review of the status of land-based birds in Australia.[48] The warning is given that about 250 species will become extinct by the end of this century, unless measures are taken to halt habitat loss and other key threatening processes.

Perhaps the main obstacle that this legislation will need to overcome is the power given to the states under the Australian Constitution to take primary responsibility over land management. While the Federal Government does not have any explicit powers to intervene in state land issues, there is increasing acceptance of national approaches to environmental issues, such as biodiversity and land degradation problems. The Federal Government has also ratified various international treaties, like the Convention on Biodiversity, through which it has used its external affairs powers to list world heritage areas.

Further international agreements exist specifically for the protection of migratory bird species and wetlands considered to be of international importance, especially as waterfowl habitat. The need to protect wetland habitats received worldwide recognition through the *Ramsar Convention on Wetlands of International Importance* (1971), which provides a framework for inter-governmental cooperation in the protection and sustainable use of wetlands.[49] One of the original motivations for the establishment of this Convention was the noted decline in migratory waterfowl populations (mainly ducks), and the desire to conserve their habitats. As such, the Convention emphasises that wetland systems are often used by migratory species of waterbirds that regularly cross national boundaries.

Australia is credited as being the first Contracting Party to the Ramsar Convention, which has inspired both Commonwealth and state governments to develop wetland strategies and policies for the conservation of wetlands and waterbirds.[50, 51, 52, 53, 54] Particularly at the national level, the focus of wetlands policy has been directed at the conservation of migratory waterbird species and the protection of specific habitats.

Formal agreements which involve migratory waterbirds include the 1974 *Japan–Australia Migratory Bird Agreement* (JAMBA), and the 1986 *China–Australia Migratory Bird Agreement* (CAMBA). These migratory bird agreements overlap with the Ramsar Convention as they are also concerned with the wetland environment of the birds. In all, there are more than thirty species of shorebirds that travel from their Northern Hemisphere breeding habitats to summer feeding grounds in Australia. Under these agreements the taking of listed species is prohibited. However, Conacher and Conacher suggested that not only the hunting of birds is illegal, but that any activity which is directly related to the death of protected birds may result in prosecution.[55] The ambiguity of the term 'taking' has been used in the United States to prosecute where chemical spills and pollution have caused the death of protected species.[56] In the same sense, dryland salinity in south-western Australia could be viewed as a form of 'natural' pollution in fresh-water aquatic environments that is the direct result of land clearance for agriculture.

Australia's obligations under the Ramsar Convention are coordinated by the Council of Nature Conservation Ministers, with Environment Australia being responsible for the listing of wetlands; although many of the Ramsar obligations are now part of state legislation. A *Wetlands Policy of the Commonwealth Government of Australia* was released in 1997. Unfortunately, Ramsar guidelines for the listing and 'wise use' (as well as Commonwealth and state legislation) of wetlands are not always clear, adequate or enforceable.[57] Australia's poor record for wetland conservation has been highlighted in a World Wildlife Fund position paper,[58] and is further evidenced at state level by the fact that only Western Australia and New South Wales have a wetlands policy.

The *Wetlands Conservation Policy of Western Australia* supports the objectives of the Ramsar Convention, the migratory bird agreements (JAMBA and CAMBA), and the National Biodiversity Strategy. This Policy also provides an overarching framework for the development of regional wetland protection policies. The threatened ecological communities in Lake Toolibin are given recognition by Commonwealth, State and regional wetlands policies. This high level of attention by governments is due to the fact that this wetland is considered to be of international importance and is listed under the Ramsar Convention. Three migratory shorebird species—the Greenshank, Sharp-tailed Sandpiper, and Oriental Plover—that are protected by JAMBA and CAMBA, have also been recorded at Lake Toolibin.[59, 60] Lake Toolibin is subject to major efforts by State government agencies, including the Department of Conservation and Land Management, to preserve the wooded swamp and its waterbird breeding habitat. In 1998, Lake Toolibin was the only ecological community in the Wheatbelt to be entered onto the Department of Conservation and Land Management's 'Threatened Ecological Communities Database', where it has been assessed as critically endangered.[61] Since 1998, a number of other threatened ecological communities have been added to this database.

While providing a potentially effective legislative framework for protecting biodiversity, these positive developments should not disguise the enormousness of the challenge facing the nation, nor the patchy record of governments in acting upon the principles contained in the range of international agreements. A recent review of Australia's National Biodiversity Strategy concluded, in part, that:

> The cumulative impact of widespread on-going land clearing and habitat degradation, together with other threats such as inappropriate water and fire management practices, salinity and disease, have led to the extinction of some species and continue to threaten many other species and ecological communities with the same fate. The protection of threatened species will continue to be an on-going task requiring a long-term commitment by all levels of government and the wider community.[62]

STATE GOVERNMENT ACTION

Western Australia is in the process of responding to Australia's international biodiversity responsibilities. It was the first state to sign up to the *National Strategy for the Conservation of Australia's Biological Diversity* which, in turn, embodies the principles contained in the *International Convention on Biological Diversity*. This commitment is paving the way for biodiversity to come to the forefront of environmental policy. Importantly, it is enabling the issue to assume a major priority for the State's Environmental Protection Authority (EPA) which is able to invoke this commitment in their current efforts to provide advice to government on drafting biodiversity legislation; develop specific environment policy documents; and, where necessary, protect individual species.

Nevertheless, the efforts of the EPA will need to be reinforced by wider State Government action which has been limited. Recent changes to the *Soil and Land Conservation Act* (1945–1992), to protect remnant vegetation and to limit land clearing, have gone some way towards ensuring a protective framework but wider policy action has encountered a lack of political urgency. For example, even though biodiversity was a theme included in the *Salinity Strategy 2000*, a close examination of the actual commitments shows little new activity was being developed beyond existing programs. Few of these programs carried specific targets and levels of funding.

Much was made in the Strategy of protecting Carnaby's Cockatoo, promoted as a 'flagship' species which typifies the dependence of native fauna on landscape health.[63] This cockatoo prefers to nest in Salmon Gum and Wandoo, which are now quite rare in the Wheatbelt due to land clearing for agriculture and secondary salinity, and feeds in nearby banksia heathlands. The *Action Plan for Australian Birds 2000* indicates that this species' abundance has at least halved over the past forty-five years, and that this decline is likely to continue. Therefore, the protection of existing remnant vegetation, as well as replanting of important natives like the Salmon Gum, is essential for the survival of the endangered Carnaby's Cockatoo and for wildlife conservation in general. However, it must be stressed that any number of species could be elevated to such 'flagship' status, and it cannot be confidently asserted that a particular focus on this species will necessarily guarantee the protection of others which are equally vulnerable. This is especially the case in view of the large number of species about which little is known.

The Salinity Strategy did foreshadow the introduction of biodiversity legislation and an accompanying implementation plan but both have been long-standing commitments without having materialised in draft form. This long delay suggests the State Government has had difficulties resolving some of the complex issues involved in such action: conflicts about the rights of private landholders versus the public good; the issue of compensation for landholders; and the broader need to commit significant levels of funding.

The commitment of state governments will also be further tested in their willingness to fund local governments which carry much of the ultimate responsibility for ensuring protective works and public education on biodiversity are carried out. To date, Western Australia lags behind other states in this regard. This finding emerged from the recent *National Local Government Biodiversity Survey* by Environment Australia and the Australian Local Government Association.[64] Whereas 30 per cent of councils nationally have conducted awareness, education and training, the figure in Western Australia is less than 15 per cent. The issue of resourcing biodiversity conservation was regarded as particularly important as local councils were well placed to play an active and leading role. However, in most cases funding was offered 'on a short-term basis through specific program funding with no on-going guarantee'. In Western Australia, only 28 per cent of councils have employed a 'dedicated environmental officer', compared to 35 per cent of councils nationally. In terms of planning, 54 per cent of councils in the State participated in regional planning, significantly down on the national figure of 71 per cent. The State did not fare any better in the ability of local government to use regulatory and planning powers—through council by-laws—to influence the way biodiversity is managed at the local level (see Table 4 below).

TABLE 4: Use of local by-laws by councils to protect biodiversity in Western Australia and nationally

By-laws	Western Australia (No.)	(%)	National (%)
Domestic species control	20	24	44
Clearing	13	16	25
Tree preservation	12	14	35
Weeds	11	13	35
Coastal planning	7	8	14
Vegetation management plans	6	7	16
Feral species	4	5	15
Wetlands	3	4	11
Threatened species	1	1	10
Covenants	1	1	5
Migratory species	–	–	2
Coastal acid sulfate soils	–	–	5

Source: National Local Government Biodiversity Survey, July 2000—www.alga.com.au

An example of the sort of constructive action that can happen when local governments act in partnership with the community to protect biodiversity is provided by Mullewa Shire in the northern Wheatbelt, whose work was identified for its best practice principles by the *National Local Government Biodiversity Survey*. The Shire offers financial support to landholders to relocate fence lines away from roadways to increase the extent of roadside vegetation corridors. Both landholders and Council contribute to this scheme, with the landholder handing the land over to the Council and removing the old fence. In return, Council pays the farmers for the materials to construct a new fence and pays for upkeep. Landholders and community groups carry out the replantings.

CONCLUSION

The Wheatbelt is a tragic lesson in the nation's loss of biodiversity. The extent of the potential losses is of international significance. If too little effort is made to redress these potential losses, the State could earn itself an unfavourable worldwide reputation. While a constructive start has been made to ensure the State abides by the spirit and the letter of its biodiversity responsibilities, the very recency of this effort underlines the urgency of the task. Moreover, it is not yet certain whether the efforts of environmental officials and local communities will be supported with a commensurate level of political commitment to ensure planning and legislative frameworks are in place and working effectively. Until this is clear, the potential for a catastrophic level of species loss remains a distinct possibility.

Solutions to the Salinity Crisis

Governments face an enormous challenge in trying to save the large part of the Wheatbelt under threat from salinity. The legacy of decades of indifference to the salinity threat is now manifest in a lack of detailed information about, and understanding of, the various options. Moreover, little consensus has been built up in either the farming or broader communities about the viability and cost-effectiveness of the various options. The fragmentation and sometimes sharp divisions within the scientific community about the ways to deal with salinity have hindered progress, especially in developing viable solutions. In this regard, salinity is little different from any other contentious area of government policy. The options will need to be weighed, priorities identified, and a framework for implementation developed. At the time of writing, this work was only in the commencement phase. Just how difficult the task is emerges from a critical evaluation of the strengths and weaknesses of each of the available options; key salinity strategies include revegetation and preservation of existing native plants, commercial tree plantations, productive use of salt-affected land, engineering solutions, and changes to farming practices.

REVEGETATION WITH NATIVE PLANTS AND PROTECTION OF REMNANT BUSH

Among the most hardworking advocates of the need for revegetation in the Wheatbelt is the Western Australian chapter of the international organisation, Men of the Trees. Every winter dedicated members of this community organisation brave frosty mornings in the Wheatbelt in their quest for a greener environment. Since 1979, the organisation has coordinated the planting of nearly five million trees. President Barrie Oldfield explains:

> Our vision for the Wheatbelt is to restore the balance in the ecosystem. We understand that we cannot fully restore the original vegetation because the environment has been dramatically changed by farming, especially the soil biology and its associated micro-organisms and fungi. These essential components have been substantially damaged by chemical farming. Perennial vegetation must be put back over the widest area possible. In my view the land must be returned to an open woodland for a considerable period after ten or fifteen years of cropping. Farming is not incompatible with such revegetation so long as it fits into rotation with perennial trees and shrubs. But farmers need financial and moral support to revegetate. Currently farmers are operating in an uneconomic way; the harvest is being paid for but there is no attempt to factor in the cost of land care. Too much of the current debate on salinity is focused on the science and the economics. We need to factor in the human element as well. This refers to how we, as a society, view the landscape. The human will to succeed prevailed at wartime as everybody rallied to the cause. Similarly, if salinity is seen as sufficiently serious, people will put their hearts and hands into the task of helping farmers with revegetation. We don't want the Wheatbelt to stand as testimony of our neglect for our environment.

Not only is there an urgent need for revegetation with native species to combat salinity and conserve biodiversity, but it is also important to protect existing native vegetation from the impacts of salinity. Such revegetation needs to include not only the larger trees and shrubs, but also a variety of understorey plants that form natural habitats. This option emphasises the use of rainwater as it falls on the land surface, before it infiltrates to the groundwater system. The obvious response is therefore to replant the original native vegetation, and to protect that which remains. This option is based on restoration of the natural hydrological balance of the environment; rainwater falling on the land surface is soaked up by deep-rooted vegetation before it infiltrates the water table, causing it to rise. Simple and attractive as such an option sounds, it carries several shortcomings, not the least being that, if adopted on a large scale, the livelihoods of many Wheatbelt farmers would be threatened.[1]

Ideally, revegetation should occur on as broad a scale as possible, as herbaceous and woody perennials are known to have little or no effect on water tables more than 10 to 30 metres from the planted area.[2] While it is generally accepted that establishment of native perennials is likely to help reduce the rate of rise of saline water tables, insufficient information is available to provide farmers with quality advice on where in the landscape, and at what density on a particular farm, a given number of trees should be planted to maximise their impact on the water table.[3]

Furthermore, a major difficulty exists in the considerable uncertainty about the actual extent of replanting that is required to solve the problem. Some researchers have suggested that as much as 80 per cent of catchments need to be replanted to eliminate salinity completely.[4] Others consider that strategic planting in the landscape may be sufficiently effective and that the small amount of salinity in the landscape may be acceptable.[5] Moreover, recent analyses perpetuate this uncertainty. On the one hand, there are those researchers who argue that planting native tree species in groundwater recharge areas (that is, where water infiltrates into the groundwater table) will only lead to significant reductions in water levels, and eventually salinity, if more than 50 per cent of the catchment is revegetated.[6] In discharge areas (that is, areas where water has come to the surface from the rising of the underground water table), the probability of achieving reduced water levels is lower, the magnitude of the response smaller, and the risk of tree mortality high.[7] To this end, Pannell has pointed out that hydrologists have estimated that if revegetation were the sole option, at least half of the

Wheatbelt landscape would need to be replanted with trees.[8] This would require an investment of up to $1 million per farm. Farmers are unlikely to invest such a sum in non-commercial trees. In any event, a figure of 50 per cent revegetation is thought not to be consistent with the total elimination of salt.

However, another more optimistic assessment based on trials in Katanning has revealed that trees can use water in excess of rainfall—meaning that they are more effective than previously acknowledged. On the basis of this fact, it may be possible to reduce salinity by replanting less than 50 per cent of the landscape and perhaps even only 10 to 20 per cent.[9] This on-going uncertainty within the scientific community has major ramifications for the development of effective salinity strategies.

Nevertheless, the limitations inherent in revegetation as a single option do not, of course, mean that revegetation efforts should cease. Well-planned revegetation implemented by farmers, community groups and government agencies has significant benefits for wildlife and biodiversity conservation, erosion control (water and wind), stock shelter, and recharge management. The re-integration of native species into agricultural systems will require further substantial research and development into direct seeding techniques (especially in low-rainfall areas) and will depend on the availability of major new seed resources.[10] For example, in those areas that have been extensively cleared, there may not be enough seed available for revegetation from existing bush remnants.

Although many farmers now recognise the value of replanting trees and shrubs, there is relatively little information on how to imple-ment such an option, including where to plant and which species to use. In recognition of the paucity of quality information on this topic, a revegetation guide to the central Wheatbelt has been prepared by Lefroy, Hobbs, and Atkins.[11] This practical and worthwhile reference contains notes on flowering times and seed production in eighty-two local plant species; however, there is still considerable work to be done in a region that supports 3,000 to 4,000 native species. Over half of the native plants described are from the understorey, which is an important group in the ecology of the Wheatbelt that is often overlooked. Above ground these plants protect the soil surface and provide food and shelter for wildlife, while below the surface they sustain soil micro-organisms and assist with the movement of air and water. More recently, Greening Australia and Bushcare have also become responsible for disseminating much-needed information to landholders and community organisations engaged in revegetation.

In 1998, the Living Landscapes project, funded and managed by Greening Australia (WA) and Alcoa World Alumina Australia, introduced an important change in the science and philosophy of rebuilding the Wheatbelt by integrating native conservation planning into the farming landscape. This project added another dimension to salinity control, so that there is now greater awareness of the need to incorporate native conservation actions into farm plans and landcare activities.

In particular, imaginative approaches are required for the development of bush corridors that not only contribute to the control of salinity, but also meet the requirements of different fauna. Isolated remnants of native vegetation are particularly endangered when they are not buffered and joined by appropriate bush corridors. Many small animals and birds will not cross open ground, so providing for their needs of food and shelter can make most planting useful as corridors. This usefulness is greatest when remnants to be connected are large (for example, 50 hectares) and they are fairly close together, although any provision of links between remnants is beneficial. The corridors themselves are more effective if they are wide (10 to 20 metres) rather than narrow.[12] Revegetation along streams and around wetlands with local native species is an integral part of establishing such bush corridors. In addition, it is possible to develop corridors by widening and revegetating road reserves.

The quest to revegetate parts of the Wheatbelt may, over time, receive a boost from the agreement reached at the 1997 Kyoto Climate Change Conference, which sanctioned the use of carbon credits; that is, the planting of trees as a trade-off for polluting industries. *The National Greenhouse Strategy* recognises that increasing vegetation cover is an important means of enhancing Australia's greenhouse gas 'sinks' for atmospheric carbon dioxide.[13] Wheatbelt farmers may be able to sell credits for the carbon uptake from trees on their property to organisations such as Western Power, Woodside Petroleum and BHP, as well as many overseas companies producing greenhouse gases.[14, 15] There is a need for a body, presumably a company, to undertake the role of negotiating with those who need the carbon credits. In turn, the same body would negotiate with farmers for areas of saline land for revegetation.[16]

Recent figures show that the market is paying between $US5 and $US20 per tonne of carbon sequestered.[17] Carbon credits and greenhouse gas emission trading, coordinated at national and international levels, can add extra returns to commercial tree crops on large parcels of land.[18] Locally, cooperative or corporate entities, such as the Western Australian Landcare Trust and the Oil Mallee Association, are well positioned to invest in greenhouse tree-plantings in high-priority catchments that contain valuable public assets or natural ecosystems. There is a double return in saving such assets by using more water, while at the same time attracting greenhouse credits. While this sounds promising, the framework in which carbon sequestration projects utilising Mallee Oil projects can operate is still unclear and returns are difficult to predict. However, Shea suggested that as a most conservative estimate the annual return to an Oil Mallee carbon owner could be in the range of $10 to $30 (Australian dollars, that is) per hectare.[19] Overall, the development of an Oil Mallee industry appears worthwhile, though Pannell cautioned that even if such a venture is highly successful, it will only be suitable for certain niches within the farming system.[20] Moreover, doubts now surround the entire international commitment to the Kyoto agreement—and hence to future commitment to reducing greenhouse gas emissions—following the new Bush administration's 2001 decision to withdraw the United States from the agreement.

In any event, revegetation is not a straightforward process. There are pitfalls such as the selection of correct species (preferably local genetic material), replanting costs, and the survival of plantings in more saline parts of the landscape. Whatever scale of revegetation emerges, there is also no escaping its impact on existing agriculture: native perennials divert farmland from its current uses for cropping and pastures and, therefore, threaten farm viability and, ultimately, could cause significant social dislocation. Therefore, as a first step in recharge control it is easier to retain and conserve remnant vegetation than to revegetate.[21]

Existing native vegetation provides vital wildlife habitats, and as such forms the basis of ecosystems that are needed for the maintenance of biodiversity. This vegetation also regulates the water balance and is valued for salinity control on a catchment scale, or as smaller stands in high-recharge areas (for example, rocky outcrops and deep sands) and discharge zones along drainage lines and wetlands. Remnant vegetation is also an important genetic resource for the development of new commercial crops, and as a seed source for the propagation of plants to be used in future revegetation.

Clearing regulations have been progressively tightened by the State Government since their introduction in 1986, with additional measures implemented early in 1999. The removal of native vegetation under normal circumstances is no longer acceptable given the issues of salinity, biodiversity, and global warming.[22] This view is supported by the State's Environmental Protection Authority, which in a position statement on the protection of native vegetation, declared that 'from an environmental perspective any further reduction in native vegetation through clearing for agriculture cannot be supported'.[23] The Authority must not waver from this position in its advice to existing Western Australian Governments, or succumb to political pressures of the kind that are currently most evident in Queensland.

Satellite imagery of Queensland has revealed that panic land clearing accelerated to 340,000 hectares per year in the period 1995 to 1997; this represents the equivalent of nearly 80 football fields of native vegetation cleared every hour.[24] Native bushlands are being bulldozed to make space for agricultural expansion, as farmers race to beat proposed new land-clearing laws relating to freehold land. Meanwhile, conservationists are urgently lobbying to protect rapidly shrinking ecosystems in the face of condemnation by some politicians who have labelled the new laws as draconian and too restrictive. Queensland MP Dr Peter Prenzler of Pauline Hanson's One Nation Party provided the most colourful and vehement denunciation, stating that 'the "evil" legislation, urged on by "the rabid and racist environmental day dreamers"', promised to 'establish a new ecosystem for the one-eyed, left leaning, mouldy green extremists, like the hippy with the Greenpeace T-shirt and the cockroach infested hair'.[25] This clearing is occurring despite the legacy of excessive clearing in the southern states, which has manifested itself as major salinity problems and a decline and extinction of species.

In Western Australia, the degree of State Government commitment to enforce the protection of existing native vegetation in the Wheatbelt still remains to be confirmed by further on-the-ground action. Evidence of significant inequities in the enforcement of clearing controls continues to emerge through the media. On the part of the State Government there appears to be a general reluctance to prosecute all farmers in violation of clearing controls. This has created a climate of considerable uncertainty for some farmers in regard to their rights as private landholders. Such inequities do not only apply to the treatment of individual farmers, but also to the accountability expected of government agencies involved in land clearing. At present, government agencies can clear native vegetation on public land without undergoing the same level of justification required of private landholders. Unless inequities such as these are resolved by State Government action, inappropriate and often illegal clearing will continue to occur on a limited scale in the Wheatbelt. This tragic disappearance of remnant patches of bushland is obvious to even the most casual observer. Any motorist regularly travelling outside of Perth's metropolitan area can testify to the on-going clearance of native vegetation from road verges.

The Native Vegetation Working Group was established in 1999 to develop mechanisms for the retention (and eventual protection) of privately owned bushland in agricultural areas. While real estate advertisements in *The Countryman* newspaper show that cleared land can sell for as little as $400 per hectare, the final report of this Working Group detailed the costs involved in revegetation for hydrological purposes as being between $800 and $2,000 per hectare. Replanting for biodiversity purposes is considerably more expensive at a minimum cost of $4,000 per hectare, and can be as high as $15,000 to $20,000 per hectare. This suggests that the true value of standing native vegetation is generally far more than the market value of the land.[26] Consequently, a strong case exists for providing farmers with added incentives that affect their ability and willingness to own and manage large areas of bushland. This can only be achieved through mechanisms that address the true costs of such initiatives.

The Working Group identified the need for greater acceptance by farmers that having areas of well-managed bush on their property is an integral part of operating a productive and sustainable farm. Barbara York Main described how remnant bushland can add a special quality to a cultivated landscape:

> To climb through a wire fence out of a ploughed and sown paddock into a wild wind raked stretch of bushland is to tumble into an order of life unmoulded by man but one which can jolt the mind into a deeper wonderment, not only of this ungarnered territory, but of the whole natural world.[27]

To protect such special areas, services provided to landholders by the State Government include the Land for Wildlife Scheme, Remnant Vegetation Protection Scheme, voluntary conservation covenants, and cooperation with Natural Heritage Trust programs such as Bushcare. The Commonwealth Bushcare program, with almost $350 million in funding over six years, has identified two main goals: a revegetation rate that is greater than vegetation loss, and an improvement in the quality and condition of Australia's native vegetation. However, these goals cannot be met by Landcare groups and committed individual landholders in the absence of effective controls on land clearing in all states; this is the business of state governments.[28] As well as providing advisory and support services to private landholders, Federal and State governments have responsibility for protecting and managing native vegetation on their own lands.

In addition to salinity, the value of remnant vegetation to the long-term conservation of biodiversity depends on appropriate management of a range of threats and destructive events, including weeds, feral animals, flood or drought, fire, and dieback disease. There is also increasing evidence that commercial activities like livestock grazing are a major cause of degradation of native vegetation through destruction of the understorey, lack of native species recruitment, and invasion of exotic species. Therefore, best practice management should exclude all livestock grazing in remnant vegetation.[29]

2 COMMERCIAL TREE PLANTATIONS

It has already been established that broad-scale, strategic planting of woody perennials is required to control salinity. Woody perennials include both trees (for example, pines and gums) and shrubs (for example, Oil Mallees).

This strategy will only be effective if the large area of revegetation required for most catchments can be efficiently integrated into the agricultural system. Due to the obvious agricultural disadvantage of replanting exclusively with native trees, the alternative, and more attractive, proposition is to find commercially useful plants that perform the same hydrological role as native vegetation. Such plants could be farmed as part of the wheat growers' rotational patterns, or as fodder in mixed farming operations. Moreover, the substantial investment involved in the development and establishment of new commercial tree crops, products and industries means that economic returns are essential to achieve large-scale adoption. Woody perennials such as Blue Gum, pines (such as Maritime Pines), Tagasaste, and Oil Mallees have each required many millions of dollars of capital to develop as commercial crops. As Bartle has pointed out:

> For revegetation to have an impact on salinity it will need to be measured in millions of hectares and be of long duration. Species and products should therefore be selected for their large potential market volume and strong, enduring demand.[30]

Further increasing the area of commercial tree plantations is viewed by the State's Sustainable Land Management Technical Panel as a priority action.[31] There is also considerable merit in searching more widely overseas for other hydrologically appropriate and commercially useful plants (including trees and shrubs, as well as crops).

Early work on the use of trees with commercial value that perform the same hydrological task as native vegetation was conducted in water supply catchments, particularly tributaries of the Collie River which supply Wellington Dam. More than one-third of cleared areas in the Wellington Dam Catchment were replanted on the slopes and valley floors between 1979 and 1989. As a consequence, the groundwater table dropped by 1.5 metres and groundwater salinity decreased by 30 per cent.[32] In general, groundwater levels immediately beneath treated areas, near discharge areas, or in high-rainfall catchments, have shown a falling trend. Presently, commercial tree crops of Tasmanian Blue Gums have emerged in higher rainfall areas, on what was formerly farmland, to support a woodchip export industry. In intermediate rainfall areas, Maritime Pine and the fodder shrub Tagasaste can make a contribution to salinity control. However, more emphasis needs to be directed to the development of a range of tree crops for the low-rainfall areas.

However, there is an urgent need for careful, long-term research to examine the environmental and socio-economic consequences of this type of extensive commercial tree-planting. This form of land use, as well as changing the aesthetics of the landscape, is likely to contribute to further depopulation and decline in rural communities, and the trees themselves are not matched with local ecological and hydrological conditions. Blue Gums provide minimal habitat for the support of local biodiversity, and come with all the risks of failure associated with any monoculture. This species is also not adapted to the Wheatbelt, being a high user of water that requires 700 to 800 millimetres of rainfall annually, deep permeable soils with few root impediments and excess soil water. Consequently, commercial Blue Gum plantations cannot be viewed as a solution with broad applications to the salinity problem.

However, trials are currently under way to assess the suitability of Blue Gums for phase farming in medium to low (300 to 600 millimetres) rainfall areas.[33] Trees are being grown at high planting densities in very short rotations (three to five years). These are expected to rapidly remove water from farming catchments at risk of salinity, by depleting soil water while producing utilisable products such as wood fibre and biomass suitable for 'green' electricity generation. It is intended that the tree phase would be followed by an agricultural phase of a length defined by the persistence of the hydrological buffer to recharge created by the trees drying out the soil profile to depth.

Potentially the most exciting commercial perennials—especially for low-rainfall areas—are widely thought to be the Oil Mallee species, ironically being prominent among the original native vegetation cleared during the development phase of the Wheatbelt. Oil Mallees have three distinct commercial applications:

– The twig and leaf residues can be converted to a combustible material for use in electricity generation as an adjunct to the use of coal.
– The oil from the leaf can be refined into a biodegradable and highly effective solvent for a range of industrial solvents as a replacement for existing oil-based products.
– The wood stems can be converted into ethanol and methanol for use as transportation fuel in combination with, and potential replacement for, fossil fuels.

The market for these Oil Mallee products rests on an understanding of the emerging 'green economy'. The advent of global warming is creating a growing demand for renewable sources of energy. It is estimated that these energy forms could provide half the world's energy needs by 2050.[34] Adoption of renewable energy based on the harvesting of plant material is referred to as 'biomass farming' or a 'carbohydrate economy'. It has only recently received limited Commonwealth Government support through the requirement that 2 per cent of the nation's energy should be derived from renewable energy as a contribution to lowering Australia's output of greenhouse gases. However, as the above predictions show, this commitment is out of step with future predictions for renewable energy.

Already in Western Australia, there have been steady developments in the creation of a future Oil Mallee industry. Since 1994, some 900 growers have planted trees on nearly 7,000 hectares. In addition, Western Power has announced that it will construct a 20 per cent scale demonstration plant using fuel derived from Mallee residue (after oil extraction). Yet, these developments represent a fraction of the potential that CSIRO researchers hold out for biomass farming: they predict that there could be between 1,200 and 1,600 bioethanol plants in Australia producing between 10 million and 100 million litres annually, leading to the production of 85 per cent of all transport fuels by 2040.[35] On this scale, the industry would require between $60 billion and $90 billion in investment over twenty to thirty years.

The developments in Western Australia represent important, but limited, steps in this larger vision. However, impediments to the growth of the industry remain, including the availability of specialised harvesting and processing technology, the full confidence of the farming community, and the development of growth markets. This is especially the case in the rapidly evolving technology of the motor car industry where a variety of fuel options are being developed.

It is also important to recognise that the mallee oil industry, while offering a potential commercial alternative to the grains and sheep industries, will not fully address the biodiversity aspects of salinity discussed in the previous chapter. While reduced salinisation will help to protect remnant bushland, commercial plantations will not provide additional wildlife habitat. Moreover, the very promise of a mallee oil industry should not deter the search for other potential commercial crops which currently centre around trials in Sandalwood, native bush foods and medicines, and olives.

3 IMPROVED FARMING SYSTEMS

Recharge to catchments can be reduced by altering existing farming systems to practices that use more water. New cropping options may include a considerable area of deep-rooted perennial species and plants with a longer growing season. Recent research indicates that there is only limited potential to decrease recharge by manipulating existing annual crop and pasture systems. For example, a doubling of yield can be achieved with high-performance annual crops on fine-textured soils in the medium- to low-rainfall areas, but recharge may only decrease by 5 per cent.[36]

Warm-season cropping, that is, trying to grow crops in the drier summer months, has the potential benefit of not only reducing recharge, but also of recycling nutrients, breaking down 'hard pans' and assisting weed control. At present these systems are most suited to higher rainfall areas and waterlogged sites, but are being trialled throughout the Wheatbelt. The Western Australian No Tillage Farmers' Association is committed to the establishment of warm-season cropping over 15 per cent of the Wheatbelt within five years, and is supported in this initiative by both the Natural Heritage Trust and the Salinity Council.[37] The development of more salt-tolerant crops would delay the onset of salinity and provide extra time and income for the implementation of new farming systems.

In addition to cropping initiatives, the development of new farming systems based on perennial pastures (for example, deep-rooted lucerne) can also contribute to the reduction of recharge. What this option attempts to do is to convert profitable but unsustainable production of annuals, such as wheat, to at least equally profitable and sustainable production of perennial trees, shrubs and pastures.[38] For example, perennial pastures and fodder shrubs (for example, Tagasaste) are best suited to sheep grazing in the medium-rainfall areas. There is significant scope for combining the grazing of livestock, using a perennial pasture base, with commercial tree crops for agroforestry.

However, it is unrealistic to expect farmers to make sacrifices to prevent salinity without simultaneously providing economically viable treatments offered by better perennial options. Even if such options eventuate, many farmers will be cautious and sceptical about adopting such innovations.[39] In any event, known improvements to farming systems are likely to make less than a 10 per cent reduction in recharge.[40]

The fundamental challenge is therefore to develop sustainable farming systems that mimic natural ecosystems, and will be developed and maintained by farmers.[41] Given the critical importance of this activity, it has been grossly underfunded by governments in the past.[42] A significant research and development effort is only now about to commence through a Cooperative Research Centre based at The University of Western Australia for plant-based management of dryland salinity, which was recently awarded $22.5 million by the Commonwealth Government. These funds are part of a $325 million allocation to nineteen such projects across Australia, to develop new commercially viable farming systems.[43]

According to the Director of the Centre, Professor Phillip Cocks, its role is to facilitate a 'sea change in agriculture', based around the cooperative research efforts of key scientists from government agencies and universities throughout Australia. Commenting on the significance of the project, Professor Cocks explained that although the problem of salinity is serious,

> it's certainly not hopeless. And even though it will take a long time to fix the problem, there has to be progress in the short term. Some people think that we should have found solutions by now, but, in fact, there has been a lot of research done into the causes of salinity but not much into the answer to it.[44]

The Centre envisages commercial perennial shrubs and trees replacing much of the current wheat industry.

4 ENGINEERING SOLUTIONS

Among the most controversial options to deal with salinity are various proposals to move saline water off the landscape via drainage systems. Many farmers like John Hall of Narembeen believe that the answer to salinity on their properties lies in the construction of drains which move salt water into nearby rivers and collection ponds. As he explains:

> We have to move salt out of the landscape and put it back in

the sea. The drains have worked magnificently. All land that previously grew vegetation, whether it be 30 or 40 years ago, and is now salt-affected—I have no doubt if the water can be moved, all these lands can be turned back into viable productive farmland. This is rather exciting, what one can do with these lands. Drainage is the beginning of an encompassing reversal of salt degradation and presents the opportunity to take productive enterprises far and beyond the present-day thinking. I started my drainage project in 1989 and I have now bought neighbouring salt-affected farms and am also converting those. The drains really fixed this area up. Before, we would not even be able to crop half the area, and it hardly grew a crop at all. Productivity has more than doubled where nothing used to grow before. Definitely we have got our money back from the works we did. I don't believe that you are going to find a case that we are damaging the environment. People say what about the salt that you are moving downstream. But in about twelve months most of these drains really slow down. The salts have been going down the stream systems for thousands of years, and we might be speeding it up a bit. For every obstacle one puts up there are ways of getting around things so that you don't do damage.

Many farmers share John Hall's confidence in drainage as a solution to dryland salinity on their properties. Drainage offers a direct, unilateral action that farmers can adopt in situations where a recharge approach is considered to be ineffective. However, the widespread adoption of this solution is constrained by environmental considerations and construction costs (especially if schemes were to be sponsored by government). Farmers also perceive the application process as being onerous to the point that many either do not lodge an application, or else they construct their own drains without approval. In such cases, drains may be environmentally unsound. Drains have become one of the most contentious solutions to salinity because of the clash of interests involved. Farmers wish to pursue their own options on their land and governments want to ensure that the environment, the interests of neighbouring farmers, and community infrastructure and assets (for example, roads) are protected.

Engineering options—which include the use of various drainage and pumping systems—have generated a great deal of uncertainty in the community, which has caused confusion, and in some cases conflict. Part of the attractiveness of drainage schemes, in particular, to some farmers lies in the belief that drains will deliver a more immediate solution to salinisation on their property than other options, such as extensive tree-planting and alternative farming systems. This view is supported by government hydrologist Dr Richard George who believes that so far recharge management options have not been shown to be effective. Currently the issue of drainage has polarised the debate on salinity management, which will only hinder acceptance of a strategy that involves the use of a variety of different tools in different situations.

Drainage in salinity management is about redirecting saline water by means of deep or shallow drains to other parts of the landscape in order to allow current land use to continue, or to facilitate the establishment of new land uses. Assuming a rising groundwater table, this response sets out to address the mechanisms causing the problem.[45] Table 5 on page 238 describes the major types of shallow (surface) and deep (sub-surface) drainage.[46] Shallow drainage mostly operates on surface and topsoil water, while deep drainage serves to intercept groundwater at considerably higher cost.

Engineering options are recognised by the State Salinity Council as being complementary to other available options, such as revegetation, within the framework of a catchment plan. In reality, it is doubtful that they will play a large part in the eventual solution due to high cost and undesirable environmental impacts. Furthermore, recharge control through revegetation and high-water-use farming systems will slow, but not prevent, the spread of salinisation in the medium- to low-rainfall areas of the Wheatbelt.[47]

During the late 1970s and early 1980s interest in saltland drainage increased in the northern Wheatbelt due to some local farmers promoting successes on their own farms; for example, in the Buntine and Watheroo areas. While in the 1990s, large-scale drainage works occurred

Table 5: Summary of types of surface and sub-surface drainage

Type	Construction	Options	Use	Problems
(i) Shallow (Surface)				
V, W, spoon, raised beds, mounds	Tractor, grader, scraper	Many variations	Surface water control, improved leaching	Low volumes, storm damage, little water table control
Waterways, floodways	Scraper, grader, dozer	With/without walls, connected (or not) on a catchment basis	Valley floor, stream or flood control	Storm damage, little water table control, relative cost
Banks	Dozer, grader, (e.g. WISALTS)	Level, grade, interceptor, reverse, sills, gap spreaders	Hillsides	Design and lay-out, workability of farm, cost
(ii) Deep (Sub-surface)				
Deep open drains	Excavator	Open, with or without banks, connected (or not) on a catchment basis	Extensive agriculture, valley floors	Clays, low permeability, unstable soils, run-off, velocity, poor lateral connectivity, cost, disposal, storm damage
Tile drains	Trench diggers, excavators	With gravel, moles, tyres	Valley floors, protecting high-value assets, lower water tables	Clays, low permeability, poor lateral effect, cost, construction, expertise
Pumping	Drilling rig, excavator	Relief wells, syphons, single or multiple wells	Protecting high-value assets, lower water tables	Low permeability, cost, disposal, energy, radial impact, water balance

Source: Adapted from Coles, George and Bathgate, 1999.

throughout the State, particularly in the Belka Valley and Narrembeen in the Merredin District. These works were controversial and provoked conflict between the groups involved and government agencies. In 1992, in response to ongoing interest in drainage and concern about the impacts, Regulation 5 was established under the *Soil and Land Conservation Act* (1945–1992). The Regulation requires that if

> an owner or occupier of land proposes to drain or pump water from under the land surface because of salinity and to discharge that water onto the land, into other water or into a watercourse, the owner or occupier shall, at least 90 days before commencing the drain or pumping commences, notify the Commissioner [for Soil and Land Conservation].[48]

The present Notice of Intent to Drain Process is perceived to be slow and unclear by many farmers and drainage proponents. For this reason, the Minister for Primary Industry and Fisheries had already established the Deep Drainage Taskforce in August 1999 to develop a protocol that

> coordinates deep drainage (including underground pumping of saline water and relief wells) practices within catchment areas to maximise the benefits in treating salinity and waterlogging whilst taking into account the possible negative impacts of fresh or saline water disposal.[49]

This protocol considers how deep drainage can be combined as part of the landcare tool kit at a catchment level in the most effective manner, while minimising the impact of water disposal. In order to implement this protocol, the Taskforce recommended a whole-of-government approach through a Memorandum of Understanding between relevant agencies. The intention is to provide an integrated 'one stop shop' regulatory process for assessing proposals against specific drainage design and assessment criteria. It was also proposed that approvals should be fast tracked for cooperative group proposals and low-risk plans to meet deficiencies in current procedures, which favour individual actions. This could be viewed as a reaction to the considerable lobbying and pressure that various farmers, contractors, and politicians have directed at relevant government agencies and the media.

Farmers are finding it difficult to secure the agreement of all landowners (both private and government) within an area that is proposed to be drained, and to identify acceptable and agreed upon disposal points. This is especially the case for catchment-scale proposals, where a large number of parties are involved and a substantial volume of water is to be drained. Uncertainties and concerns about the impact of deep drainage relate to downstream agricultural land, streams and wetlands, conservation reserves, and the cumulative impact of many drains within a catchment, especially in regard to flooding. The Deep Drainage Taskforce estimated that between 200 and 300 kilometres per year of drains are now being constructed, many without government approval.[50] However, recent modifications (Drains 1 Policy, 1999) to the process facilitate a shorter assessment period for group proposals made on a catchment planning basis.

Under suitable hydrological conditions, engineering options can be useful in the protection or recovery of high-value assets, such as areas of high agricultural productivity, areas of biological significance (including wetlands such as Lake Toolibin), town buildings or other infrastructure (for example, Merredin townsite). However, engineering options must be implemented with full knowledge of their on-site and off-site impacts and practicality. Conversely it is also important to consider what might happen to the environment if no action is taken.

A new approach to engineering options identified by the Deep Drainage Taskforce, and adopted in the Salinity Strategy, concerns a best practice environmental management package designed to assist landholder groups to develop their own catchment-based drainage proposals. Such an approach involves careful consideration of the amount of discharge of salt and water required, identification of water management practices for different areas in the catchment, calculation of the cumulative impacts of all drainage works on the catchment, and demonstration that downstream environmental impacts (for example, on wetlands and remnant vegetation) are minimal. A more effective and appropriate authorisation process is needed to ensure that private engineering proposals are consistent with government water management practices, such as maintenance of public water supply.[51] Consultation must take place with all potentially affected landholders and relevant government agencies, particularly where one area is sacrificed in order to save another area. All drainage proposals should incorporate the cost of salt control and disposal, as well as the cost-effectiveness of this measure in comparison to other available management strategies.

Surface water management offers a means of changing the hydrological balance on a farmer's property. Accumulation of water on the soil surface, and waterlogging in the soil profile, can be addressed by directing water along grade lines using drains, banks or cultivation rows. These measures have the potential to reduce erosion and groundwater recharge, particularly in wet years when these problems are greatest. Examples of such systems are shallow drains built along contour lines that channel water into a series of dams, and may also include several rows of trees or shrubs planted on the downslope side of the drains.

The interceptor bank method adopted by Brookton farmer Harry Whittington (see Chapter Three) assumes that the secondary salt problem is caused by throughflow (that is, seasonal shallow, lateral, subsurface soil–water movement), instead of rising groundwater tables. If throughflow is responsible, this method serves to intercept downslope water movement and to divert, or use, the water before it reaches low-lying areas to cause waterlogging and eventually salinisation. Whittington had previously tried salt-tolerant plants, as advised by agricultural agency officers, but would not accept that there was nothing else he could do to solve the severe salt problem on his property.[52] He gradually extended his interceptor bank system until by the 1980s it covered the entire property. The water that is intercepted by such a contour bank evaporates or infiltrates vertically and laterally into the soil. Some of that water is used by crops or pastures, although some of it must also infiltrate to a greater depth.[53]

Neighbouring farmers observed the results of Whittington's work and began to construct their own systems. As discussed in Chapter

Three, this led in 1978 to the formation of WISALTS (Whittington Interceptor Salt-Affected Land Treatment Society). Examples of farmer despair over the limited productive potential of saltland are contained in WISALTS newsletters published in *Elders Weekly* in Western Australia between 1983 and 1988.[54] The official position of the agency was that interceptors may, in fact, add to the salt problem by increasing infiltration to the deep groundwater system and, as a result, raise groundwater tables in the valley floor. Understandably, this method generated considerable conflict between agriculture agency staff and farmers advocating the use of contour interceptors. In particular, WISALTS was highly critical of strategies for combating salinity based on reducing recharge.

Farmers constructing interceptor bank systems in the early 1980s had mixed results, with the greatest reported impact being in reduced waterlogging. Success was largely determined by the care with which interceptor banks were constructed and the extent of their coverage and degree of control over the catchment of the salt-affected land. Later detailed hydrological research showed that both throughflow and the deep groundwater system were contributing water and salts to salt-affected land.[55] By the 1990s government scientists were able to demonstrate that large increases in recharge could result from these banks. There are however still a considerable number of properties with Whittington-style drains (especially around Brookton), but uncertain results and the high cost of this technique compared with other shallow drains (for example, grade banks to direct overland flow away from seeps) limits their acceptance and widespread adoption.

Surplus water harvested from a catchment can also be redirected into water storages as a means of drought-proofing the property, or used to support new farm enterprises, such as aquaculture (for example, trout farms). Otherwise, the disposal of such water into nearby streams and wetlands requires careful planning to ensure that any impacts on the environment or downstream property are within acceptable limits. Management of surface water requires the adoption of strategies that complement engineering works by maximising water use and reducing discharge of saline groundwater.

A common engineering option, which has generated considerable controversy, is to excavate deep drains on salt-affected land in order to drain groundwater away from the site and lower the water table. However, there are a number of fundamental problems with this approach, including the lack of success in impermeable soils; the need for closely spaced ditches to achieve groundwater drawdown (unsuitable for areas used to graze stock or move machinery); the high cost (treatment may exceed land value); and the concerns about the disposal of saline groundwater.[56] Unlike surface water, the management of permanent groundwater systems involves methods such as deep drains (open or closed), pumping, relief and syphon wells. Deep drains are constructed at depths of 1 to 2 metres depending on site conditions, and are most effective in permeable landforms, such as limestone, that resist slumping and erosion. Many Wheatbelt soils are unstable (loose sands) or have low permeability (clays), and therefore an evaluation of land capability and site responsiveness is essential before construction. Sites with a low permeability have a very small zone of influence on the groundwater. However, in places like Narembeen, where in valleys there is a cementation of sandy soils (alluvium), the use of drains has resulted in better than expected outcomes.[57]

Well-designed deep drains have a role in salinity management, but disposal of drainage water off-site needs to meet specific criteria in relation to the risk of increased flooding and sedimentation downstream, and the potential for damage to other properties, public assets and nature reserves.[58] In situations where water may be discharged into natural streams and wetlands, it is essential that current and future water supplies are not compromised and there are no significant impacts on ecosystems receiving water that is different in quality or quantity. Another option for disposal of drainage water is the use of evaporation basins, which may also be used for other purposes, such as aquaculture, energy production using solar ponds, or commercial harvesting of salt.

An altogether separate engineering solution has been advocated by Belford,[59] who criticised the Salinity Strategy for not taking the necessary actions to make any progress on desalinating the Wheatbelt. He argued that State Government and community support for tree-planting as a tool to overcome salinisation could be challenged on the basis that no substantial vegetation would grow in the valleys because of future salinity and waterlogging. He regarded the usefulness of revegetation as being limited to rectifying small hillside seeps, and for reducing the amount of water added annually to underground stores in the valleys. Instead, Belford advocates the pumping of groundwater to the surface for storage, and eventual evaporation, in existing salt lakes or purpose-built ponds. In wet years, these evaporation basins may also function as flood mitigation ponds. Issues central to this project that are still being debated include the pumping rates required to achieve the desired drawdown in groundwater, the amount of energy consumed in this task, and the running costs.

Since 1980, there has been considerable pumping of saline groundwater with as many as a hundred pumps being installed, of which only ten are still in operation.[60] Groundwater pumping involves the drilling of bores and use of electric or compressed air pumps to protect high-value assets. This option is usually costly to install and maintain. The effectiveness of pumping is largely dependent on soil permeability, which determines how many pumps and how much power is needed to achieve the outcome. As with deep drains, the same problems with disposal of water and off-site impacts must be considered. Groundwater pumping is usually used in conjunction with other strategies, but may need to be implemented at the start of an overall program of management if the salinity risk is severe. For example, groundwater pumping is presently being evaluated at Lake Toolibin and in some rural towns.

Bores drilled to bedrock can be used to naturally discharge groundwater held under pressure, through polythene pipes into waterways. Relief wells and syphons may be the most easily managed of the engineering options, but as with all drains the off-site impacts of saline water disposal need to be considered. This technique is being evaluated in the Gordon River Focus Catchment by Agriculture Western Australia and the Water and Rivers Commission.[61]

Agriculture Western Australia conducted a Wheatbelt survey in 1999 to determine the efficiency of deep drainage works from a landholder's perspective.[62] The results highlighting advantages and disadvantages of deep drains constructed in the Wheatbelt are shown in Table 6.

Engineering options, particularly deep drains, are unlikely to be adopted by farmers on a broad scale due to high costs of installation and maintenance, as well as community concerns about environmental impacts. In particular, engineering options should be directed to the protection of discrete, localised, well-defined assets, including country towns threatened by salinity and some of the native reserves that contain threatened species.[63] In these cases, the community benefits of such treatments may be so high that it is worth adopting salinity treatments that otherwise would be considered unviable. Until the mid-1980s, there was little State Government support for drainage works on farmland, but this has increased in response to growing community interest in both recharge- and discharge-based approaches. The Department of

TABLE 6: Summary of the outcomes of drainage case studies from the landholder's point of view

Advantages	Disadvantages
– Reduced soil salinity through leaching (mainly lateral tube drains)	– Not cost effective
	– Limited water table drawdown
	– Poor construction and design
– Reduced waterlogging and inundation period	– Increased saline and sediment discharge
– Increased discharge	– High maintenance costs (with few drains maintained)
– Increased productivity	
– Effective at break of slope and in combination with other treatments	– Downstream flooding and inundation
	– Other solutions may have been just as effective
– Reclaimed marginal land	– Spoil and drains restrict access to areas of the property
– Reduced the rate of salinity spread	– Low gradients and hydraulic heads

Source: Adapted from Coles et al., 1999.

Agriculture, in particular, was preoccupied for many years in disproving the claims made by WISALTS on the operation and success of Whittington contour banks:[64] the Department's position was eventually exonerated. This controversy has been largely responsible for hindering progress in the development of more cost-effective and efficient drainage techniques that would also prove to be environmentally acceptable. For these reasons, some farmers still advocate drainage for incorrect and inappropriate applications. This issue has also become highly political, which has polarised the debate even further.

5 PRODUCTIVE USE OF SALT-AFFECTED LAND

Revegetation of a substantial proportion of the Wheatbelt with native vegetation would clearly displace many farmers. The early response to the salinity problem suggested that farmers should 'learn to live with it'.[65] This response was also promoted for many years by Agriculture Western Australia (formerly the Department of Agriculture), which recommended that farmers fence off their salt-affected land and establish salt-tolerant plants (known as halophytes). For example, wheat (a non-tolerant plant) has a 50 per cent decrease in growth at salt concentrations equivalent to about 6 per cent of sea water (2,100 mg/L). In contrast, River Saltbush has a 50 per cent decrease in growth at salt concentrations equivalent to 80 per cent of sea water (28,000 mg/L), and is still alive at concentrations equivalent to 140 per cent of sea water (49,000 mg/L).[66] Research by Barrett-Lennard and Galloway has shown that stands of River Saltbush have the added benefit of being able to use up to 0.7 millimetres of water per day and reduce shallow water tables by 60 centimetres over a summer.[67]

Yet, even though productive uses can be found for salt-affected land, these must be viewed as very much a last resort in the policy toolbox. Ideally, using salt-affected land productively should be reserved for those areas already badly salt-affected and where alternatives lack feasibility. After all, the very existence of salt-affected parts of the landscape stands as a permanent reminder of our failure to protect the natural environment.

Nevertheless, Australian researchers have been major innovators in the introduction of plants to saltland for productive use. There were introductions of Tall Wheat Grass and Salt Water Couch in the 1940s, *Puccinellia* in the 1950s, and halophytic forage shrubs in the 1960s.[68] A considerable body of research was also established on plant species that grow in naturally saline soils in other parts of the world, including North America, Israel and the Middle East, to determine their suitability for the Wheatbelt. There have even been attempts to breed for salt tolerance in cereals, but these efforts have had little practical benefit due in part to the associated problem of waterlogging.[69] It is now recognised that waterlogging on saltland affects the growth and survival of all but the most waterlogging-tolerant plants.

Such a strategy had unfortunate consequences for future relationships between farmers and government agencies.[70] Some farmers believed that the establishment of salt-tolerant plants was intended to rehabilitate the saltland, although Agriculture WA (at that time known as the Department of Agriculture) has indicated that this was not the intention. As a result many farmers became disillusioned and felt 'let down' once it became apparent that saltland vegetation was not having the anticipated result. The effect of Saltbush pastures on sheep was also poorly understood by some farmers who believed that Saltbush could provide an alternative source of feed. However, the view of agriculture agency researchers had always been that Saltbush pastures were only good for 'maintenance' of sheep during the dry autumn period. At this time, green feed is no longer available and farmers often rely on grain as an alternative. According to former agricultural scientist Clive Malcolm, misinformation about the role of saltland pastures by media eventually led to a reduction in priority for this field of research in Western Australia.[71]

The situation had changed considerably by the 1990s. By then most farmers understood that the use of salt-tolerant vegetation was unlikely to return the land to its former productivity. For this reason, Conacher and Conacher interpreted this option as largely a 'band-aid' response,[72] although, some benefits of using salt-tolerant vegetation do exist, such as improvement to the aesthetics of bare, salt-encrusted soil surfaces; reduced erosion by wind and water; and limited grazing of sheep (rarely for more than six weeks in any one year). For example, farmer Michael Lloyd, on a property north-east of Lake Grace, has shown that the establishment cost of a saltland pasture need not be prohibitively high and returns are significantly higher than doing nothing to saltland.[73] For this reason there exists a practical guide to the best pasture plants for saltland in Australia, although species from areas beyond the Wheatbelt should be treated with caution as potential environmental weeds.[74] Presently Agriculture Western Australia has a shortage of staff with expertise in the productive use of saline lands, and this has serious implications for on-going research in this area.

The Saltland Pastures Association promotes revegetation of saltland in low- and medium-rainfall areas with salt-tolerant annuals and grasses, herbs and woody perennials. Presently three types of saltland pasture are available: natural regeneration of saltland using existing plants, sown shrub pastures, and sown mixed shrub/grass pastures.[75] There is a realisation that the grazing value of Saltbush-based pastures needs to be re-assessed, and in some cases revised downwards to more realistic levels than those reported about fifteen years ago. Saltbushes are now recognised as being only of low nutritive value to sheep.[76] Current research suggests that sheep can maintain body condition on saltland pastures for four to five weeks at stocking rates of 10 sheep per hectare. In other words, saltland pastures support stocking rates of 280 to 350 sheep-grazing-days per hectare per year.[77]

However, the productive use of saline land is still strongly on the agenda both locally and nationally. At a local level, the Saltland Pastures Association was formed in 1997 to promote opportunities for use of saline lands, particularly as pasture suitable for maintenance of livestock (mostly sheep). This Association has initiated a project for the revegetation of about one million hectares, or 50 per cent, of land currently affected by salinity with saltland pastures or salt-tolerant vegetation over the next decade.[78] In 2000, the project was included as part of the *State Salinity Strategy 2000*, and will be implemented with cooperation from Agriculture Western Australia and the Department of Conservation and Land Management.

Various benefits can be derived from productively managed saline land, including improved economic returns for landholders with large areas of saltland, reduced land degradation, local drawdown of saline water tables and reduced flood risk, improved nature conservation, and improved visual and landscape amenity. There is also a potential for the development of new saline agricultural industries, such as saltland pastures, seed harvesting, wood for pulp, fuel-wood, specialist timbers, sequestered carbon, essential oils, organic chemicals, and aquaculture. Some believe that all salt-affected land in the Wheatbelt is capable of some productive and profitable use.[79] Yet, this is likely to be too optimistic an assessment in light of the unknown economics of most of these industries. Most are unlikely to be more than niche industries making relatively small contributions to the overall problem.

One of the most promising of these industries is aquaculture, which has been one of the world's fastest growing food production systems for the past decade, largely due to wild fish harvests having now reached their sustainable limits and the increasing popularity and demand for fish products.[80] Inland saline waters offer a range of opportunities for commercial aquaculture and seaweed production; however, little research and development has occurred in Western Australia for such enterprises.[81] For example, trout can tolerate a wide range of salinities, and therefore provide a productive use for saline water that has been redirected from on-farm drainage works into collection ponds. Furthermore, large amounts of saline water can be removed from the system by evaporation in an environmentally sustainable manner.

Aquaculture offers an opportunity of diversification into a growing market, providing increased farm profitability. At present, Rainbow Trout are the only fish being farmed commercially, but the scale of this industry should be increased to include other species, such as Black Bream.[82] In addition, large-scale harvesting of a range of seaweed species grown in near-stagnant, low-salinity ponds for food and chemicals is already occurring in other parts of the world, particularly in China.[83] When determining the most appropriate use of saline lands and water, it needs to also be recognised that naturally saline wetlands are diverse ecosystems in their own right and have important conservation values.

At a federal level, the National Program for Productive Use and Rehabilitation of Saline Lands provides a forum for the exchange of ideas and research results at regularly held national conferences and workshops. The conference proceedings are a valuable source of information in regard to the most recent developments in the productive management of saltland. At the 1999 National Conference, the need was identified for defining market capability to enable saltland industries to flourish. There is an urgent requirement for assessment of the relative marketability of saline agricultural options. Barrett-Lennard was not aware of any such analysis having ever been done for prospective saline agricultural products.[84] This field of enquiry is especially important as it is the selling of products that generates the revenue stream that provides farmers with the incentive to invest in new agricultural systems.

6 INTEGRATED CATCHMENT MANAGEMENT (ICM)

A strategic approach is essential to the management of salinity as the problem occurs on such a broad scale. To this end, a Natural Resources Management framework policy is proposed in the Salinity Strategy, from which the development and implementation of regional strategic plans will flow. Such an approach treats salinity in the broader context of natural resource management, and may lead to a diminished focus on salinity as a crisis issue in its own right. This is not to say that salinity should not be viewed as inter-related with other aspects of land degradation.

Ideally, salinity management should be addressed in the landscape at the whole-of-catchment level, based on the principle of ecologically sustainable development. For this to occur there needs to be a strengthening of links between land-use planning and catchment planning. To this end, the problem of salinity is best tackled through Integrated Catchment Management. This approach shifts the focus of land management away from the individual farm, district, or sub-catchment levels and towards integrated catchments and regional scales. The federal Inquiry into Catchment Management, completed in 2000 by the

Standing Committee on Environment and Heritage, unanimously endorsed the acceptance of a catchment-based approach to the management of land and water in Australia, and recommended that a National Catchment Authority be established. This position is supported by recent developments in south-eastern Australia, where the Murray–Darling Basin Ministerial Council released in the same year a draft statement of commitment to ICM as a way forward into the future.[85] A similar approach should be considered for the rehabilitation of salt-affected land in the Western Australian Wheatbelt.

Already in the Wheatbelt various government agencies have identified priority catchments (that is, focus catchments and recovery catchments) for more intensive management, including the use of salinity rehabilitation programs. As this structure is currently in place, the notion of adopting ICM on a broader scale has considerable merit. In the first instance, this would require a greater degree of cooperation between relevant government agencies, and between the State Government and local municipalities throughout the Wheatbelt. Agency roles often overlap in areas of natural resource management, which makes a coordinated effort towards the management of salinity even more necessary. A commitment to ICM for the Wheatbelt would require all levels of government, rural communities, landholders, Landcare groups, special-interest groups and indigenous people to work in partnership. Only through a true partnership between government and communities can the difficult choices concerning salinity be made to achieve the desired changes in the landscape. The involvement of rural communities is of particular importance, as any decision on the use and management of natural resources as part of a salinity strategy will also affect the economic and social values of those communities.

In order to move progressively to managing salinity at a catchment scale, it is necessary to strengthen institutional arrangements with-in catchments. This will require catchment management organisations that can be responsible for delivering change with the support of all stakeholders. For these organisations to have the capacity to deliver change, the support of government policy and legislation is essential, along with delegated responsibility and accountability. A key responsibility of these organisations will be the development of catchment strategies and local salinity action plans. These initiatives will then need to be implemented, followed by a process of monitoring, evaluation and reporting to ensure that delivery of on-ground investment.

In 1987, the State Government adopted an ICM policy as a management system for the natural environment, and established the Office of Catchment Management as an umbrella organisation.[86] This important initiative did not have the support of ICM legislation, and as a consequence the role of the Office was weakened and eventually lapsed following the creation of the Water and Rivers Commission in 1995. Conacher and Conacher reported that several subsequent attempts to strengthen the ICM strategy failed.[87] Adequate statutory and institutional backing still does not exist, and strong resistance persists among not only Agriculture WA but also other relevant State agencies. Moreover, Pannell reported difficulties in cooperation between farmers in a catchment.[88] Few farmers appear to be working effectively with their neighbours to address salinity problems collectively. While most farmers perceive salinity as a catchment issue, they still continue to make independent management decisions on their own properties.[89] The State Government's challenge for the future of salinity management in the Wheatbelt is to reaffirm its commitment to ICM policy, supported by appropriate legislation, in line with progress being made in eastern Australia.

CONCLUSION

There is still a lack of certainty about the effectiveness of many of the tools proposed as solutions to the salinity problem. The problem is complex and needs a variety of solutions that can be adopted in the most appropriate combination for each different geographical location. Considerable research effort is still required to evaluate the effectiveness of each tool separately, and in combination with others, to determine the most cost-effective and efficient methods to tackle the problem in different parts of the landscape. For these reasons, some researchers offer little optimism in their prognosis for the future of the salinity-prone areas of the Wheatbelt, based on current levels of understanding and refinement of these options. The undeniable reality may be that viable treatments, from which farmers can generate long-term benefits, are only available for a small proportion of the area where salinity is developing.[90] Support for this view was offered by Lefroy, who asserted that presently there were no solutions for managing salinity that are both biophysically and economically viable for approximately two-thirds of the cleared land in the Wheatbelt.[91] Furthermore, recent studies based on computer modelling of catchments indicate that the likelihood of the majority of the salinity treatment options being adopted is currently low.[92] Results suggest that these options are not well developed, or are not as economically attractive as the current farming systems.

As each locality is different, the relative importance of the mecha- *Variance* nisms leading to salinisation varies from one location to another. Only when the mechanisms at a particular locality have been identified and measured is it possible to design the best combination of remedial measures. This approach requires not only strategic planning and management at the farm level, but also recognition of the importance of ICM in a whole-of-landscape context. In the past, ICM has enjoyed mixed successes due largely to the implicit understanding that all stakeholders in a catchment wish to cooperate in the initiative. In the event that some farmers choose not to join a catchment group, the implementation of Landcare programs for saltland restoration becomes complicated and less effective. Furthermore, the declining population of many rural communities undermines the necessary voluntary labour force required to undertake salinity actions within the framework of ICM. Notwithstanding this problem, the ICM approach is ideally suited as an overarching approach for the implementation of the various tools for salinity management. This will, however, require additional commitment and allocation of resources by all levels of government.

Many of the current tools used in salinity restoration programs are still experimental, and little consideration has been given to the way in which they can be incorporated into new farming systems. Furthermore, the reality may be that viable treatments for salinity are only available for a small proportion of the area where the problem is developing.[93] For this reason, a more concerted effort needs to be made to develop new agricultural systems based on commercial tree crops.

Given that an unlimited pool of funds for controlling and managing salinity does not exist, there is a need to be strategic with the allocation of resources. In response to this constraint, Pannell, Lefroy and McFarlane[94] developed a framework for prioritising government investment in salinity. This framework is based on the principle of 'triage', which recognises that some parts of the Wheatbelt are not practicably saveable, some are saveable with additional incentives from government, and there are those that are either not threatened or are in the process of being saved without additional incentives (for example, commercial tree plantations are providing a solution). Such an approach has the unfortunate implication that some areas and some landholders will miss out on the allocation of strategic funds for salinity rehabilitation. Some areas have already progressed to the point where they are no longer considered to be recoverable with currently available technology, or at reasonable cost.

PART —Ⅳ—

CONCLUSION

'... available information shows a steady
decline in the condition of the environment
and an increase in the pressure humans place
on the environment.'

'The State of the Environment Report',
WA Department of Environmental Protection, 1998

CHAPTER — 8

Towards a Sustainable Future

Evidence is mounting from around Australia that the nation faces a crucial choice: we must either change land management practices substantially, or face the fact that it may be too late to save much of our environment. For a large part of the Wheatbelt, it may already be too late. In fact, many experts are becoming increasingly pessimistic about the ability of governments and the community to make a significant impact on salinity. One recent assessment undertaken for the National Dryland Salinity Program concluded that 'dryland salinity has all the hallmarks of an intractable policy problem'.[1] This conclusion flowed from a judgement that strategies such as better communication with farmers about farming methods tended to be ineffective, while more drastic strategies such as regulating what forms did tended to be practically infeasible. In the event that much of the region does succumb to salinity, the tragedy of the Wheatbelt must serve a larger purpose—to re-inforce some serious questions: What lessons are to be learnt from its degradation by salinity, and how might they be applied in the future? Reflecting on these questions at least offers a chance that future environmental disasters on the scale of salinity can be prevented.

The lessons of the Wheatbelt are for everyone to reflect upon. The key issue is the Euro-Australian attitude to the land which allowed this crisis to unfold. What do we, as a community, need to understand about this relationship in order to change it? In Chapter Three, the appeal of developmentalism was raised as the driving force behind the wholesale clearing of the region. While this concept explains much of the political momentum surrounding the opening of the Wheatbelt area to agriculture, it does not explain how such a policy became so deeply embedded in the social and political structure of Western Australia (and elsewhere in Australia for that matter). To understand these deeper questions, the policy of land clearing in the Wheatbelt needs to be placed in the cultural context of the Western tradition of subordinating nature. A telling illustration of these cultural attitudes can be found in the 1906 dairies of the Italian Consul in Western Australia, Leopoldo Zunni, who wrote that

> it is pleasing to the traveller to observe that almost all the land along the way between Northam and Goomalling is cultivated; whereas, on the section between Perth and Northam, because of the sandy and rocky nature of the soil, there is little to see besides the monotonous bushland. Instead in this area [Northam/ Goomalling] the work of man has completely transformed the landscape. Vast fields of wheat, oats and rye extend as far as the eye can see.[2]

Only by appreciating the depth of this tradition is it possible to explore the extent of cultural change now needed to forge a different relationship with the environment; one based more on harmonisation rather than exploitation and degradation.

Subordinating nature to the needs of humans is one of the most ancient of Western traditions. Yet, at regular intervals it has been revived by new strands of philosophical thought so that the counter idea of humans as guardians of nature has never emerged beyond a minority tradition. Writers such as Ponting,[3] and Thomas,[4] have explained how classical and medieval thought placed humans in a position of dominance over the rest of nature, a view expressed in and given credence by the rise of Christianity. The creation myth in the Bible in Genesis (chapter one) decreed that God created humans as the climax of his previous five days' work and, with divine blessing, humans were granted dominion over the rest of nature. For centuries, this was taken to mean that humans' authority over the natural world was virtually unlimited, a view justifying civilisation as a conquest of nature. In Aristotle's system of thought, for example, man stood at the apex of nature: 'Plants exist to give substance to animals, and animals to give it to men … Accordingly, as nature makes nothing purposeless or in vain, all animals must have been made by nature for the sake of men.'[5]

New waves of philosophical thought refurbished this foundation stone of Western society. The work of seventeenth-century philosophers further entrenched the split between humans and nature. John Locke, the most influential thinker in the development of liberalism, devised the ideas behind the 'right' to private property as one of the fundamental rights possessed by humans. Locke argued that when people mixed their labour with the land, the resulting improvements became the exclusive property of the individual. In terms of the environment, two main consequences flowed from this theory: it justified the claim that society had little or no right in the management of the land and, consequently, it encouraged the view that landowners had no moral obligation to the land itself.[6]

Meanwhile, Francis Bacon advocated a human-centred world view based on the mastery of nature through science. For him,

> knowledge of the world acquired through scientific endeavour was not to be the mere object of contemplation, but should be put to work so that the human race could ultimately assume mastery and control over nature in pursuance of its own interests ... so nature had to be treated as an antagonist and 'bullied' into submission.[7]

Flowing from the belief in the virtues of scientific inquiry, upon which the industrial age was built, was the idea of progress which captured thinkers and popular opinion from the seventeenth century. Based on a wave of optimism about humanity, this idea held that history was a chronicle of improvement in every field, showing humans had unlimited potential. Almost any change became equated with progress, including the quickening pace of environmental exploitation which was viewed 'as perfectly natural and a way of improving a rough, unfinished, natural environment'.[8]

The idea of progress was an even more potent belief when it fused with the emerging capitalist ethic of the eighteenth century. The influential eighteenth-century philosopher of capitalism, Adam Smith, extolled wealth creation as a new national enterprise 'where the flow of goods and services consumed by everyone constitutes the ultimate aim and end of economic life'.[9] In fact, to Smith and the great economists who followed him, the interests of society as a whole were equated with individuals freely competing to create their own wealth.

In this way, the rise to prominence of the discipline of economics added a powerful new element to the way Western societies view the world, and, increasingly, just about every part of the world. Achieving economic growth is the central aim of government policy and the assumption behind this growth is the value system of 'individual consumption'.[10]

Over the past two decades, the resurgence of free-market ideas associated with Adam Smith, and known as the New Right (or neo-liberalism), have added another layer in the response of modern government towards the environment. At the core of this philosophy is the idea that the needs of the environment complement the free market: what is good for business is good for the environment. According to Doyle:

> Due to this rationale, much environmental legislation and national and state-based environmental protection agencies have been gutted in recent times. Furthermore many of these agencies have changed their focus from monitoring industrial excesses to helping business jump through the regulatory hoops.[11]

Most recently, free-market ideas have been the driving force behind the spread of global capitalism characterised by an energy-intensive, export-oriented model of development. The values behind global capitalism are argued by environmentalists to be at odds with ecology because of the encouragement given to economic growth, mass consumption, and large-scale economic activity. Despite rising standards of living in many parts of the world, economic globalisation 'is further distancing humans from an awareness of the environmental consequences of their behaviour'.[12]

There is an important point to be drawn from this 'brief tour' of Western thought on the environment. The attitudes which led both governments and farmers to view the wholesale removal of the natural environment of the Wheatbelt, and to pursue environmentally unsustainable farming practices to the present day, represent a deeply ingrained cultural attitude towards the environment. If as a community we are to learn the lesson of the Wheatbelt, it is to appreciate how our views towards the environment have been shaped, the depth to which these views have taken root and the corresponding difficulty in shifting our cultural attitudes towards nature to reflect a new relationship between economics and environmental values. To date, Ecologically Sustainable Development (ESD) is the only concept around which some degree of political consensus exists to forge this new relationship. The ambiguity of the term was discussed in Chapter One, yet failure to comes to terms with its meaning for policy-makers risks leaving the environment without any framework around which to resolve the inevitable conflicts between proponents of continued growth-at-any-cost and those ecologists opposed to the very concept of growth.

The barriers in the way of realising any meaningful application of ESD principles are considerable. For example, many commentators point to the opposition from well-organised industry groups which either oppose sustainable development in general or at least campaign for less stringent measures. Governments, it is argued, 'will ordinarily be unwilling, indeed politically unable, to jeopardise present and palpable economic advantage to avoid future and uncertain environmental costs'.[13] This was certainly the conclusion of an independent assessment presented to the Commonwealth Government in 1996, in which the Government's policies covering ESD and biodiversity were described as only affecting decision-making in 'the most perfunctory way'.[14] Moreover, there was 'little sign that economic planning takes serious account of the ecological impact of the options available at any time; it is assumed that the first priority is a healthy economy'. A more recent report by the Productivity Commission in 1999 came to a similar conclusion: 'that ecological sustainability has been incorporated into policy in an ad hoc, incomplete and tentative manner'.[15] The success which attended the Howard Government's opposition to legally binding international greenhouse gas emission targets and, indeed, for increased emission levels to apply to Australia, is, perhaps, among the most compelling indicators of this reluctance. It shows the power exerted by the energy industry on government policy and in contravention of public opinion in support of reductions.[16]

Yet, amid this general criticism there are signs of change. The efforts of the State Government to take its biodiversity responsibilities more seriously were noted in Chapter Six. There is also movement in the attitudes of some corporations. The recent release of the Australian Conservation Foundation's *Natural Advantage: A Blueprint for a Sustainable Australia* was supported by BHP, whose Chief Executive, Mr Paul Anderson, explained that the energy industry 'is starting to realise that this is the way forward—no one can hide from responsibility'.[17] The far-reaching nature of the reforms called for in the Blueprint, including the introduction of a carbon tax and widening the powers of government to intervene to protect the environment, illustrates the extent of the cultural shift currently being debated.

At the State level, the struggle to achieve sustainable development is clearly evident from recent State Government reports. A 1990 Discussion Paper prepared by the Select Committee into Land Conservation questioned the extent to which government departments had been able to resolve ESD's conceptual ambiguities. The Committee noted that the meaning of the term 'sustainability' could be interpreted in at least three ways: productivity, stewardship, and community views. Each interpretation involves different objectives for land management and the development of different strategies. The productivity view of sustainability is concerned with maintaining the profitability of agriculture, and economics becomes the primary concern. The stewardship, or ecological, view sees sustainability as an ecological phenomenon, and maintaining the environment becomes the primary factor of concern. The community view of sustainability is concerned with the maintenance of existing rural and regional settlement patterns and the threats to the viability of farming families and country towns become the main concern.[18]

According to the members of the Select Committee, the productive view prevails in Western Australia with the Department of Agriculture encouraging profitable use of the land without diminishing the quality or quantity of land. To this end, landowners may have to 'adopt new practices on the basis of increased long-term profitability'.[19] *The State of the Environment Report*, issued in 1998 by the Western Australian Department of Environmental Protection, contained stern warnings about the continuing steady decline in the quality of the State's environment:

> In general, available information shows a steady decline in the condition of the environment and an increase in the pressure humans place on the environment … The continued decline in the condition of the environment will result in increasing social costs. With few exceptions the social costs are not being accounted for.[20]

The Report goes on to state that there is currently 'no mechanism to examine fundamental questions about the sustainability of our population and consumption patterns', warning that 'some difficult questions need to be debated':

- Are there limits to growth in Western Australia?
- Is there an optimum population size for the State?
- Should we be planning to limit the size of our cities?
- Are we better off managing population growth, consumption levels, or both?
- How will society incorporate full environmental costings and population options into its development decisions?[21]

Such fundamental concerns about sustainable development expressed by a government department underline the extent of the challenges lying ahead. It is not the purpose of this book to discuss these wider issues, but simply to draw out the obvious conclusion that much needs to be done at the community level to ensure that future large-scale environmental problems do not further erode quality of life. The parallels with the Wheatbelt are equally obvious: governments know the dimensions of the potential problems of unsustainable economic practices but are still not able to respond systematically to them. The same cultural attitudes that led to the widespread clearing of the Wheatbelt remain an underlying force, despite the substantial growth in public and political support for environmental principles. As *The State of the Environment Report* explains: 'Given the strong growth ethos in Western Australia these issues [that is, those mentioned immediately above] are difficult issues for some individuals even to contemplate.'[22]

Farmers should be in the forefront of embodying a new environmental ethic. Indeed, as previous chapters have shown, many farmers have drawn from the lessons of the Wheatbelt and embraced considerable changes in their farming practices. However, many have not. Governments and farmer organisations face substantial challenges in convincing those who, for whatever reason, have been unwilling to change. The *State of the Environment Report* provides a summary of these challenges. While noting the 'significant progress' in developing more sustainable farming systems, the Report was still critical of the continuing rate of land degradation through poor farming practices:

Soils are becoming acid more quickly as a result of farming practice. This means applied fertiliser is less effective and crop yields are lower. Soil structure declines, subsoil compaction and water repellent soils are widespread, affecting up to 34 per cent of agricultural land ... herbicide resistance is making it increasingly difficult to control weeds in cropping areas. Weeds pose a threat to the biological diversity of remnant vegetation and conservation reserves ... In pastoral areas, some management practices are ecologically unsustainable. There has been widespread soil erosion and loss of perennial grasses and shrubs. Uncontrolled access of stock has caused damage to critical wildlife habitats and siltation of rivers.[23]

As the Report explains, the traditional view of farming as purely a business is no longer appropriate; seeking improvements in farm profits by increasing crop yields, and animal weight gains is short term because it fails to factor in the long-term effects on the land or the waterways: 'New ways of farming are required which consider these on-site and off-site effects and allow farmers to make a living.'[24]

It is a noteworthy sign of the impact which the concept of sustainability is having that Agriculture WA rates sustainable management as one of its strategic objectives.[25] The key performance targets are worth noting:

– Environmental sustainability criteria for all major farming systems should be established.
– All land of key agricultural significance should be identified for protection in land-use plans.
– An increasing proportion of farmers should have a current business plan.
– Fifty per cent of graduates from agency-sponsored leadership courses should hold influential positions on state and/or national agriculture-related committees or boards.
– At least 75 per cent of farmers should adopt high-water-use farming systems.
– There should be an increasing upward trend in the condition of rangelands and pastoral leases.
– Baseline information should be established and a framework for monitoring and reporting on resource conditions in the agricultural areas should be implemented.
– More than 80 per cent of landholders should be aware of the standards for sustainable land management.

However, the current Director of the Department, Dr Graeme Robertson, is under no illusions about the challenges in achieving sustainable agriculture. Reporting in 1996 on a survey of farmers' views on sustainability, he noted:

> It was somewhat of a shock that many farmers felt that sustainability was not relevant. Despite a decade of debate and discussion on the issue, farmers had the view that sustainability was a pseudonym for conservation and that conservation was something quite different from production. Sustainability was seen to cost money, not produce it.[26]

Moreover, the terms of trade for agriculture are judged by Robertson to be a significant hurdle to the efforts to change farmers' views:

> The evidence suggests that the profitability of agriculture will be a key constraint to achieving a sustainable agricultural system. If the profit outlook for agriculture is low or expected to continue to decline, there is both little incentive or capacity for the industry to invest in resource conserving practices. That is, low net returns to agriculture are placing a very low value on the land resource.

Robertson notes the adverse impact of salinity on sustainability: 'It is clear that current agricultural systems are incompatible with reversing salinity in many areas.' Whether or not he had the Wheatbelt industry in mind in the following comment is unclear, yet it is clearly applicable to it:

> It is unacceptable for any industry to degrade the resource on which it is based. Agriculture must be profitable enough to invest in systems and technology that avoid resource degradation. If it cannot do this it will not have any long-term use of the resource either because the resource condition will decline or the community will withdraw the access.[27]

Government has a special responsibility to consider the lessons of the Wheatbelt. It has to try to resolve some of the challenges outlined throughout this book. Prominent among these is the claim that the salinity crisis represents a weakness in our democratic system of government, because our institutions and political parties failed to act in the long-term public interest. Improving the capacity of government to plan for, and deal with, issues of ecological sustainability must, on the evidence assembled here, be a priority. Part of this process will be the need to integrate science into policy-making more effectively. After all, the separation of these two realms was responsible for the creation of the current crisis in salinity. Integrating science into policy provides a potentially stronger platform to seize the opportunities outlined in Chapter Seven for the creation of new industries in the Wheatbelt with prospects to lessen our reliance on fossil fuels. Such a development would represent a major commitment to placing the overall economy on a more sustainable basis. Yet, the difficulties involved in shifting to ESD cannot be underestimated.

Some of these difficulties have been highlighted in Western Australia by the work of the Legislative Council's Standing Committee on Ecologically Sustainable Development. The establishment of this Committee—its membership is drawn from all political parties represented in Parliament—is, in itself, a positive sign of progress towards a new environmental ethic in government. Broadly, the Committee aims to report on the extent to which Western Australia accords with the concept of ESD as defined in the *National Strategy for Ecologically Sustainable Development*. It can initiate an inquiry into any matter relating to planning or the environment in the State and it is given a special watching brief on the implementation of the Salinity Action Plan. The Committee has already undertaken several inquiries, notably into the forestry and uranium issues.

At a general level, the pressures—both political and personal—involved in the work of the Committee have been described by Committee member, Mr Norm Kelly:

> Conservation groups really wanted us to hammer the Government. But members of the committee are aware of the long-term future of such a committee and we have to be wary about how we

go about our work so that we can establish our credibility. There are limitations on our workloads. Three of our five members are country-based, which makes it difficult to organise meetings outside non-sitting hours. We also have to consider the other committee workloads of members.[28]

The Committee's report into the controversial and complex issue of forestry highlights some of the conceptual difficulties involved in working with ESD principles and the potential impact these can have when applied. The Committee's deliberation on this issue covered two reports running to several hundred pages. It notes at the outset the polarised nature of the debate over forestry in Western Australia:

A number of witnesses endorsed the concept of the multiple use forest, but believed that the current management regime failed to achieve an appropriate balance where different uses were incompatible. Others took the extreme view that harvesting of timber is destructive to the point that it can never be ecologically sustainable.[29]

Within these very different perspectives, the Committee first had to decide what 'sustainability' actually meant when applied to logging practices. The Committee considered three definitions. The first is the lower threshold; that is, sustaining gross volume of wood fibre. The second is a higher threshold—a long-term yield of sawlogs of a consistent quality. The third is ecologically sustainable forest management; that is, 'sustaining the eco-system … [which] requires that not only is the wood harvest sustainable but also that water quality, flora and fauna, soil characteristics and so forth are maintained'.[30]

However, this last approach has not characterised the forestry industry in this State. In fact, the Committee found a history of overcutting from the 1920s until recent times:

Under the 1987 Timber Strategy the cut was supposed to drop back in two stages, in 1990 and 1996. However, the reductions did not occur. On the basis of social and employment considerations, the FMP [Forest Management Plan] postponed the planned decrease to sustainable levels until 2003. History suggests that at that time there will be pressure from industry to maintain the level of over-harvest for a further period, and that the government of the day will be tempted to allow this to occur, justifying the decision as a short term measure to assist the industry.[31]

The Committee was aware that its call for a reduction in cubic metres cut from 490,000 to 300,000 'will significantly affect timber businesses and workers currently relying on the Jarrah resource'.[32] The years of contentious debate about sustainable forestry in Western Australia were partially concluded when the State Labor Party won office in February 2001 on a bold plan to end forestry in 'old growth' forests. However, sustainably managing re-growth forests remains an issue.

This brief 'case study' of ESD and forestry—the first industry in Western Australia to be examined systematically according to these principles—has some important insights into the application of ESD principles to the broader economy. Shifting to a more sustainable economy is an immensely complex task because it is aimed at making ecology and the environment more compatible. As the Standing Committee's report into forestry noted:

> The standard approach in the past has been to regard the financial and employment benefits of development as a legitimate trade-off for a resultant deterioration of the environment. Still today this trade-off is often considered as inevitable.[33]

The challenge—which is of great significance to the salinity crisis—is to develop new models which can deliver on both jobs and the environment; a task which the Committee frankly acknowledges as far more challenging than the traditional approach which is based on locking away relatively small areas of the environment and making available most of the rest to some degree of exploitation. However, as the Chairman of the ESD Committee, Dr Christine Sharp, noted: 'If applied with rigour and imagination ESD can provide environmental protection, employment and resource availability. Everyone uses the term but who is actually making the tough decisions to apply it?'.[34]

Applying the 'tough decisions' is clearly the next stage if the ESD process is to continue to have meaning. Currently, there is no State Government policy on ESD. The challenge for policy, according to Dr Sharp, is to apply ESD principles in the same way that competition policy is applied to all areas of the economy for compliance.[35]

More practically, there is an absence of agreed, specific, on-the-ground outcomes and targets for the sustainable management of natural resources for farm and regional levels. Such indicators 'should be capable of monitoring change in the condition of the natural resource base, other environmental values, non-economic returns, and social well-being'.[36]

While agriculture is one area where the State Government is trying to respond with improved land management practices, there is still the need to examine the ecological sustainability of the cereal and pastoral industries, as well as reviewing what can be achieved to address salinity. In the end ESD will only succeed if the community as whole appreciates the need for a cultural shift in attitudes towards the environment—and not just 'icon' issues such as forestry—and if the political system can respond to the challenge of managing this change.

For this reason, some people believe that a more holistic response should underpin our relationship with nature. One of the earliest and most influential voices among Western writers of an 'ecocentric' perspective was Aldo Leopold, an American forester, and later conservationist and professor, who became concerned about the impact of humans on the land. His 1949 book, *A Sand County Almanac*, soon became a classic text of the conservation movement. Claiming that the environment was important beyond the well-being of humans, Leopold argued for a radical rethinking of our ethical response to nature. Humans, he said, needed to be transformed from conquerors of nature to the status of but one member of the 'biotic' community. Within this community, 'rights' should be extended to birds, soil, waters, plants and animals. His view is most concisely summarised in the following celebrated but controversial statement:

quit thinking about decent land-use as solely an economic problem. Examine each question in terms of what is ethically and
esthetically right, as well as what is economically expedient. A
thing is right when it tends to preserve the integrity, stability, and
beauty of the biotic community. It is wrong when it tends otherwise.[37]

Leopold's book sparked the emergence of an intellectual movement based around 'environmental ethics'. It is a way of thinking which
tries to establish the moral relationship between human beings and their
natural environment. Using established theories about ethics, 'environmental ethics' asks questions such as: What are humans' responsibilities
towards nature?; What rights does nature possess?; What is justice for
the environment?; and What is the common good linking humans and
the environment?[38] Naturally, it is a contentious area.

Advocates of an 'environmental ethics' perspective will see in the
rise of salinity in the Wheatbelt a significant case study of the need for
a renewed commitment to the health of the land as advocated by
Leopold. The absence of such a commitment is the fundamental cause
of its degradation. Moreover, the perspective of environmental ethics is
an important one in considering policy responses to the current salinity crisis: too little attention to such an ethic, in favour of strictly economic outcomes, will see precious biodiversity diminish and some
species lost forever.

Yet, not everyone will agree that ecology and ethics should co-
exist so closely or that we have some special responsibility towards
nature above our own interests. In the case of the Wheatbelt, for example, there may be limits to the capacity of the community to afford to
save all wildlife and people's need for livelihood needs to be considered.

Nevertheless, adding environmental ethics to the equation of our
response to salinity is an important exercise. Salinity is a complex and
multifaceted problem deserving a broadly based response. The lessons
of the Wheatbelt will not have been lost if they help to stimulate thinking on bridging the gap between meeting human needs and protecting
the environment

Appendix: Common and Scientific Names for Plants, Animals and Birds Mentioned in the Text

COMMON NAME	SCIENTIFIC NAME

Plants (native and cultivated)

COMMON NAME	SCIENTIFIC NAME
Acacia	*Acacia spp.*
Balansa Clover	*Trifolium michelianum*
Banksia	*Banksia spp.*
Black Morrel	*Eucalyptus melanoxylon*
Casuarina	*Casuarina spp.*
Christmas Tree	*Nuytsia floribunda*
Cyprus	*Callitris spp.*
Flat-topped Yate	*Eucalyptus occidentalis*
Flooded Gum	*Eucalyptus rudis*
Gimlet	*Eucalyptus salubris*
Hakea	*Hakea spp.*
Jarrah	*Eucalyptus marginata*
Karri	*Eucalyptus diversicolor*
Lucerne	*Medicago sativa*
Maritime Pine	*Pinus pinaster*
Monterey Pine	*Pinus radiata*
Oil Mallee (local examples)	*Eucalyptus plenissima*
	Eucalyptus lissophloia
Pine	*Pinus spp.*
Puccinellia	*Puccinellia ciliata*
Raspberry Jam	*Acacia acuminata*
Red Morrel	*Eucalyptus longicornis*
River Saltbush	*Atriplex amnicola*

COMMON NAME	SCIENTIFIC NAME
Salmon Gum	*Eucalyptus salmonophloia*
Salt Water Couch	*Paspalum vaginatum*
Saltbush	*Atriplex spp.*
Sandalwood	*Santalum spicatum*
Sheoak	*Casuarina spp.*
Sugar Gum	*Eucalyptus cladocalyx*
Swamp Paperbark	*Melaleuca spp.*
Swamp Sheoak	*Casuarina obesa*
Tagasaste	*Chamaecytisus proliferus*
Tall Wheat Grass	*Thinopyrum elongatum*
Tasmanian Blue Gum (or local derivative, Western Blue Gum)	*Eucalyptus globulus*
Wandoo	*Eucalyptus wandoo*
Wheat	*Triticum aestivum*
White Gum (or Salmon White Gum)	*Eucalyptus lane-poolei*
York Gum	*Eucalyptus loxophleba*
Yorrel	*Eucalyptus gracillis*

Animals (including mammals, reptiles, fish and insects)

Boodie	*Bettorgia lesneri grayi*
Black Bream	*Acanthopagrus butcheri*
Brush-tailed Rat Kangaroo (or Woilie/Woylie)	*Bettongia penicillata*
Echidna	*Tachyglossus aculeatus*
Numbat	*Myrmecobius fasciatus*
Rainbow Trout	*Salmo gairdnerii*
Red-tailed Wambenger	*Phascogale calura*
Rock Wallaby (or Black-footed Rock Wallaby)	*Petrogale lateralis*
Sand Monitor	*Varanus gouldii*
Shingle-back Lizard	*Trachydosaurus rugosus*

COMMON NAME	SCIENTIFIC NAME
Tamar Wallaby (or Tamar, Tamma, Tammar)	*Macropus eugenii*
Termite	*Drepanotermes rubriceps*
Western Brush Wallaby (or Brush Kangaroo)	*Macropus irma*
Western Grey Kangaroo (or Mallee Kangaroo, Grey Kangaroo, Great Grey Kangaroo, Black-faced Kangaroo, Sooty Kangaroo, Stinker)	*Macropus fuliginosus*
Western Mouse	*Pseudomys occidentalis*

Birds

Australasian Grebe	*Tachybaptus novaehollandiae*
Australasian Shoveler	*Anas rhynchotis*
Australian Shelduck	*Tadorna tadornoides*
Australian Wood Duck	*Chenonetta jubata*
Black Swan	*Cygnus atratus*
Blue-billed Duck	*Oxyura australis*
Carnaby's Cockatoo (or White-tailed Black Cockatoo)	*Calyptorhynchus latirostris*
Chestnut Teal	*Anas castanea*
Egret	*Egretta spp.*
Eurasian Coot	*Fulica atra*
Freckled Duck	*Stictonetta naevosa*
Great Cormorant	*Phalacrocorax melanoleucos*
Great Crested Grebe	*Podiceps cristatus*
Greenshank	*Tringa nebularia*
Grey Teal	*Anas gibberifrons*
Hoary-headed Grebe	*Poliocephalus poliocephalus*
Honeyeater	*Meliphagidae family*
Little Black Cormorant	*Phalacrocorax sulcirostris*
Little Pied Cormorant	*Phalacrocorax melanoleucos*

COMMON NAME	SCIENTIFIC NAME
Musk Duck	*Biziura lobata*
Oriental Plover	*Charadrius veredus*
Pacific Black Duck	*Anas superciliosa*
Pink-eared Duck	*Malacorhynchus membranaceus*
Rufous Night Heron	*Nycticorax caledonicus*
Sharp-tailed Sandpiper	*Calidris acuminata*
Waterfowl (these incl. ducks)	Anatidae family
White-faced Heron	*Ardea novaehollandiae*
White-necked Heron	*Ardea pacifica*
Yellow-billed Spoonbill	*Platalea flavipes*

Notes

Chapter 1

[1] International Food Policy Research Institute, 2001, p. 1.
[2] Hillel, 1991, p. 81.
[3] Ibid.
[4] McC. Adams, 1981, p. 20.
[5] Ibid.
[6] *The West Australian,* 16 February 2001.
[7] George, 1978, p.115.
[8] Hillel, 1991, p. 138.
[9] Roberts, 1989, p. 23.
[10] *The Australian,* 19 October 2000, Media.
[11] Industry Commission, 1998, p. 53.
[12] *The West Australian,* 5 February 2000.
[13] Beale, 2000.
[14] *The Australian.* 20 December, 1999.
[15] Mackay and Eastburn, 1992, pp. ix-x.
[16] Ibid., p. 225.
[17] Industry Commission, 1998, p. 35.
[18] Australian Conservation Foundation, 2000(a), p. 2.
[19] Conacher, 1986, p. 114.
[20] Pannell, 2000(a), p. 4.
[21] Short and McConnell, 2000, p. 7.
[22] Marsh et al., 2000.
[23] Laurie, 2000, p. 8.

24 *The West Australian,* 16 February, 1999.
25 Burvill, 1979.
26 York Main, B, 1967, pp. 2-3.
27 Bindon and Walley, 1992, p. 30.
28 Ibid.
29 Bindon and Walley, 1992.
30 Pate and McComb, 1981.
31 Barrett and Dent, 1991.
32 York Main,1967.
33 O'Brien, 1991.
34 Colebatch, 1929, p. 230.
35 Burvill, 1979.
36 Taylor, 1990.
37 Department of Environmental Protection, 1996.
38 Burvill, 1979.
39 Ibid.
40 Colebatch, 1929, p. 228.
41 Burvill, 1979.
42 Armstrong, 1985, p. 27.
43 *The Swan River News,* 11 August 1847.
44 Royal Commission, 1917, p. xiv.
45 Linkletter, 1971, p. 55.
46 Laurie, 2000, p. 8.
47 Ibid.
48 Loh and Stokes, 1981.
49 State Salinity Council, 1998, p. 5.
50 Short and McConnell, 2000, p. 50.
51 State Salinity Council, 1998, p. 4.
52 Short and McConnell, 2000, p. 53.
53 Ibid.
54 Pannell and Kington, 1999, p. 11.
55 Virtual Consulting Group et al., 2000, p. 20.
56 The Industry Commission, 1996, p. xii.
57 McKenzie, 1999 p. 41.
58 Pannell, 1999, p. 5.
59 Robertson, 1982, p. 5.
60 Industry Commission, 1998, p. 56.
61 Haworth, 1996 p. 21.
62 Industry Commission, 1998, p. 134.
63 Brasden, 2000, p. 295.
64 Ibid.

[65] Ibid.
[66] State of the Environment Report, 1998, p. 13.
[67] Short and McConnell, 2000, p. 57.
[68] Ibid., p. 52.
[69] McKenzie, 1999 p. 70.
[70] Hammill, 2000.
[71] *The Sunday Times*, 17 October 1999.
[72] Jones and Tonts, 1995.
[73] McCabe, 1998, p. 48.
[74] Ibid., p. 48.
[75] Senate Select Committee, 1970, p. 55.
[76] *Greener Times*, August 1995, p. 14.
[77] Richards, 1984(c), p. 17.
[78] LeFroy, 1999, p. 2
[79] Crowley, 1999, p. 58.
[80] Pannell, 2000(a), p. 5.
[81] Bartle, 2001, p. 118.
[82] Foran and Mardon, 1999, p. 4.
[83] Industry Commission, 1998, Chapter 6.
[84] Martin, 1997, p.129.
[85] State Salinity Council, 2000.

Chapter 2

[1] Water Authority of WA, 1989, p. 1.
[2] Sutton, 1952, p. 3.
[3] Crowley, 1960, p. 156.
[4] Cited in Mercer, 1955, p. 49.
[5] Snooks, 1974, p. 26.
[6] Bolton, 1972, p. 28.
[7] Sutton, 1952, p. 4.
[8] Glynn, 1975, p. 3.
[9] The Agricultural Bank Royal Commission, 1933, p. 25.
[10] Glynn, 1975, p. 18.
[11] Kellow and Niemeyer, 1999.
[12] Layman, 1982, p. 234.
[13] Ibid., p. 20.
[14] Sutton, 1952, p. 4.
[15] Colebatch, 1929, p. 227.
[16] Greble, 1979, p. 47.
[17] Burvill, 1979, p. 3.
[18] Wadham, 1964, p. 117.

19 Glynn, 1975, p. 144.
20 Wood, 1924, p. 35.
21 Cited in Bennett and Macpherson, nd, p. 3.
22 Burvill Interview, Battye Library, File OH 924.
23 Report of Royal Commission on Mallee Belt and Esperance Lands, 1917, p. 5.
24 Ibid., p. 68.
25 Ibid., pp. 86-92.
26 Ibid., p. xiv.
27 Wood, 1924, p. 37.
28 Royal Commission into Agricultural Industries of WA, 1917, p. vi.
29 Ibid., p. xi.
30 Ibid., p. vii.
31 Ibid., p. xi.
32 Agriculture Department, Annual Report, 1925, p. 3.
33 Report of Royal Commission on Group Settlement, 1925, p. iii.
34 Ibid., p. iv.
35 *The Western Mail*, 20 April 1950.
36 Report of Royal Commission on Group Settlement, p. 10.
37 Ibid, p. 12.
38 Ibid., p. 10.
39 Snooks, 1974, p. 24.
40 The Agricultural Bank Royal Commission, 1933, p. 1.
41 Ibid., p. 18.
42 Ibid., p. 2.
43 Ibid., p. 10.
44 Ibid., p. 17.
45 Ibid., p. 14.
46 Ibid., p. 22.
47 Forests Department Annual Report, 1920, p. 3.
48 Ibid., 1925, p. 10.
49 Ibid., p. 9.
50 Burvill Interview, Battye Library, File OH 924.
51 Sutton, 1952, p. 21.
52 Ibid.
53 Sutton, 1952, p. 21.
54 Ibid, pp. 16-17.
55 Agricultural Bank Royal Commission, 1933, p. 98.
56 Ibid., p. 105.
57 Ibid., p. 115.
58 Ibid., p. 123.
59 Ibid., p. 131.

60 Transcript, Interview G.H. Burvill, 19 August 1981, p. 4, (Burvill Papers) in possession of Dr David Bennett.
61 Teakle, 1939, p. 205.
62 Ibid., p. 207
63 Teakle, 1938, p. 437.
64 Cited in Bolton, 1972, p. 70.
65 Ibid., p. 71.
66 Ibid.
67 *The West Australian*, 5 May 1936.
68 Transcript G.H. Burvill, Interview, 19 August 1981, p. 6. (Burvill Papers).
69 *The West Australian*, 5 May 1936.
70 Annual Report of the Department of Agriculture, 1946, p. 45.
71 *The Western Mail*, 23 March 1950.
72 Ibid.
73 Rural Reconstruction Commission, 1944, p. 22.
74 Ibid., p. 8.
75 Ibid., p. 15.
76 Ibid., p. 7.
77 Ibid., p. 31.
78 Annual Report of the Department of Agriculture, 1946, p. 3.
79 Whitwell and Sydenham, 1991, p. 135.
80 Twigg, nd, p. 5.
81 Ibid., p. 5.
82 Shier, 1962, p. 701.
83 *Hansard*, 1965, Vol. 167, p. 1659.
84 Transcript, G.H. Burvill, op cit., p. 8.
85 Annual Report of the Land Settlement Board, 1949, p. 24.
86 Ibid,. 1950, p. 22.
87 Industries Assistance Commission, 1975, pp. ii, 6.
88 Parliamentary Debates *(PD)*, Assembly, 1965, Vol. 167, pp. 1567-1677.
89 Ibid., pp, 1656, 1661.
90 Land Settlement Board, Annual Report, 1951, p. 21.
91 Ibid., p. 24.
92 Ibid., p. 24.
93 *The Western Mail*, 18 May 1950.
94 Land Settlement Board, Annual Report, 1951, p. 25.
95 Ibid.
96 *The Western Mail*, 1 November 1951.
97 Ibid., 15 November 1951.
98 Interview, Colin Nicholl, November 2000.
99 Land Settlement Board, Annual Report, 1952, p. 32.

[100] Reflections of Colin Cameron, in possession of Mr Keith Bradbury, Albany.

[101] Cited in *The Western Farmer*, 7 October 1982.

[102] Ayris, 1989.

[103] *The West Australian,* 29 May 1954.

[104] Land Settlement Board, Annual Report, 1951, p. 28.

[105] Jasper, 1984, p. 8.

[106] Ibid., p. 9.

[107] Ibid.

[108] Twigg, nd, p. 9.

[109] Grainger, 1983, p. 52.

[110] Oliver, 1983, p. 44.

[111] First Report of the Committee Appointed to Investigate the Salt Land Problems in the Lake Grace, Newdegate and Pingrup Districts, Burvill Papers, pp. 221-222.

[112] Burvill, 1950, p. 174.

[113] Burvill, 1945, p. 90.

[114] *The Western Mail,* 1 June 1950.

[115] Ibid., 12 July 1951.

[116] Ibid., 25 May 1950.

[117] Ibid., 20 April 1950.

[118] Land Settlement Board, Annual Report, 1951, p. 22.

[119] Reflections of Colin Cameron, op. cit.

[120] Transcript, G.H. Burvill, op. cit., p. 12.

[121] Department of Agriculture, 1949, p. 3.

[122] Ibid., 1956, p. 3.

[123] *PD,* Assembly, 1954, Vol. 1, pp. 514-515.

[124] Cited in Bennett and Macpherson, nd, p. 11.

[125] Ibid.

[126] Sandford, 1955, p. 53.

[127] Transcript C.V. Malcolm, 23 October 1981, in possession of Dr David Bennett.

[128] *PD,* Assembly, 1965, Vol. 167, p. 1656.

[129] *The West Australian* 9,10 June 1966.

[130] Ibid., 9 June 1966.

[131] Public Works Department, 1951, p. 2.

[132] Public Works Department., 1963, Appendix 2, pp. 2-3.

[133] Letter from D.C. Munro, 21 December 1961, in possession of C.V. Malcolm, Denmark.

[134] *PD,* Assembly, 1967, Vol. 176, p. 13.

[135] Burvill papers, op. cit.

[136] Interview with Bill Benson, 22 March 1982, in possession of Dr David Bennett.

137 Salt Land Advisory Committee, Burvill Papers.
138 Ibid.
139 Bennett and Macpherson, nd, p. 3.
140 Murphy, 1999, p. 3.

Chapter 3

1 Hughes, 1991, p. 3.
2 Men of the Trees, active in the fight against salinity and land degradation, was formed in Western Australia in 1979.
3 Rundle, 1997(b), p. 14.
4 *The West Australian,* 8 March 1970.
5 Ibid., 13 February 1970.
6 Rundle, 1997, p. 14.
7 Churchwood, 1991, p. 36.
8 Ibid., pp. 34-36.
9 Main, 1991, p. 19.
10 Ibid.
11 McKinnon, 1991, p. 26.
12 Forrest, 1979, p. 20.
13 Interview with Keith Bradby, February 2001.
14 Main, 1991, p. 19..
15 Parliamentary Debates (*PD).*, Assembly, 27 October 1970, p. 1540.
16 Ibid., p. 1540.
17 *PD*, Assembly, 27 October 1971, p. 1540.
18 Ibid., 3 November 1970, p. 1784.
19 Chittleborough, 1991, p. 154.
20 Ibid., p. 154.
21 *PD*, 23 September 1971, p. 1739.
22 *PD*, Assembly, 23 September 1971, p. 1739.
23 O'Brien, 1991, p. 6.
24 Ibid.
25 Main, 1991, pp. 21-2.
26 Ibid.
27 Ibid., p. 22.
28 Ibid.
29 Kellow and Niemeyer, 1999, p. 213, and Penrose, 1981, p. 93.
30 Court, 1991, p. 27.
31 *The West Australian*, 17 March 1976.
32 EPA, Annual Report, 1977/78, p. 5.
33 Porter, 1991, p. 57.
34 Main, 1991, p. 21.

35 Readhead, 1991, p. 3.
36 Churchwood, 1991, p. 39.
37 Ibid., p. 40.
38 Environmental Protection Authority, Annual Report, 1972, p. 5.
39 Chittleborough, 1991, p. 155.
40 Ibid.
41 Interview, Bill Benson, in possession of Dr David Bennett.
42 *Collie Mail*, 10 June 1971.
43 *Sunday Times*, 21 October 1973.
44 *The West Australian*, 14 March 1975.
45 Ibid,, 12 February 1975.
46 Ibid., 22 July 1978.
47 *The Countryman*, 24 July 1978.
48 *The West Australian*, 12 July 1978.
49 Ibid.
50 *The West Australian*, 13 July 1978.
51 Ibid., 19 July 1978.
52 *The Countryman*, 24 July 1978.
53 Ibid.
54 Ibid.
55 *The West Australian*, 22 July 1978.
56 *Western Farmer and Grazier*, 11 November 1979.
57 Ibid.
58 *The West Australian*, 9 March 1979.
59 *Western Farmer and Grazier*, 3 June 1983.
60 Ibid., 18 April 1982.
61 Goss, 1983, p. 36.
62 Ibid., p. 37.
63 *Farmers Weekly*, 27 October 1979.
64 Transcript of ABC TV's *Nationwide* program, 22 July 1982.
65 *Western Farmer*, 1 February 1979.
66 Friends of the Earth, 1983.
67 *The Countryman*, 3 February 1983.
68 1988, p. 100.
69 Ibid.
70 *Elders Weekly*, 21 October 1982, p. 57.
71 *Esperance Express*, 26 September 1981.
72 Ibid., 25 November 1981.
73 *Western Farmer and Grazier*, 22 October 1981.
74 *The Countryman*, 15 October 1981.
75 Ibid., 10 September 1981.
76 *The Australian I, 28 April, 1982.*

77 Transcript ABC TV's *Nationwide*, 26 July 1982.

78 Ibid., 30 June 1982.

79 Scholz and Smolinski, 1996.

80 *Esperance Express*, 2 September 1981.

81 Conacher and Conacher, 2000, p. 62.

82 Legislative Council Select Committee on Salinity, Transcript of Evidence, 1988, p. 2.

83 Ibid.

84 Ibid., pp. 63-64.

85 Whittington, 1975, p. 1.

86 Macpherson and Bennett, nd, p. 25.

87 *The West Australian*, 20 November 1978.

88 *The Countryman*, 8 January 1976.

89 *The Daily News*, 29 October 1981.

90 Conacher and Conacher, 2000, p. 75.

91 Ibid., p. 76.

92 *Daily News*, 29 October 1981.

93 *The Countryman*, 23 November 1978.

94 *Daily News*, 29 October 1981.

95 Interview, Associate Professor Arthur Conacher, November 2000.

96 Department of Agriculture, Archive Acc. No. 3515, Box 2, No. 0004, p. 154.

97 Letter dated 18 June 1985, in the Whittington papers, in possession of the Whittington family.

98 *Farmer and Grazier*, 17 August 1978.

99 Letters dated 18 August 4, December 1981, contained in the Whittington papers in possession of the Whittington family.

100 *The West Australian*, 20 November 1978.

101 *The Farmer and Grazier*, 7 September, 1978.

102 Interview, Colin Nicholl, November 2000.

103 Letter, C.V. Malcolm, 2 August 1977, in possession of C.V. Malcolm, Denmark.

104 The Salt Problem—Background Notes on a Controversy, Agricultural Department Memo, in possession of C.V. Malcolm, Denmark.

105 Duff, 1980, p. 19.

106 Conacher, 1979, p. 41.

107 Duff, 1980, p. 19

108 *Western Farmer and Grazier*, 11 May 1979.

109 Select Committee, 1988(a), p. 24.

110 Richards, 1984(b), p. 17.

111 Department of Agriculture Legislation, Soils, Acc. No. 3515, No. 4, Vol. 1, p. 30.

112 Ibid., p. 31.

[113] Ibid., p. 30.
[114] Ibid., p. 22.
[115] Ibid., p. 26.
[116] Ibid., p. 58.
[117] Environmental Protection Authority, Annual Report, 1980/1981, p. 14.
[118] *PD*, Assembly, 20 April 1982, p. 816.
[119] Environmental Protection Authority Annual Report, 1980/1981, p. 14.
[120] *PD*, Assembly, 5 May 1982, p. 1407.
[121] Ibid., Council, 12 May 1982, p. 1660.
[122] Ibid., Assembly, 6 May 1982, p. 1505.
[123] Ibid., Assembly, 11 May 1982, p. 1597.
[124] Ibid., 5 May 1982, p. 1407.
[125] Robertson, 1988, pp. 91-92.
[126] Johnson, 1991, p. 93.
[127] K. Bradby, Interview, March 2001.
[128] Cited in Chittleborough, 1991, p. 156.
[129] Ibid.
[130] Ibid.
[131] Kellow and Niemeyer, 1999, p. 213.
[132] Chittleborough, ibid., p. 157.
[133] Ibid., p. 158.
[134] EPA, Annual Report, 1986-87, p. 5.
[135] Chittleborough, 1991, p. 157.
[136] Ibid., p. 156.
[137] Preface, Chittleborough and Keating, 1987, p. iv.
[138] Ibid.
[139] Newby, 1983, p.45.
[140] Interview, Keith Bradby, February 2001.
[141] Richards, 1984, p. 19.
[142] Ibid., p. 17.
[143] Bradby, 1984, p. 34.
[144] Working Party Assisting the Agricultural Land Release Review Committee, 1985, p. 82.
[145] Select Committee on Financial Hardship in the Rural Sector, 1984, p. 64.
[146] Select Committee on Salinity, 1988(a), p. iv.
[147] Ibid., p. ii.
[148] Ibid., p. 53.
[149] Dr G. Robertson, Transcript of evidence, 14 April 1988.
[150] Select Committee on Salinity, 1988(a), p. 45.
[151] Letter dated 27 August 1988, contained in Whittington papers, in possession of the Whittington family.
[152] Select Committee on Salinity, 1988(a), p. 37.

153 Select Committee on Land Conservation, 1991, p. 150.
154 Ibid., p. 10.
155 Ibid., p. 45.
156 Ibid., p. 21.
157 Ibid., p. 81.
158 Ibid., p. 111.
159 Select Committee on the Right to Farm, 1991, p. 25.
160 Ibid., p. 29.
161 O'Connor, 1991, p. 62.
162 *The West Australian*, 1989.
163 O'Connor, 1991, p. 62.

Chapter 4

1 Crowley and Walker, 1999, p. 4.
2 *The West Australian*, 22 November 1995.
3 Figure supplied by the Environmental Protection Authority.
4 Interview, Harvey Morrell, February 2000.
5 Curtis, Keane, DeLacy, 1993, p. 2.
6 Ibid., p. 1.
7 Ibid., p. 7.
8 *The West Australian*, 3 April 1995.
9 Curtis, Keene and DeLacy, 1993, p. 9.
10 *The West Australian*, 3 April, 1995, p. 4.
11 Ibid., 20 March 1995, p. 14.
12 Interview, Marty Ladyman, May 2000.
13 Report of the House of Representatives Standing Committee on Environment and Heritage, 2000, p. 65.
14 *The West Australian,* 21 March 1995, p. 14.
15 McKenzie, 1999, p. 41.
16 Curtis, Keane, and DeLacy, 1993, p. 7
17 Report Australian Bureau of Agricultural and Resource Economics, 1998, p. 6.
18 *The West Australian*, 1 September 1995, p. 14.
19 Ibid., 28 January 1997.
20 Interview, Marty Ladyman, May 2000.
21 Morrisey, 1999, p. 25.
22 *The West Australian*, 5, 6 January 1994.
23 Ibid., 8 January 1994.
24 Ibid., 11 November 1996.
25 Ibid.
26 Ibid., 16 February 1996.
27 Interview, Keith Bradby, June, 2000.

28 *The West Australian*, 17 November 1999.

29 Ibid., 24 December 1999, p. 12.

30 *The West Australian*, 10 July 2000.

31 Ibid., 2 March 2001.

32 *The West Australian*, 2 March, 2001.

33 *Sunday Times*, 4 March 2001.

34 *The Australian*, 8 March 2001.

35 Liberal Party WA, 1993, p. 68.

36 Interview, Phillip Pendal, 16 October 2000.

37 *The West Australian*, 22 November 1995.

38 Ibid., 23 November 1995.

39 Ibid., 21 December 1995.

40 Ibid., 5 February 2000.

41 Ibid., 18 February 2000.

42 Ibid., 1 March 2000.

43 Ibid.

44 Ibid.

45 Ibid., 12 November 1996.

46 Ibid.

47 Pendal and Constable, 2000.

48 Ibid.

49 State Salinity Council, 1998, p. xiv.

50 Interviews with Alex Campbell and Colin Nicholl, November 2000.

51 Pannell, 2000(b), p. 1.

52 Ibid., 2000/01, p. 1.

53 *The Weekend Australian*, 18-19 March, 2000.

54 Letter to the editor from J.P. Cunneen, *The West Australian*, 6 December 2000.

55 State Salinity Strategy, 2000, p. 26.

56 Interview, Marty Ladyman, May 2000.

57 Pannell, 1997, p. 1.

58 Toyne and Farley, 2000.

59 Brasden, 2000, p. 282.

60 Salinity Forum Inc., 2000, p. 3.

61 State Salinity Council, 1998, p. 11.

62 Ibid., p. xv.

63 *The West Australian*, 23 May 1997.

64 Ibid., 11 February 1999.

65 'National Heritage Trust Review Exposes Serious Flaws'. In *Environment Business*, February 2000, p. 1.

66 Report of the House of Representatives Standing Committee on Environment and Heritage, 2000, p. 77.

67 Ibid.
68 'Our Vital Resources. A National Action Plan for Salinity and Water Quality in Australia', p. 2.
69 Brenchley, 2001.
70 House of Representatives Standing Committee on Environment and Heritage, 2000.
71 *The West Australian*, 27 February 2001.
72 Ibid.
73 *The Australian*, 12 July 2000.

Chapter 5

1 According to the Katanning Salinity Management Strategy (KSMS 1999, p. 3), this estimation varies considerably. Some sources suggest that as many as 20,000 people rely on the town for services and infrastructure.
2 *Great Southern Herald*, 6 December, 1998.
3 *Great Southern Herald*, 8 October, 1997.
4 Since 1974 Muslim men and women and their families have been coming to Katanning from Christmas Island to work in the abattoir (Bignell 1981, p. 309).
5 Bignell, 1981.
6 It is interesting to note that one of the locations considered for the town site was the top of a nearby hill. However, because the trains were unable to stop and unload on a slope, the town of Katanning was finally located on the valley floor. (Ainslie Evans, April 2001, pers. comm.)
7 Bignell, 1981, p. 75.
8 Ibid., p. 89.
9 Ibid., p.102.
10 Read, 1988, pp. 2-3.
11 Bignell, 1981, p. 308.
12 KSMS, 1999, p. 2.
13 Ibid.
14 Ibid.
15 Lynne Coleman, June 2000, pers. comm.
16 Ainslie Evans, June 2000, pers. comm.
17 John Blythe, June 2000, pers. comm.
18 Fly-like insects whose larva feed on the leaves of trees.
19 *Great Southern Herald*, 4 March, 1998.
20 Quoted in Dodds, 1997, p. 2.
21 The Whittington Interceptor Salt Affected Land Treatment Society was established in Quairading in 1978. See Chapter 3.
22 Unfortunately, examples of farmers situated high in the landscape who are undertaking extensive actions to prevent the increase of salinity on their

properties, such as the Rundles, are rare, while examples of farms located in flatter parts of the landscape and suffering severe salinity-related degradation, such as that of the Dixons, are a lot more common. (Margaret Scott, March 2001, pers. comm.)

23 Soil salinity becomes a problem when the underground water table is less than 2 metres from the surface.

24 The Rural Towns Program, initiated by Agriculture Western Australia, is part of the State Government's 1997 Salinity Action Plan. Towns selected to participate are required to contribute funds equal to those that they receive through the Program (*Great Southern Herald*, 15 March, 2000).

25 Groundwater is discharged at the bottom of the catchment and recharged in the higher parts of the catchment. The valley floor, where the town of Katanning is located, is both a discharge and a recharge zone, meaning that while surface water is draining into the water table here, underground water is seeping out onto the surface at the same time (KSMS, 1999, p. 7).

26 KSMS, 1999, p. 2.

27 Ibid.

28 Ibid., p. 6.

29 Ibid., p. 8.

30 Ibid., p. 12.

31 Ibid., pp.12-16.

32 In 1997/1998 financial year, Katanning imported 902 megalitres of Water Corporation scheme water (KSMS, 1999, p. 5); estimates indicate that 50 per cent of this water was used for watering lawns and gardens (p. 6).

33 KSMS, 1999, p. 12.

34 Ibid., p. 16.

35 In April 2001 the possibility of building a desalinisation plant in Katanning was also being discussed subject to economic viability. (Norman Reed, April 2001, pers. comm.)

36 KSMS, pp. 18-26.

37 Kate Jefferies, June 2000, pers. comm.

38 Lynne Coleman, the President of the Katanning Land Conservation District Committee in 2000, also emphasised the importance of individual farm plans as pre-requisites for larger scale catchment plans. She pointed out that many farmers couldn't afford to hire consultants to prepare individual farm plans to help them address salinity problems on their properties and few had the technical knowledge necessary to do it themselves (June 2000, pers. comm.).

39 Agriculture WA ran a one-day seminar in Katanning, in March 2001, on basic groundwater hydrology. What would have otherwise been an excellent opportunity for local farmers to increase their understanding of hydrology, and thus salinity, was inaccessible to most because of the $220 registration cost. (Margaret Scott, March 2001, pers. comm.)

40 Pride and shame are also factors that need to be considered in developing culturally appropriate strategies for information transfer. Many farmers may not feel comfortable asking questions in a group situation. They may feel that to do so would indicate weakness or ignorance in the eyes of their neighbours and peers. For some farmers, such feelings could also be linked to the fact that they left school at an early age to work on their parents' properties.

41 This Landcare worker also described one new farming practice that had an unusually rapid uptake amongst farmers in the area in the mid-1990s, namely the no-tillage seeding system. Others suggested that the success of this particular technology was due to its immediate and beneficial economic impact.

42 Jill Richardson, September 2000, pers. comm.

43 This is a criticism that many of the interviewees in Katanning made of urban-based bureaucrats and politicians. They reported feeling misunderstood and marginalised by government departments and officials, in Perth or in Canberra, whom they perceive as being entirely removed from the realities of day-to-day rural life.

44 Jill Richardson, September 2000, pers. comm.

45 This supports Dr Chapman's observation that mental health issues are an especially taboo area of men's health.

46 Rob White, September, 2000, pers. comm.

47 It is important to note that Landcare programs and the Rural Towns Program have actively sought to involve all Katanning school children in environmental work. This has included monitoring water quality in Katanning Creek and growing and planting trees around the town site and on surrounding farms. See for example articles in the *Great Southern Herald*, 11 June, 23 July, 23 and 20 August, 1997.

48 Dr Ralph Chapman, September, 2000, pers. comm.

49 Douglas Cherry, June 2000, pers. comm.

50 Norman Reed, June 2000, pers. comm.

51 Jill Richardson, September 2000, pers.comm.

52 The water table under Prosser Park was only 40 centimetres from the surface before rehabilitation work was undertaken. In some other parts of the town the water table is actually at surface level.

53 First World War Australian and New Zealand Army Corps. Anzac Day is an annual celebration of Australian involvement in international military conflicts.It is equivalent, if not superior, to Australia Day in its national significance.

54 *Great Southern Herald*, 30 April, 1997.

55 One resident also suggested that the Shire's decision to rehabilitate Prosser Park may have been related to its attempts to beautify Katanning in order to increase its tourist appeal.

[56] 'The purpose of the Katanning Community Charrette was to help the citizens, business operators, civic leaders, town and Shire to 'rediscover and more fully understand the community of Katanning; develop short-term goals and objectives and help visualise them; utilise a citizen-based input process; develop specific recommendations for projects, policies and programs; and educate and involve members of the community and visiting planning professionals in the planning process.' (Katanning Community Charrette Handbook, 1997, p. 5). Given these goals, and given the potential extent of the salinity problem, the relative lack of focus on addressing environmental damage in these documents seems remarkable.

[57] Katanning Community Charrette Handbook (KCCH), 1997, p. 36.

[58] Peddie and Kins 1999, p. 13.

[59] Ibid., pp. 11-13.

[60] Trigger, 1996, 1999.

[61] For further discussion of the popularity of European gardens in Australian settings see Cerwonka (1998), Seddon (1995), especially Chapter 19, and Morton and Smith (1999).

[62] Some residents also suggested that one of the noticeable impacts of salinity on the community was the depressing effect of living in a landscape that was visually degraded, where one was constantly confronted with the presence of dead trees and barren salt scalds.

[63] Katanning resident, September 2000, pers. comm.

[64] Margaret Scott, September, 2000, pers. comm.

[65] These agencies are also major employers in the town.

[66] Thirty per cent of this landscape has already been degraded and recent biological surveys indicate that about 450 plant species are in the process of becoming extinct (Bruce Bone, June 2000, pers. comm.).

[67] Agriculture Western Australia, 2000.

[68] In fact, some Landcare workers reported that they had experienced resistance from the Shire Council when they attempted to follow up on some of the actions listed in the KSMS.

[69] Less than 10 per cent of ratepayers paid the voluntary levy in 1997 (*Great Southern Herald*, 15 October, 1997).

[70] *Great Southern Herald*, 4 March,1998.

[71] One Landcare worker emphasised the importance of the Shire taking a proactive approach in terms of lobbying for funding from State and Federal governments.

[72] One Landcare worker commented that while some of the agencies sent representatives to LCDC meetings on a regular basis, others rarely participated. She felt that directives for agency representatives to participate in community Landcare needed to come from the top of the bureaucratic

hierarchy, rather than from regional managers, to ensure that factors such as personality clashes and individual priorities did not interfere with actions and processes undertaken in the interests of the larger community.

73 *Great Southern Herald*, 3 September, 1997.

74 When combined with the funds contributed by the local community, the total amount spent on Landcare in Katanning during this period was over $6 million.

75 Several Landcare workers emphasised the importance of this kind of recognition and celebration for maintaining morale amongst Landcare workers, most of whom were involved on a voluntary basis.

76 *Great Southern Herald*, 25 March, 1998.

77 Gardner, 2000, p.11. Landcare workers pointed out, however, that very few townspeople visited the centre. Almost all of its clients were farmers and others involved in agriculture.

78 Margaret Scott, September 2000, pers. comm.

79 Neale Bradford, June 2000, pers. comm.

80 With this exception, the RTP has resisted funding the employment of officers to coordinate salinity management strategies within individual towns. The implication is that this work can be done by people already employed by the Shire or the LCDC. In many cases this is an unrealistic assumption given that those individuals are already likely to have full-time workloads.

81 One government employee interviewed discussed the problems of 'burnout' volunteers often encountered. He believed the capacity of voluntarism in natural resource management had already been reached in June 2000.

82 Landcare worker, September 2000, pers. comm.

83 Several people mentioned the tax deductions available to farmers who spent money on Landcare work. Most of them believed that these deductions were of little or no benefit to farmers on very low incomes. A report in *The Countryman* on 10 July, 1997, claimed otherwise; 'The new incentives, which took effect from 1 July, 1997, mean low-income farmers implementing Landcare work will receive taxation benefits'. On 20 May, 1998, the *Great Southern Herald* carried an article entitled 'Landcare rebate "no help" to majority' which recorded the WA Farmers' Federation as asserting that '[f]armers in the Great Southern will have little incentive to continue Landcare work despite the announcement of a Landcare tax rebate in last week's Federal budget'. According to Neil O'Keefe, the Opposition spokesman for primary industries, the rebate would 'only [be] available to those whose incomes are so low that they probably have no money to spend on [Landcare]'. One farmer in Katanning suggested that this situation was part of a pattern in which farmers often discovered on close examination, due to unrealistic criteria, that they were ineligible to apply for many of the rebates that the Government supposedly offered them.

84 In 1997 Wendy Craik, the executive director of the National Farmers Federation was reported as saying that Australian farmers were spending close to $300 million per year on 'protecting and rehabilitating the rural environment—an average of around $2,500 per farmer from their own pockets' (*The Countryman*, 10 July, 1997). Katanning compares impressively with this national estimate.

85 Jenny Gardner, September 2000, pers. comm.

86 As Jenny Gardner pointed out in January 2001, farmers in some of the areas in Western Australia that are most badly affected by salinity, and hence most in need of funding, no longer have any money to match against grant dollars, despite their willingness to undertake Landcare work.

87 Katanning resident, September, 2000, pers. comm.

Chapter 6

1 Myers et al., 2000.
2 Lambert et al., 1995.
3 Myers et al., 2000.
4 Bell and Froend, 1990.
5 Riggert, 1977.
6 Taylor, 1990, p. 42.
7 Commonwealth of Australia, 1998(a).
8 Turner et al., 1994.
9 Kohen, 1997.
10 Government of Western Australia, 2000.
11 Dovers, 2000, p. 38.
12 Fitzpatrick, 1958.
13 Austin, 1855.
14 Environmental Protection Authority, 1999.
15 York Main, 1967.
16 Leake, 1951(a).
17 Leake, 1951(b).
18 Leake, 1951(a).
19 Taylor, 1990.
20 Department of Environmental Protection, 1998.
21 Ibid.
22 Taylor, 1990.
23 Ibid.
24 Mollemans, 1992, p. 15.
25 Ibid., p. 3.
26 Department of Conservation and Land Management, 1999, p. 11.
27 Newbey, 1999.

28 Froend and McComb, 1991.
29 During the study group's June 2000 public seminar the following sites were announced as likely choices for recovery catchments: Lake Warden System, Lake Toolibin (one of only a few freshwater wetlands left in the Wheatbelt), Lake Muir-Unicup System, Lake Bryde System, Northern Braided Saline Drainage Line, Drummond Nature Reserve, Eastern Saline System, Wandoo Valley System, Southern Riverine System, and possibly another recovery catchment yet to be decided. These Biological Recovery Catchments will complement the twenty-two Agriculture WA Focus Catchments (including twenty-nine country towns) and the Potable Water Supply Recovery Catchments identified by the Water and Rivers Commission.
30 Water Authority of Western Australia, 1987, p. 1.
31 Halse, 1987.
32 Northern Arthur River Wetlands Committee, 1987.
33 Hearn, 1988.
34 Water Authority of Western Australia, 1987, p. 8.
35 Halse,1987.
36 Ibid.
37 Ibid.
38 Bell and Froend, 1990.
39 Blackley et al., 1996.
40 Information supplied by Dr Richard George, Agriculture WA.
41 George et al., 2000.
42 Information supplied by CALM officer, Ken Wallace, Narrogin District.
43 Conacher and Conacher, 2000.
44 Commonwealth of Australia, 1996.
45 Ibid., p. 8.
46 Ibid., p. 5.
47 Lunn, 1999.
48 Recher,1999.
49 Davis, 1994.
50 Western Australian Environmental Protection Authority, 1993.
51 Pittock et al., 1996.
52 Environment Australia, 1997.
53 Bunn et al., 1997.
54 Williams, 1998.
55 Conacher and Conacher, 2000.
56 Lyster, 1985.
57 Conacher and Conacher, 2000.
58 Pittock, et al., 1996.
59 Halse, 1987.

[60] Jaensch et al., 1988.
[61] Blyth, 1998.
[62] Australia and New Zealand Environment and Conservation Council, 2000, p. 28.
[63] Ibid.
[64] Environment Australia/Australian Local Government Association, 2000.

Chapter 7

[1] Conacher and Conacher, 2000.
[2] George, Nulsen, Ferdowsian and Raper, 1999.
[3] Pannell, 1997, p. 5.
[4] See Conacher and Conacher, 2000 for a summary of research.
[5] McFarlane and George, 1992.
[6] George, Clarke and Hatton, 2000, p. 2.
[7] George, Nulsen, Ferdowsian and Raper, 1999.
[8] Pannell, 2000(b), p. 2.
[9] White et al., 2001.
[10] State Salinity Council, 2000.
[11] Lefroy, Hobbs, and Atkins, 1991.
[12] Ibid.
[13] Commonwealth of Australia(b), 1998(b).
[14] Francis, J., 1998.
[15] Francis, P., 1998.
[16] Saltland Pastures Association, 2000.
[17] Borough and Burke, 1998.
[18] Borough, Burke and Bennett, 1998.
[19] Shea, 1999. Dr Syd Shea, upon his resignation as the influential Head of the Department of Conservation and Land Management, had a role as key Salinity Adviser (Consultant) to the Coalition Government.
[20] Pannell, 1998, p. 2.
[21] State Salinity Council, 2000, p. 45.
[22] Ibid., p. 46.
[23] Environmental Protection Authority, 1999, p. 7.
[24] Glanznig, 1999.
[25] Sherwin, 2000, p. 8.
[26] Native Vegetation Working Group, 2000.
[27] York Main, 1967.
[28] Government of Australia, 1999.
[29] Strawbridge, 1999.
[30] Bartle, 2001, p. 119.
[31] Sustainable Land Management Technical Panel, 1999.

32 Conacher and Conacher, 2000.
33 Harper et al., 2000
34 Foran and Mardon, 1999, p. 9.
35 Ibid., p. 19.
36 State Salinity Council, 2000, p. 38.
37 Ibid., p. 39.
38 Pannell, 2000(b), p. 3.
39 Pannell, 1999, p. 2.
40 Interview with Dr Richard George, Department of Agriculture hydrologist.
41 Pannell, 1997, p. 1.
42 Pannell, 1999, p. 7.
43 Anon, 2001, pp. 1-2.
44 Brophy, 2001.
45 Conacher and Conacher, 2000, p. 70.
46 Hatton, Clarke, George, and Reggiani, 1999.
47 Deep Drainage Taskforce, 2000, p. 1.
48 Ibid., p. 10.
49 Ibid., p. 1.
50 Ibid., p. 10.
51 State Salinity Council, 2000, p. 48.
52 Conacher and Conacher, 2000, p. 75.
53 Ibid.
54 Ibid., p. 76
55 Ibid., p. 78.
56 Ibid., p. 71.
57 Interview with Dr Richard George, Department of Agriculture hydrologist.
58 State Salinity Council, 2000, p. 50.
59 Belford, 2000.
60 Deep Drainage Taskforce, 2000, p. 11.
61 State Salinity Council, 2000, p. 51.
62 Coles, George and Bathgate, 1999.
63 Pannell, 2000(b), p. 3.
64 Senior Government Scientist, pers. comm., 2001.
65 Conacher and Conacher, 2000, p. 69.
66 Barrett-Lennard and Malcolm, 1995.
67 Barrett-Lennard and Galloway, 1996.
68 Barrett-Lennard, 1999.
69 Barrett-Lennard and Malcolm, 1995.
70 Conacher and Conacher, 2000, p. 69.
71 Interview, Clive Malcolm, November, 2000.
72 Conacher and Conacher, 2000, p. 70.

73 Ghauri and Westrup, 2000.
74 Barrett-Lennard and Malcolm 1995.
75 Ibid.
76 Barrett-Lennard, 1999.
77 Barrett-Lennard and Malcolm, 1995.
78 Saltland Pastures Association, 2000.
79 Barrett-Lennard, 1999.
80 Lacey, 1999.
81 State Salinity Council, 2000, p. 44.
82 Ibid.
83 Ibid.
84 Barrett-Lennard, 1999.
85 Murray-Darling Basin Ministerial Council, 2000.
86 Conacher and Conacher, 2000, p. 310.
87 Ibid.
88 Pannell, 2000(b).
89 Kington and Pannell, 1999, p. 11.
90 Pannell, 2000(b), p. 1.
91 Lefroy, 2000, p. 1.
92 George, Clarke and Hatton, 2000, p. 2.
93 Pannell, 2000(b), p. 7.
94 Pannell, Lefroy and McFarlane, 2000.

Chapter 8

1 Vertical Consulting Group et al., 2000, p. 4.
2 Melia and Bosworth (eds), 1997, p. 86.
3 Ponting, 1992.
4 Thomas, 1984.
5 Barker, 1960, p. 25.
6 Hargrove, 1998, pp. 179-181.
7 Jones, 1987, p. 236.
8 Ponting, 1992, p. 151.
9 Heilbroner, 1987, pp. 41-41.
10 Ponting, 1992, p. 151.
11 Doyle, 2000, p. 145.
12 Helleiner, 2000, p. 61.
13 Blowers and Glasbergen, 1995, p. 178.
14 State of the Environment Advisory Council, 1996, pp.10-28.
15 Productivity Commission, 1999, p. 63.
16 Beder, 2000, p. 234.

[17] *The Australian,* 20 October 2000.

[18] Select Committee on Land Conservation, 1990, Discussion Paper No. 2, 1990, p. 150.

[19] Ibid., p. 150.

[20] Department of Environmental Protection, 1998, p. 7.

[21] Ibid., p. 14.

[22] Ibid.

[23] Department of Environmental Protection, 1998, p. 102.

[24] Ibid., p. 100.

[25] Agriculture Western Australia, 1998.

[26] Robertson, 1996, p. 2.

[27] Ibid., p. 6.

[28] Standing Committee on Ecologically Sustainable Development, 1998, Report No. 3, p. 12.

[29] Ibid., 1999, Report No. 4, p. 1.

[30] Ibid.

[31] Ibid., p. 43.

[32] Ibid., Report No. 2, p. 80.

[33] Ibid., Report No. 4.

[34] Ibid., p. 15.

[35] Interview, Dr Christine Sharp, November 2000.

[36] House of Representatives Standing Committee on Environment and Heritage, 2000, p. 78.

[37] Leopold, 1974, p. 224.

[38] Des Jardins, 1997: Rolston, 1988.

Bibliography

State Archives

Department of Agriculture: Soil Conservation: Legislation, Acc. No. 3515, No. 4, Vol. 1.

Interview with G. H. Burvill, File No. OH 924.

Western Australian Parliamentary Debates (PD), House of Assembly and Legislative Council. Selected years, 1950–2000.

Books/Articles

Anon (2001). 'Salinity Research Funded.' *CALM News*, January/February.

Armstrong, P. (1985). *Charles Darwin in Western Australia: A Young Scientist's Perception of an Environment*. Nedlands, University of Western Australia Press.

Austin, R. (1855). *Journal of Assistant-Surveyor R. Austin, Commanding an Expedition Sent by the Government to Explore the Interior of Western Australia, North and East of the Settled Districts, for Extensive Tracts of Fertile Lands*. Perth, Government Printer.

Ayris, C. (1989). 'How the West was Lost.' *The West Australian, Big Weekend*, 18 March.

Barker, E. (Translator) (1960). *The Politics of Aristotle*. Oxford, Clarendon Press.

Barrett, R. and Dent, P. (1991). *Australian Environments: Place, Pattern and Process*. South Melbourne, Macmillan Education Australia.

Bartle, J. (2001). 'New Perennial Crops. Mallee Eucalypts—A Model, Large Scale Perennial Crop for the Wheatbelt.' Australian Bureau of Agricultural Resource Economics, Outlook 2001 Conference, Papers and Proceedings.

Beale, B. (2000). 'Salvation of a Continent.' *Bulletin*, 13 June.

Beder, S. (2000). *Global Spin. The Corporate Assault on Environmentalism*. Melbourne, Scribe Publications.

Bell, D. T. and Froend, R. H. (1990). 'Mortality and Growth of Tree Species Under Stress at Lake Toolibin in the Western Australian Wheatbelt.' *Journal of the Royal Society of Western Australia*, 72 (3), pp. 63–66.

Bignell, M. (1981). *A Place To Meet: A History of the Shire of Katanning, Western Australia*. Nedlands, University of Western Australia Press.

Bindon, P. and Walley, T. (1992). 'Hunters and Gatherers.' Landscope, Spring.

Blowers, A. and Glasbergen, P. (1995). 'The Search for Sustainable Development.' In P. Glasbergen and A. Blowers (Eds), *Environmental Policy in an International Context*. London, Arnold.

Bolton, G. (1972). *A Fine Country to Starve in*. Nedlands, University of Western Australia Press.

Borough, C. and Bourke, M. (1998). 'Carbon Trading.' *Australian Forest Grower, Special Liftout Section, 45*.

Borough, C., Bourke, M., and Bennett, D. (1998). 'Forests as CO_2 Sinks—An Opportunity for Forest Growers?' *Australian Forest Grower, Special Liftout Section, 43*.

Bradby, K. (1984). 'A Rationale for Respect', Conference Proceedings. Diversity or Dust: A Review of the Impact of Agricultural Land-clearance Programmes in the South West of Australia. Hawthorn, Australian Conservation Foundation, pp. 33–37.

Bradsen, J. (2000). 'Soil Conservation: History, Law and Learning.' In S. Drovers *Environmental History and Policy. Still Settling Australia*. Oxford, Oxford University Press.

Brenchley, F. (2001). 'Salt Block'. In *The Bulletin*, 29 May.

Brophy, L. (2001). 'Radical Change to Rural Landscape Predicted.' In *UWA News*, 20 (6).

Burvill, G. H. (1947). 'Soil Salinity in the Agricultural Region of Western Australia', *Journal of the Australian Institute of Agricultural Science*.

Burvill, G. H. (1950). 'The Salt Problem in the Wheat Belt.' *Journal of Agriculture WA*, June.

Burvill, G. H. (1979). 'The Forward Move, 1889-1979.' In Burvill, G. H. *Agriculture in Western Australia 1829–1979*. Nedlands, University of Western Australia Press.

Chittleborough, R. (1991). 'Government, Science and Environment.' In Allan Peachment (Ed.), *The Business of Government: Western Australia 1983-1990*. Leichhardt, The Federation Press.

Christidis, L. and Boles, W. E. (1994). 'The Taxonomy and Species of Birds of Australia and its Territories.' *Royal Australian Ornithologists Union, Monograph* 2.

Churchward, B. (1991). 'A Conservationists View.' In Hughes, R. (Ed.), *Reflections on 20 Years*. Perth, Environmental Protection Authority.

Colebatch, H. (1929). *A Story of a Hundred Years*. Perth, Government Printer.

Coles, N., George, R. and Bathgate, A. (1999). 'Assessment of the Efficiency of Deep Drains Constructed in the Wheatbelt of Western Australia.' *Agriculture Western Australia Bulletin 4391*, November.

Conacher, A. (1980). 'Environmental Legislation in Western Australia.' *Australian Geographical Studies*, 18.

Conacher, A. (1986). 'Dryland Agriculture and Secondary Salinity.' In W. Hanley and H. Cooper (Eds). *Man and the Australian Environment*. Sydney, McGraw-Hill.

Conacher, A. and Conacher, J. (1995), *Rural Land Degradation in Australia*. South Melbourne, Oxford University Press.

Conacher, A. and Conacher, J. (2000). *Environmental Planning and Management in Australia*. South Melbourne, Oxford University Press.

Court, Sir Charles (1991). 'The Politics of Environmental Protection in the Beginning', In Hughes, R. (Ed.), *Reflections on 20 Years*. Perth, Environmental Protection Authority.

Crowley, F. (1960). *Australia's Western Third: A History of Western Australia from the First Settlements to Modern Times.* London, Macmillan.

Crowley, K. (1999). 'Explaining Environmental Policy: Challenges, Constraints and Capacity.' In Walker, K. and Crowley, K., *Australian Environment Policy 2.* Sydney, University of New South Wales Press.

Crowley, K. and Walker, K. J. (1999). *Australian Environmental Policy 2. Studies Decline and Devolution.* Sydney, University of New South Wales Press.

Davis, T. J. (Ed.) (1994). *The Ramsar Convention Manual: A Guide to the Convention on Wetlands of International Importance Especially as Waterfowl Habitat.* Gland, Switzerland, Ramsar Convention Bureau.

Des Jardins, R. (1997). *Environmental Ethics. An Introduction to Environmental Philosophy.* Boston, Wadsworth.

Dilworth, R., Gowdie, T. and Rowley, E. (2000). 'Living Landscapes: The Future Landscapes of the Western Australian Wheatbelt', *Ecological Management and Restoration*, 1 (3).

Dodson, J. R. and Westoby, M; (1985). *Are Australian Ecosystems Different?* Proceedings of the Ecological Society of Australia, 14.

Dovers, S. (Ed.) (2000). *Environmental History and Policy; Still Settling Australia.* South Melbourne, Oxford University Press.

Doyle, T. (2000). *Green Power. The Environment Movement in Australia.* Sydney, University of New South Wales Press.

Fitzpatrick, K. E. (1958). *Australian Explorers. A Selection from Their Writings, with an Introduction.* London, Oxford University Press.

Forrest, M. (1979). 'Public Administration and the Executive.' In R. Pervan and C. Sharman (Eds). *Essays on Western Australian Politics.* Perth, University of Western Australia Press.

Francis, J. (1998). 'Carbon Credits: New Source of Farm Income.' *Australian Farm Journal*, July.

Francis, P. (1998). 'Greenhouse-friendly Farms Present New Opportunities.' *Australian Landcare*, June 1998, pp. 8–11.

Froend, R. H. and van der Moezel, P. G. (1994). 'The Impact of Prolonged Flooding in the Vegetation of Coomalbidgup Swamp,

Western Australia.' *Journal of the Royal Society of Western Australia* 77: pp.15–22.

Froend, R. H., McComb, A. J. (1991). An Account of the Decline of Lake Towerrinning, A Wheatbelt Wetland. *Journal of the Royal Society of Western Australia*, Vol. 73 (4), pp. 123–128.

Gardner, J. (1997). 'Towns Important in Salinity Reduction.' *Great Southern Herald*, 13 August.

Garnett, S. T. and Crowley, G. M. (2000). *The Action Plan for Australian Birds*. Canberra: Environment Australia.

Gentilli, J. (Ed.) (1979). *Western Landscapes*. Nedlands, University of Western Australia Press.

George, P. (1978). 'The Dryland Salinity Problem in North America.' *Journal of Agriculture*, 19 (4).

George, R. J., Dogramaci, S., Smith, A. and Wallace, K. (2000). *Toolibin: A Life and Death Struggle for the Last Freshwater Wheatbelt Lake*. Conference paper presented at Hydro 2000, Perth.

George, R., McFarlane, D., and Nulsen, B. (1997). 'Salinity Threatens the Viability of Agriculture and Ecosystems in Western Australia.' *Hydrogeology Journal*, 5 (1).

George, R., Nulsen,R., Ferdowsian, R and Raper, P. (1999). 'Interactions Between Trees and Groundwaters in Recharge and Discharge Areas: A Survey of Western Australian Sites.' *Agricultural Water Management*, 39.

Ghauri, S. and Westrup, T. (2000). 'Saltland Pastures: Changing Attitudes Towards Saline Land.' *Farmnote*, 47/2000 (Agdex 330).

Glanznig, A. (1995). 'Native Vegetation Clearance, Habitat Loss and Biodiversity decline: An Overview of Recent Native Vegetation Clearance in Australia and its Implications for Biodiversity.' *Department of the Environment, Sport and Territories, Biodiversity Series, Paper 6*.

Glanznig, A. (1999). 'Striking a Balance for the Bush.' *Life Lines*, 5 (3): pp.1–2.

Glynn, S. (1975). *Government Policy and Agricultural Development. A Study of the Role of Government in the Development of the Western Australian Wheatbelt 1900-1930*. Perth, University of Western Australia Press.

Greble, W. (1979). *A Bold Yeomanry. Social Change in a Wheat Belt District, Kulin 1848-1970*. Perth, Creative Research.

Guy, D., Kalajzich, J. and Nelson, J. (1991). *Landscapes and Land Uses: Studies in Australian Geography*. Sydney, McGraw-Hill.

Halse, S. A. (1987). 'Probable Effect of Increased Salinity on the Waterbirds of Lake Toolibin.' *Department of Conservation and Land Management, Technical Report 15*.

Halse, S. A. Jaensch, R. P., Munro, D. R. and Pearson, G. B. (1990). 'Annual Waterfowl Counts in South-western Australia—1988/89.' *Department of Conservation and Land Management, Technical Report 25*.

Halse, S. A. Jaensch, R. P., Munro, D. R. and Pearson, G. B. (1992). 'Annual Waterfowl Counts in South-western Australia—1989/90.' *Department of Conservation and Land Management Technical Report 29*.

Hargrove, E. (1998). 'Anglo-American Land Use Attitudes'. In Botzler, R. and Armstrong, S. *Environmental Ethics. Divergence and Convergence*. Boston, McGraw Hill.

Haworth, R. (1996). 'Fine Sentiments vs Brute Actions: the Landcare Ethic and Land Clearing in Contemporary Australia.' *Rural Society*, 6 (2).

Hearn, S. J. (1988). 'Soil Conservation and Management Strategies for the Toolibin Catchment.' *Department of Agriculture, Division of Resource Management, Technical Report 75*.

Heilbroner, R. (1981). *The Worldly Philosophers*. New York, Penguin.

Helleiner, E. (2000). 'New Voices in the Globalisation Debate: Green Perspectives on the World Economy'. In R. Stubbs and G. Underhill, *Political Economy and the Changing Global Order*. New York, Oxford University Press.

Higgins, P. J. and Davies, S. J. J. F. (Eds) (1996). *Handbook of Australian, New Zealand and Antarctic Birds: Volume 3—Snipe to Pigeons*. Melbourne, Oxford University Press.

Hillel, D. (1991). *Out of the Earth: Civilization and the Life of the Soil*. Berkeley, California University Press.

Hughes, R. (Ed.) (1991). *Reflections on 20 Years*. Perth, Environmental Protection Authority.

Jaensch, R. P. and Vervest, R. M. (1988a). 'Ducks, Swans and Coots in South-western Australia: The 1986 and 1987 Counts.' *Royal Australian Ornithologists Union, Report 31.*

Jaensch, R. P. and Vervest, R. M. (1988b). 'Ducks, Swans and Coots in South-western Australia: The 1988 Count and Recommendations.' *Royal Australian Ornithologists Union, Report 46.*

Jaensch, R. P., Vervest, R. M. and Hewish, M.J. (1988). 'Waterbirds and Nature Reserves of South-western Australia, 1981–1985: Reserve Accounts.' *Royal Australasian Ornithologists Union, Report 30.*

Jasper, R. (1984). 'An Historical Perspective', Conference Proceedings Diversity or Dust: A Review of the Impact of Agricultural Land-clearance Programmes in South West of Australia. Hawthorn, Australian Conservation Foundation, pp.7–15.

Johnson, P. (1991). 'Environmental Protection and the Law.' In R. Hughes, *Reflections on 20 Years.* Perth, Environmental Protection Authority.

Jones, A. (1987). 'From Fragmentation to Wholeness: A Green Approach to Science and Society, Part One.' *The Ecologist*, 17 (6).

Jones, R. and Tonts, M. (1995). 'Rural Restructuring and Social Sustainability: Some Reflections on the Western Australian Wheatbelt.' *Australian Geographer*, 26 (2).

Kellow, A. and Niemeyer, S. (1999). 'The Development of Environmental Administration in Queensland and Western Australia: Why Are They Different?' *Australian Journal of Political Science*, 34 (2).

Kington, E. and Pannell, D. (1999). 'Dryland Salinity in the Upper Kent River Catchment of Western Australia: Farmer Perceptions and Practices.' *Sustainability and Economics in Agriculture, Working Paper 99/09.*

Kington, E. and Smettem, R. (2000). 'Evaluations of Policy Approaches to Dryland Salinity Management in the Kent River Catchment.' *Sustainability and Economics in Agriculture, Working Paper 00/07.*

Kirkpatrick, J. (1999). *A Continent Transformed: Human Impact on the Natural Vegetation of Australia.* South Melbourne, Oxford University Press.

Kohen, J. (1997). *Aboriginal Environmental Impacts*. Sydney, University of New South Wales Press.

Laurie, V. (2000). 'Salt 'n' Science', *The Weekend Australian*, 15–16 April, Review.

Layman, L. (1982). 'Development Ideology in Western Australia, 1933–1965.' *Historical Studies*, 40, (79).

Leake, B. (1957). 'Eastern Wheatbelt Wildlife.' *The Western Mail*, 14, 21, 28 June.

Lefroy, E.C., Hobbs, R.J. and Atkins, L.J. (1991). 'Revegetation Guide to the Central Wheatbelt.' *Department of Agriculture Western Australia, Bulletin 4231*.

Lefroy, T. (1999). 'Why marketing won't help if you've got nothing to sell: A response to the Salinity Action Plan'. In *Sustainability and Economics in Agriculture*, Issue 1.

Leopold, A. (1974). A Sand County Almanac. Oxford, Oxford University Press.

Linkletter, A. (1971). *Down Under*. Sydney, Ure Smith.

Loh, I. and Stokes, R. (1981). 'Predicting Stream Salinity Changes in South-Western Australia'. *Agricultural Water Management*, 4.

Lunn, S. (1999). Ecology Library is our Preserve. *The Weekend Australian*, 11–12 September 1999. Science and Technology, p. 7.

Lyster, M. (1985). *International Wildlife Law*. Cambridge, Grotius Publications.

Marchant, S. and Higgins, P. J. (Eds) (1990). *Handbook of Australian, New Zealand and Antarctic Birds: Volume 1—Ratites to Ducks, Part B, Australian Pelicans to Ducks*. South Melbourne, Oxford University Press.

Marchant, S. and Higgins, P. J. (Eds) (1993). *Handbook of Australian, New Zealand and Antarctic Birds: Volume 2—Raptors to Lapwings*. Melbourne, Oxford University Press.

Marsh, S., Burton, M., and Patterson, J. (2000). 'Community Attitudes to Land Degradation and Responsibilities in Western Australia', *Sustainability and Economics in Agriculture, Working Paper 2000/02*.

Martin, P. (1997). 'Saline Politics: Local Participation and Neoliberalism in Australian Rural Environments', *Space and Polity*, 1.

McCabe, T. (1998). *Nyoongar Views on Logging Old Growth Forests*. Perth, Wilderness Society.

McC. Adams, R. (1981). *Heartland of Cities. Surveys of Ancient Settlement and Land Use on the Central Floodplain of the Euphrates*. Chicago, Chicago University Press.

McFarlane, D. J. and George, R. J. (1992). 'Factors Affecting Dryland Salinity in Two Wheatbelt Catchments in Western Australia.' *Australian Journal of Soil Research*, 30.

McKenzie, F. (1999). 'Impact of Declining Rural Infrastructure.' Canberra, Rural Industries Research and Development Corporation.

Mackay, N. and Eastburn, D. (Eds) (1992). *The Murray*. Canberra, Murray–Darling Basin Commission.

MacKinnon, G. (1991). 'Changing Attitudes.' In Hughes, R. (Ed.), *Reflections on 20 Years*. Perth; Environmental Protection Authority.

Main, D. (1991). 'Setting the Ground Rules.' In Hughes, R. (Ed.) *Reflections on 20 Years*. Perth, Environmental Protection Authority.

Melia, M. and Bosworth, R. (1997). *Western Australia As It Is Today, 1906: Leopoldo Zunni Royal Consul of Italy*. Nedlands, University of Western Australia Press.

Mercer, F. R. (1955). *On Farmers' Service. A Short History of Farmers' Organisations in Western Australia*. Perth, The Executive of the Farmers' Union.

Myers, N., Mittermeier, R. A., Mittermeier, C. G., da Fonseca, G. A. B. and Kent, J. (2000). 'Biodiversity Hotspots for Conservation Priorities.' *Nature*. 403: pp. 853–858.

'National Heritage Trust Review Exposes Serious Flaws.' In *Environment Business*, February, 2000.

Newbey, B. (1999). 'Birds Australia: Birds on Farms Project in Western Australia 1996-1999.' *Western Australian Bird Notes*, Supplement 5.

Newby, K. R. (1983). 'Principles of Land Use Planning.' In E. H. Lawson, *Land Release in Western Australia, Policies, Practices and Politics*. Perth, The Australian Institute of Agricultural Science.

O'Brien, B. J. (Ed.) (1979). *Environment and Science*. Perth, University of Western Australia Press.

O'Brien, B. (1991), 'The EPA in the Beginning.' In Hughes, R. (Ed.),

Reflections on 20 Years. Perth, Environmental Protection Authority, pp. 5–18.

O'Connor, D. (1991), 'People and the Environment.' In Hughes, R. (Ed.), *Reflections on 20 Years*. Perth; Environmental Protection Authority, pp. 61–67.

Oliver, D. G. (1983). 'Some Economic Aspects of New Land Release.' In E. H. Lawson, *Land Release in Western Australia, Policies, Practices and Politics*. Perth, The Australian Institute of Agricultural Science.

Palmer, C. B. (1945). *The Interest of Farming*. Perth, Sands and McDougall Pty Ltd.

Pannell, D. (1997). 'Social and Economic Challenges to the Development of Complex Farming Systems.' *Sustainability and Economics in Agriculture*, Working Paper 2.

Pannell, D. (1998). 'Comments on the Western Australian Salinity Action Plan.' *Sustainability and Economics in Agriculture*, Issue 1, May.

Pannell, D. (1999). 'Explaining Non-Adoption of Practices to Prevent Dryland Salinity in Western Australia: Implications for Policy.' *Sustainability and Economics in Agriculture*, Working Paper 99/08.

Pannell, D. (2000a). 'Salt Levy? The Complex Case for Public Funding of Salinity', *Sustainability and Economics in Agriculture*, Working Paper 2000/01.

Pannell, D. (2000b). 'Salinity Policy: A Tale of Fallacies, Misconceptions and Hidden Assumptions.' *Sustainability and Economics in Agriculture*, Working Paper 8.

Pannell, D. (2000c). 'Ethics in Dryland Salinity Management and Policy.' *Sustainability and Economics in Agriculture*, Working Paper 2000/04.

Papadakis, E. (1993). *Politics and the Environment: The Australian Experience*. St. Leonards, Allen and Unwin.

Pate, S. and McComb, A. (Eds) (1981) *The Biology of Australian Plants*. Nedlands, University of Western Australia Press.

Penrose, S. (1981). 'Western Australia: Political Chronicle, July 1980 to December 1980.' *Australian Journal of Politics and History*, 37 (1).

Ponting, C. (1992). *A Green History of the World*. London, Penguin.

Porter, C. (1991). 'Starting from Scratch'. In R. Hughes, *Reflections on 20 Years*. Perth, Environmental Protection Authority.

Read, V. (1988). 'Salinity in Western Australia: A Situation Statement' (submission to the Parliamentary Select Committee on Salinity, 1988), *Technical Report No. 81*. Western Australian Department of Agriculture, Division of Resource Management.

Recher, H. (1999). 'Status of Australia's Avifauna: A Personal Opinion and Prediction for the New Millennium.' *Australian Zoologist* 31: pp.11–27.

Richards, R. (1984a). 'Structure and Process.' In Conference Proceedings Diversity or Dust: A Review of the Impact of Agricultural Land Clearance Programs in South West Australia. Hawthorn, Australian Conservation Foundation.

Richards, R. (1984b). 'Economic Naivety.' In Conference Proceedings Diversity or Dust: A Review of the Impact of Agricultural Land Clearance Programmes in South West of Australia. Hawthorn, Australian Conservation Foundation.

Richards, R. (1984c). 'Agricultural Accountability.' In Conference Proceedings Diversity or Dust: A Review of the Impact of Agricultural Land Clearance Programmes in South West of Australia. Hawthorn: Australian Conservation Foundation.

Riggert, T. L. (1977). 'The Biology of the Mountain Duck on Rottnest Island, Western Australia.' Wildlife Society, USA, *Wildlife Monographs*, 52.

Roberts, R. W. (1989). *Land Conservation in Australia: A 200-Year Stocktake*. Sydney, Soil Conservation Service.

Robertson, G. A. (1988). 'Soil Conservation Districts—Land Users Solving Mutual Problems.' In P. Newman, S. Neville, and L. Duxbury (Eds), *Case Studies in Environmental Hope*. Perth, Environmental Protection Authority.

Robertson, G. A. (1993). 'Naturing the Resource', *Making it Happen: The Australian Institute of Agricultural Science National Conference*.

Robertson, G. A. (1996). 'Sustainable Agri-industry', Sustaining Agri-industry—Valuing the Environment Conference. The Australian Institute of Agricultural Science.

Rolston, H. (1988). *Environmental Ethics: Duties to and Values in the Natural World*. Philadelphia, Temple University Press.

Rundle, G. (1997a). 'The Conservation Campaign of 1970.' *The Greener Times*.

Rundle, G. (1997b). 'The 1970 Conservation Bill of Rights.' *The Greener Times*.

Sand, P. H. (Ed.) (1992). *The Effectiveness of International Environmental Agreements: A Survey of Existing Legal Instruments*. UN Conference on Environment and Development. Cambridge, Grotius Publications.

Sandford, J. (1955). *Walter Harper and the Farmers*. Perth, Westralian Farmers Cooperative Printing Works.

Sherwin, C. (2000). 'Queensland's New Law of the Land: Good, Bad, and Ugly.' *Habitat Australia*, 28 (8).

Shier, P. (1962). 'Light Lands in Western Australia, History and Future Prospects.' *Journal of Agriculture WA*, 3 (9).

Snooks, D. (1974). *Depression and Recovery in Western Australia*. Nedlands, University of Western Australia Press.

Storey, A. W., Vervest, R. M., Pearson, G. B. and Halse, S. A. (1993). *Wetlands of the Swan Coastal Plain: Volume 7—Waterbird Usage of Wetlands on the Swan Coastal Plain*. Perth, Western Australian Department of Conservation and Land Management and Royal Australasian Ornithologists Union.

Straw, P. (Ed.) (1997). *Shorebird Conservation in the Asia-Pacific Region*. Papers presented at a symposium held on 16–17 March 1996 in Brisbane, Australia. Melbourne, Australasian Wader Studies Group of Birds Australia (RAOU).

Strawbridge, M. (1999). 'The Extent, Condition, and Management of Remnant Vegetation in Water Resource Recovery Catchments in South Western Australia: Report to the Natural Heritage Trust.' *Water and Rivers Commission Technical Series, 15*.

Sutton, G. L. (1952). *Comes the Harvest. Half a Century of Agricultural Progress in Western Australia 1900-1949*. Perth, West Australian Newspapers.

Taylor, J. (1990). *Australia's Southwest and Our Future*. Kenthurst, Kangaroo Press.

Teakle, L. (1939). 'The Soils of the 3,500 Farms Scheme Area, Western Australia.' *Journal of Agriculture WA*, 16.

Teakle, L. J. H. (1938). 'Soil Salinity in Western Australia.' *Journal of Agriculture WA*, 15, (4).

Teakle, L. and Burvill, G. H. (1945). 'The Management of Salt Lands in Western Australia.' *Journal of the Department of Agriculture WA*, June.

Thomas, K. (1984). *Man and the Natural World. Changing Attitudes in England 1500–1800*. Harmondsworth, Penguin.

Toyne, P. and Farley, R. (2000). 'Work Together for Better Landcare.' *The Australian*, 27 July.

Turner, R. K., Pearce, D. and Bateman, I. (1994). *Environmental Economics*. Hertfordshire, Harvester Wheatsheaf.

Wadham, W. (1964). *Land Utilisation in Australia*. Melbourne, Melbourne University Press.

Wallace, J. and Campbell, N. (1998). *Evaluation of the Feasibility of Remote Sensing for Monitoring National State of the Environment Indicators*. Canberra, Environment Australia.

Watkins, D. (1993). 'A National Plan for Shorebird Conservation in Australia.' Royal Australian Ornithologists Union (Australasian Wader Studies Group) and World Wide Fund for Nature. *Royal Australasian Ornithologists Union, Report 90*.

Western Australian Environmental Protection Authority (1993). Strategy for the Protection of Lakes and Wetlands of the Swan Coastal Plain. *Environmental Protection Authority, Bulletin 685*.

Whittington, H. (1975). *A Battle for Survival Against Salt Encroachment at Spring Hill, Brookton*. Self-published.

Williams, W. D. (Ed.) (1998). *Wetlands in a Dry Continent; Understanding for Management*. Canberra, Environment Australia Biodiversity Group.

Wood, W. E. (1924). 'Increase in Salt in Soil and Streams Following the Destruction of the Native Vegetation.' *Journal of the Royal Society of Western Australia* 10 (7).

Worboys, G., Lockwood, M. and De Lacy, T. (2001). *Protected Area Management: Principles and Practice*. South Melbourne, Oxford University Press.

York Main, B. (1967). *Between Wodjil and Tor.* Brisbane, Jacaranda Press.

Young, A. (2000). *Environmental Change in Australia Since 1788.* South Melbourne, Oxford University Press.

Newspapers

The Australian
The Bulletin
The Collie Mail
The Countryman
The Daily News
The Daily Telegraph
Elders Weekly
Esperance Express
Farmers Weekly
The Great Southern Herald
The Sunday Times
The Farmer and Grazier
The Western Mail
The West Australian

Reports

Agriculture Bank Royal Commission (1934). Report, Perth, Government Printer.

Agriculture Western Australia (2000). *Rural Towns Program: Katanning.* Government of Western Australia (pamphlet).

Agriculture Western Australia (1998). *Focus on the Future, Agriculture Western Australia's Strategic Directions 1998–2008.*

Australian and New Zealand Environment and Conservation Council (2000). *Review of the National Strategy for the Conservation of Australia's Biological Diversity,* Canberra.

Australian Bureau of Agricultural and Resource Economics (1998). *Landcare: Promoting Improved Land Management Practices on Australian Farms.* Canberra, ABARE.

Australian Local Government Association (2000). National Local Government Biodiversity Survey. www.alga.com.au

Australian Soil Conservation Council (1988). *National Soil Conservation Strategy*. Canberra, Australian Government Publishing Service.

Barrett-Lennard, E. G. and Malcolm, C. V. (1995). *Saltland Pastures in Australia: A Practical Guide*. South Perth, Western Australian Department of Agriculture.

Belford, A. C. (2000). *A Plan to Recover Salinated Land in the South West Lands Division to Agricultural Use: A South West Lands Division Engineering Solution*. Unpublished report, Perth.

Blackley, R., Usback, S. and Langford, K. (1996). *A Directory of Important Wetlands in Australia*. Canberra, Australian Nature Conservation Agency.

Blyth, J. (1998). 'Threatened Species and Ecological Communities.' In: Government of Western Australia. *Review of Salinity Research and Development in Western Australia: Draft*. A report commissioned by the Salinity R. and D. Working Group for the Western Australian Salinity Action Plan, pp. 37–39.

Bunn, S. E., Boon, P. I., Brock, M.A., and Schofield, N. J. (Eds) (1997). *National Wetlands R and D Program: Scoping Review*. Canberra, Land and Water Resources Research and Development Corporation.

Chittleborough, G. and Keating, F. *(1986). Western Australian Environmental Review* 1986. Perth, Department of Conservation and Environment.

Commonwealth of Australia (1992). *National Strategy for Ecologically Sustainable Development*. Canberra, Australian Government Publishing Service.

Commonwealth of Australia (1996). *National Strategy for the Conservation of Australia's Biological Diversity*. Canberra, Department of the Environment, Sport and Territories.

Commonwealth of Australia (1998a). *Australia's National Report to the Fourth Conference of the Parties to the Convention on Biological Diversity*. Canberra, Environment Australia.

Commonwealth of Australia (1998b). *National Greenhouse Strategy:*

Strategic Framework for Advancing Australia's Greenhouse Response.
Canberra: Australian Greenhouse Office.

Conservation and Environment Council (1983). *A Conservation Strategy for Western Australia: Living Resource Conservation for Sustainable Development.* Perth, Department of Conservation and Environment, Report 12.

Deep Drainage Taskforce (2000). *Deep Drainage in South West Western Australia: Making it Work—Not Proving It Wrong.* Report and Recommendations to the Honourable Monty House, MLA, Minister for Primary Industries and Fisheries. Perth, Government of Western Australia.

Department of Agriculture, Annual Reports 1920–2000. Perth.

Department of Agriculture (1949). *Agriculture in the Western Australian Wheat Belt.* Perth, Western Australian Government Tourist and Publicity Bureau.

Department of Agriculture (1956) *Agriculture in the Western Australian Wheat Belt.* Perth, Western Australian Government Tourist and Publicity Bureau.

Department of Conservation and Environment: (1987). *A State Conservation Strategy for Western Australia: A Sense of Direction.* Perth, Government of Western Australia.

Department of Conservation and Land Management (1999). *CALM Biodiversity Survey of the Agricultural Zone: September 1999 Status Report.* Perth, Department of Conservation and Land Management.

Department of Environmental Protection (1998). *State of the Environment Report.* Perth, Department of Environmental Protection.

Duff, J. (1980). *A Study of Salinity Problems and Research in South Western Australia.* Victoria, Soil Conservation Authority.

Environment Australia (1997). *Wetlands Policy of the Commonwealth Government of Australia.* Canberra, Environment Australia (Wetlands, Waterways and Waterbirds Unit of the Biodiversity Group).

Environment Australia/Australian Local Government Association (2000). *National Local Government Biodiversity Survey.* www.alga.com.au

Environmental Protection Authority, Annual Reports, 1972 to 1999/2000. Perth.

Environmental Protection Authority (1999). *Environmental Protection of Native Vegetation in Western Australia: Position Statement No. 2.* Perth, Government of Western Australia.

Forests Department, Annual Reports, 1920–1930. Perth.

Gardner, J. (2000). *Katanning Landcare Co-ordination and Resource Centre Report, February 1997 to January 2000.* Prepared for the Katanning Land Conservation District Committee and the Natural Heritage Trust.

George, R. J., Clarke, L. J. and Hatton, T. (2000). *Computer Controlled Groundwater Response to Recharge Management for Dryland Salinity Control in Western Australia.* Unpublished document prepared by researchers from Agriculture Western Australia, Murdoch University and CSIRO for the State Salinity Council.

Government of Australia (1999). *Bushcare: New Directions in Native Vegetation Management.* Statement by Senator the Honourable Robert Hill, Minister for the Environment and Heritage. Canberra, Natural Heritage Trust.

Government of Western Australia (1992). *State of the Environment Report.* Perth, Department of Environmental Protection.

Government of Western Australia (1996a). *Environment Western Australia 1996: State of the Environment Report.* Perth, Department of Environmental Protection.

Government of Western Australia (1996b). *Western Australian Salinity Action Plan. Perth,* Government of Western Australia.

Government of Western Australia (1998). *Environment Western Australia 1998: State of the Environment Report.* Perth, Department of Environmental Protection.

Harper, R. J., Mauger, G., Robinson, N., McGrath, J. F., Smetten, K. R. J., Bartle, J. R. and George, R. J. (2000). 'Manipulating Catchment Water Balance Using Plantation and Farm Forestry: Case Studies from South-Western Australia.' In proceedings of a national workshop on *Plantations, Farm Forestry and Water*, 20–21 July, Melbourne.

Hatton, T., Clarke, C., George, R. and Reggiani, P. (1999). 'Controlling Salinity: The Size of Our Challenge.' *Productive Use and Rehabilitation of Saline Land*, Perth.

Holmes, J. (1979). 'The Whittington Interceptor Drain Trial.' Report to the Public Works Department, Western Australia.

House of Representatives Standing Committee on Environment and Heritage (2000). *Coordinating Catchment Management*. Report of the Inquiry into Catchment Management, Canberra.

Industries Assistance Commission (1975). *New Land Farms. Assistance to New Land Farms in Western Australia*. Canberra, Australian Government Printing Service.

Industry Commission (1996). *Land Degradation and the Australian Agricultural Industry*, Staff Information Paper, by P. Gretton, and U. Salma. Canberra, Australian Government Printing Service.

Industry Commission (1998). *A Full Repairing Lease Inquiry into Ecologically Sustainable Land Management*. Canberra, Industry Commision.

Lambert, J. A., Elix, J. K., Chenowith, A. and Cole, S. (1995). *Approaches to Bioregional Planning. Part 2. Background Papers to the Conference, 30 October–1 November 1995*, Melbourne. Canberra: Department of the Environment, Sport and Territories.

Land Settlement Board, Annual Reports, 1949–65. Perth.

Mollemans, F. (1992). *Distribution and Ecological Significance of On-farm Bush Remnants in the Southern Wheatbelt Region of Western Australia*. Perth, Western Australian Department of Agriculture.

Mollemans, F. (1993). *A Simplified Key for Assessing the Ecological Significance of On-farm Bush Remnants in the Wheatbelt*. Perth, Western Australian Department of Agriculture.

Murray–Darling Basin Ministerial Council (2000). *Integrated Catchment Management in the Murray–Darling Basin, 2001–2010: Delivering a Sustainable Future* (Draft). Canberra, Commonwealth of Australia.

Native Vegetation Working Group (2000). *Final Report of the Native Vegetation Working Group*. South Perth, Agriculture Western Australia.

Northern Arthur River Wetlands Committee (1987). *The Status and Future of Lake Toolibin as a Wildlife Reserve*. Water Authority of Western Australia Report WS2.

Parliament of Western Australia (1988). *Report on Salinity in Western Australia*. Select Committee on Salinity, Discussion Paper.

Peddie, B. and Kins, A. (1999). *Katanning Shire Cultural Policy and Plan 1999/2000–2003/2004*.

Pittock, J., Mitchell, D. and Handley, M. (1996). *Australia's Wetlands Record: Position Paper*. Sydney, World Wide Fund for Nature.

Productivity Commission (1999). *Implementation of Ecologically Sustainable Development by Commonwealth Departments and Agencies*, Report No. 5. Canberra, Productivity Commission.

Public Works Department (1951). *Salinity Problems in Western Australian Catchments with Particular Reference to Wellington Dam*. File P.W.W.S. 251/51 (Burvill Papers).

Royal Commission on the Agricultural Industries of Western Australia (1917). Votes and Proceedings, Vol 2.

Royal Commission on the Mallee Belt and Esperance Lands (1917). Votes and Proceedings of Parliament.

Royal Commission on Group Settlement (1925). Votes and Proceedings of Parliament, Vol. 1 No. 5.

Rural Reconstruction Commission (1944). *Settlement and Employment of Returned Men on the Land*. Canberra, Government Printer.

Select Committee into Land Conservation (1990). *Discussion Paper No. 2, Agricultural Region of Western Australia*. Perth, Legislative Assembly.

Select Committee of the Legislative Assembly Appointed to Enquire into Hardship in the Rural Sector. (1984). Final Report. Parliament of Western Australia, Legislative Assembly.

Select Committee on Land Conservation (1991). Final Report. Parliament of Western Australia, Legislative Assembly.

Select Committee on Salinity (1988a). Report on Salinity in Western Australia: Discussion Paper. Parliament of Western Australia, Legislative Council.

Select Committee on Salinity (1988b). Report on Salinity in Western Australia: Final Report and Recommendations Paper. Parliament of Western Australia, Legislative Council.

Select Committee on the Right to Farm: Final Report (1991). Parliament of Western Australia, Legislative Assembly.

Senate Select Committee on Water Pollution (1970). *Water Pollution in Australia*. Report. Canberra, Commonwealth Government Printing Office.

Short, S. and McConnell, C. (2000). *Extent and Impacts of Dryland Salinity*. Perth, Agriculture WA.

Soil Conservation Branch, Department of Agriculture, Annual Reports, 1945–1970.

Standing Committee on Ecologically Sustainable Development, (1998). *Management of and Planning for the Use of State Forests in Western Australia: The Regional Forest Agreement Process*. Legislative Council of Western Australia.

Standing Committee on Ecologically Sustainable Development (1999). *Management of and Planning for the Use of State Forests in Western Australia—The Sustainability of Current Practices*. Report 4, Legislative Council of Western Australia.

State of the Environment Advisory Council (1996). *Australia: State of the Environment 1996*. Collingwood, CSIRO Publishing. (Also published, Canberra, Department of the Environment, Sport and Territories.)

State Salinity Council (1998). *Western Australia Salinity Action Plan, Draft Update*. Perth, State Salinity Council.

State Salinity Council (2000). *Natural Resource Management in Australia: The Salinity Strategy 2000*. Perth: Government of Western Australia.

State of the Environment Reference Group (1998). *State of the Environment Report*. Perth, Government of Western Australia.

Stirzaker, R., Lefroy T., Keating, B., and Williams, J. (2000). *A Revolution in Land Use: Emerging Land Use Systems for Managing Dryland Salinity*. Canberra, CSIRO.

Sustainable Land Management Technical Panel (1999). *Report to Council*. Perth, Western Australian Greenhouse Council.

Virtual Consulting Group and Boorara Management and Consulting (2000). *Enhancing Institutional Support for the Management of Dryland Salinity*. A Discussion Paper. Canberra, National Dryland Salinity Program.

Water Authority of Western Australia (1987). *The Status and Future of Lake Toolibin as a Wildlife Reserve*. Perth, Water Authority of WA.

Water Authority of Western Australia (1989). *Stream Salinity and Its Reclamation in South West Western Australia.* Perth, Water Authority of WA.

Western Australian Museum (1976–1981). *Biological Survey of the Western Australian Wheatbelt, Parts 1–14.* Perth, WA Museum.

Working Party on Dryland Salting in Australia (1982). 'Salting of Non-Irrigated Land in Australia.' Published by the Soil Conservation Authority, Victoria for Standing Committee on Soil Conservation.

Unpublished

Australian Conservation Foundation (2000a). *Land Management. Fact Sheet.*

Australian Conservation Foundation (2000b). Media Release, 15 May.

Barrett-Lennard, E. G. (1999). *Plants in Saline Environments—An Australian Experience.* Proceedings of the Productive Use and Rehabilitation of Saline Lands 1999 National Conference, held 1–5 November, Naracoorte, South Australia.

Barrett-Lennard, E. G. and Galloway, R. (1996). *Saltbush for Water-table Reduction and Land Rehabilitation.* Proceedings of the Productive Use and Rehabilitation of Saline Lands 1996 National Conference and Workshop, held 25–30 March, Albany, Western Australia.

Bennett, D. and Macpherson, D. (no date). 'Where Are We Going? We Don't Know. What Will We Learn There? We Ain't Certain. The Fifth Australian Soil Conservation Conference in Historical Context.' (Copy available from Dr David Bennett, Fremantle.)

Conacher, A. (1979). *Salinity Problems in South Western Australia: A Critical Evaluation of the Holmes Report on the Whittington Interceptor Drain Trial.* Nedlands, Department of Geography, University of Western Australia.

Curtis, A., Keane, D., and DeLacy T. (1993). *Land Conservation District Committees Western Australia: An Evaluation Using LCDC Reports.* Albury, Charles Sturt University.

Cusack, V. (1999). *The Western Australian Environmental Protection Authority (EPA): Its Structure, Functions and Performance 1971–1996.*

Unpublished Politics Honours Thesis, Edith Cowan University, Western Australia.

Dodds, R. (1997). 'Nine Years of Alley Farming in WA.' *Alley Farming Network*, Update No.9. Greening Australia, Victoria.

Friends of the Earth (1983). Environment Conference, University of Western Australia.

Gardner, J. (2000). *Katanning Landcare Co-ordination and Resource Centre Report, February 1997 to January 2000.* Prepared for the Katanning Land Conservation District Committee and the Natural Heritage Trust.

Goss, K. (1963). 'Social Aspects of Development of New Land Areas.' In E. H. Lawson, *Land Release in Western Australia, Policies, Practices and Politics.* Perth, The Australian Institute of Agricultural Science.

Grainger, G. (1983). 'Farming a Fitzgerald Land Release.' In E. H. Lawson, *Land Release in Western Australia, Policies, Practices and Politics.* Perth, The Australian Institute of Agricultural Science.

Hammill, S. (2000). *Marginalisation, Resistance, Celebration—Cultural Identity Amongst Farmers in Western Australia.* Nedlands, Anthropology Department, University of Western Australia.

International Food Policy Research Institute (2001). Brief 58. Soil Degradation, www.ifpri.cgair.org

Katanning Community Charrette Handbook (1997). Prepared for the Katanning community by students from Ball State University, Indiana, USA.

Katanning Salinity Management Strategy (1999). Prepared in conjunction with the Katanning community and the Rural Towns Program (an Agriculture WA Project) by John Duff and Associates and VORAN—Managers, Planners, Engineers.

Lacey, P. (1999). 'The Outback Ocean—Inland Saltwater Aquaculture.' Proceedings of the Productive Use and Rehabilitation of Saline Lands 1999 National Conference, held 1–5 November, Naracoorte, South Australia.

Lefroy, E. C. (2000) *Why Marketing Won't Help if You've Got Nothing to Sell: A Response to the Salinity Action Plan.* Document prepared for the State Salinity Council.

Liberal Party WA (1993). *Fightback! Western Australia*, unpublished.

Macpherson, D. K. and Bennett, D. (no date). 'Osmosis in the Promised Land: The Fifth Soil Conference in Context.' (Copy available from Dr David Bennett, Fremantle.)

McCarthy, A. P. (1998). Carbon Sequestration of Two "Oil Mallee" Species, *Eucalyptus loxophleba* subsp. *lissophloia* and *Eucalyptus, kochii* subsp. *plenissima* in the Semi-arid Environment of the Central Wheatbelt of Western Australia. Bachelor of Science (Hons) (Env. Man.) Thesis, Edith Cowan University, Joondalup, Western Australia.

Morrisey, P. (1999). *Interest Groups and the Landcare Forum: How Do They Influence Sustainability in Rural Australia.* Lismore, Southern Cross University. PhD thesis.

Murphy, J. (1999). 'Salinity Our Silent Disaster', Transcript, ABC. '7.30 Report' program, 13/05/99. www.ABC.net.au/science/slab/salinity/default/htm

Pannell, D., Lefroy, T., and McFarlane, D. (2000). *A Framework for Prioritising Government Investment in Salinity in Western Australia.* Salinity Policy Plan 4. Unpublished document prepared by researchers from the University of Western Australia and the Water and Rivers Commission.

Pendal, P. and Constable, E. (2000). 'Funding Issues and the Alinta Gas Sale.' Address to the Salinity Forum's Conference, Perth.

Readhead, C. (1991). 'Legal Aspects of Environmental Issues.' *Environmental Protection Act, Where to Now?* Seminar Proceedings, 20 November 1991.

Robertson, G. (1982). Address, Esperance Civic Centre, Agriculture WA.

Salinity Forum Inc. (2000). *Salinity Forum Response to Salinity Strategy—April 2000.* Unpublished.

Saltland Pastures Association (2000). *Saltveg One Million: A Strategy For Revegetation of One Million Hectares of Wheatbelt Saltland in Western Australia.* Unpublished report by the Saltland Pastures Association.

Shea, S. (1999). 'Potential for Carbon Sequestration and Product Displacement with Oil Mallees.' Proceedings of the Oil Mallee

Profitable Landcare Seminar, held in March 1999, Perth, Western Australia. The Oil Mallee Association of Western Australia.

Soil and Land Conservation Council of Western Australia (2001). Submission to the House of Representatives Standing Committee on Environment and Heritage into Public Good Conservation. Unpublished.

Twigg, R. J. (no date). *The Impact of European Settlement on the Environment of Jerramungup*. Murdoch University, Environmental Studies Honours thesis.

Working Party Assisting the Agricultural Land Release Review Committee (1985). Final Report.

Personal Papers

Burvill Papers. The personal papers of Mr G. H. Burvill were given by him to former CSIRO scientist Dr David Bennett of Fremantle who donated them to the project. It is expected that these materials will be passed on to the State Archives.

Other personal papers were provided by Mr Clive Malcolm, the Whittington Family, and Associate Professor Glen Phillips.

Index